D0597009

Praise for *The Myth of Hitler's Pope*

"Whatever your views on the controversial issues of Pope Pius XII's papacy, you will profit from David Dalin's engagingly written and cogently argued study. Dalin provides a valuable corrective to the farrago of recent criticism leveled against Pius XII and the Catholic Church for its actions (or non-actions) during World War II and places this criticism in the context of the 'culture wars.'"

—MARSHALL J. BREGER, professor,
Columbus School of Law, Catholic University

"After the misrepresentation, slander, and prejudice that have marked books on Pope Pius XII in recent years, David Dalin's calm and judicious scholarship will do much to clarify the historical record."

—ROBERT WILKEN,
William R. Kenan Jr. Professor of the History of Christianity,
University of Virginia

"Rabbi David Dalin has written an admirable defense of Pope Pius XII from a religiously committed Jewish perspective. He effectively answers the vicious, distorted charges that portray Pius XII as a Nazi sympathizer who did nothing to help save Jews from Nazi genocide. Dalin's meticulous scholarship shows just what an effective enemy of Nazi racism Pius XII really was, both before and during his papacy, and the personal and collective risks he took to rescue as many Jews as he could under the most dangerous conditions imaginable. Jews, especially, should not only be wary of the calumny against the pope, they should remember his life and career with gratitude. Dalin's important book gives Jews good reason for such gratitude."

—DAVID NOVAK,
J. Richard and Dorothy Shiff Professor of Jewish Studies,
University of Toronto

"Courage is contagious, so clutch this book close to your heart. Righting great wrongs requires great courage, and that is what *The Myth of Hitler's Pope* delivers. With devastating effectiveness, Dr. Dalin exposes their motives and subdues the assailants who with rashness and folly attempt posthumously to assassinate Pope Pius XII. This restoration of a good man's good name is a mitzvah—a Jewish good deed."

—RABBI DANIEL LAPIN,
president, Toward Tradition

"Although he was warmly praised in his day, and upon his death, by Jewish leaders for his efforts to protect and defend the victims of Hitler's genocidal madness, Pope Pius XII's reputation as a friend of the Jewish people has suffered since Rolf Hochhuth depicted the pontiff as 'silent' in the face of Nazi atrocities in his 1964 play *The Deputy*. Today, Pius is regarded in some circles as an anti-Semite and even a Nazi sympathizer. His more fevered critics have constructed the fable that he was 'Hitler's pope.' In his superb book *The Myth of Hitler's Pope*, Rabbi David Dalin buries this slanderous tale under an avalanche of facts. Far from being condemned as an enemy of the Jewish people, Pius should be honored, the rabbi forcefully argues, as a righteous gentile."

—ROBERT P. GEORGE,
McCormick Professor of Jurisprudence and
director of the James Madison Program in American Ideals
and Institutions, Princeton University

THE MYTH OF
HITLER'S
POPE

THE MYTH OF
HITLER'S
POPE

HOW POPE PIUS XII RESCUED
JEWS FROM THE NAZIS

RABBI DAVID G. DALIN

REMOVED FROM COLLECTION

418 924

West Islip Public Library
3 Higbie Lane
West Islip New York 11795

Since 1947
REGNERY
PUBLISHING, INC.
An Eagle Publishing Company • Washington, DC

Copyright © 2005 by David G. Dalin

All rights reserved. No part of this publication may be reproduced or transmitted in any form or by any means electronic or mechanical, including photocopy, recording, or any information storage and retrieval system now known or to be invented, without permission in writing from the publisher, except by a reviewer who wishes to quote brief passages in connection with a review written for inclusion in a magazine, newspaper, or broadcast.

Library of Congress Cataloging-in-Publication Data
Dalin, David G.
  The myth of Hitler's Pope / David G. Dalin.
   p. cm.
  Includes index.
  ISBN 0-89526-034-4
1. Pius XII, Pope, 1876–1958—Relations with Jews. 2. Holocaust, Jewish (1939–1945) 3. Judaism—Relations—Christianity. 4. Catholic Church—Relations—Judaism. 5. Christianity and anti-Semitism—History—20th century. 6. World War, 1939–1945—Religious aspects—Catholic Church. 7. National socialism and religion. I. Title.
  BX1378.D35 2005
  282'.092—dc22
                2005010476

Published in the United States by
Regnery Publishing, Inc.
One Massachusetts Avenue, NW
Washington, DC 20001
www.regnery.com

Distributed to the trade by
National Book Network
Lanham, MD 20706
Manufactured in the United States of America

10 9 8 7 6 5 4 3 2 1

Books are available in quantity for promotional or premium use. Write to Director of Special Sales, Regnery Publishing, Inc., One Massachusetts Avenue NW, Washington, DC 20001, for information on discounts and terms or call (202) 216-0600.

*For my mother, Bella Dalin, and in memory
of my father, Rabbi William Dalin*

Contents

CHAPTER ONE

THE MYTH OF HITLER'S POPE AND WHY IT MATTERS

I T IS IRONIC THAT SIXTY YEARS after the Holocaust—with anti-Semitism virulent among Islamic fundamentalists and growing rapidly among secular Europeans—that the liberal media in the West has tried to blame Pope Pius XII (and even the Catholic Church as a whole) for anti-Semitism.

No one believed this at the time. From the end of World War II until at least five years after his death in 1958, Pope Pius XII enjoyed an enviable reputation amongst Christians and Jews alike. He was hailed as "the inspired moral prophet of victory," and "enjoyed near-universal acclaim for aiding European Jews." He was, as one historian has aptly put it, "universally praised by Catholics and non-Catholics alike, as the spiritual leader not only of Catholicism but of Western civilization itself."[1] Indeed, in 1951, the eminent British writer (and liberal Catholic) Graham Greene could praise him as "a pope who many of us believe will rank among the greatest,"[2] an assessment shared by many other Catholics and Jews who hailed the pope for his many efforts to save Jewish lives during World War II.

The Slander of a Pope

The rhetorical campaign against the pope's conduct in World War II began as easily dismissed Communist agitprop against the strongly anti-Communist pontiff. But the campaign of vilification became a major issue after the 1963 Berlin premiere of a play called *The Deputy*, written by a young left-wing German writer (and former member of the Hitler Youth) named Rolf Hochhuth. Hochhuth vilified Eugenio Pacelli (who became Pope Pius XII in 1939) as a Nazi collaborator and as an icy and avaricious pontiff guilty of moral cowardice and inexcusable silence as Europe's Jews were murdered by the Nazis. Promoted as "the most controversial play of our time," *The Deputy* was fictional, highly polemical, and offered no historical evidence. It never-theless became a sensation and ignited a firestorm of controversy in the media and among intellectuals.[3]

That was forty years ago. Why does this myth persist? And why is it impor-tant? It is important, first of all, because of the duty we owe to the truth. It is also important because the battle over the reputation of Pope Pius XII is one of the most historically important battles of the culture war. An increasingly left-wing intellectual class wants to denigrate not only traditional Catholi-cism, but Christianity and even Judaism. It is no coincidence that some of the most extreme of the pope's attackers—including James Carroll (author of *Constantine's Sword*) and Garry Wills (author of *Papal Sin*)—are also out-spoken critics of the late Pope John Paul II.

Very few of the many recent books about Pius XII and the Holocaust are actually about Pius XII and the Holocaust. The liberal bestselling attacks on the pope and the Catholic Church are really an intra-Catholic argument about the direction of the Church today. The Holocaust is simply the biggest club available for liberal Catholics to use against traditional Catholics in their attempt to bash the papacy and thereby to smash traditional Catholic teaching—especially on issues relating to sexuality, including abortion, con-traception, celibacy, and the role of women in the Church. The anti-papal polemics of ex-seminarians like Garry Wills and John Cornwell (author of *Hitler's Pope*), of ex-priests like James Carroll, and of other lapsed or angry liberal Catholics exploit the tragedy of the Jewish people during the Holocaust to foster their own political agenda of forcing changes on the Catholic Church today.

This hijacking of the Holocaust must be repudiated. The truth about Pope Pius XII—which the mainstream media has been content to ignore while helping to make bestsellers out of bad history—must be restored. The liberal culture war against tradition—of which the Pope Pius XII controversy is a microcosm—must be recognized for what it is: an assault on the institution of the Catholic Church and traditional religion.

It is astonishing that so little commentary exists about the extreme nature of the attacks on the Catholic Church. Books and articles attacking Catholicism have become a cottage industry of the mainstream media. One example is the January 21, 2002, issue of the *New Republic*, which published Daniel Jonah Goldhagen's essay, "What Would Jesus Have Done?"—one of the most hateful attacks against the Roman Catholic Church (and in particular, Pope Pius XII) ever printed in a major American publication. The *New Republic* devoted an unprecedented twenty-four pages to Goldhagen's anti-Catholic diatribe and featured it as the cover story.

In fall 2002, Goldhagen expanded this essay into a book-length attack on the Church, *A Moral Reckoning: The Role of the Catholic Church in the Holocaust and Its Unfulfilled Duty of Repair*, which has added new fuel to the controversy over the Vatican's role during the Holocaust.[4]

Goldhagen is no stranger to controversy. In 1996, he created an international sensation with the publication of his book *Hitler's Willing Executioners*, which received widespread media coverage and remained on the *New York Times* bestseller list for many weeks. In *Hitler's Willing Executioners*, Goldhagen's explanation for the Holocaust was remarkably simple and simplistic: Blame for the Holocaust should be placed on the ordinary Germans and their uniquely vicious brand of anti-Semitism, whose aim was the elimination of the Jews. The Holocaust, claimed Goldhagen, was attributable to a murderous or "eliminationist" anti-Semitism that was widely prevalent among the German people and intrinsic to the German character. The Nazi

extermination of the Jews could thus take place because the vast majority of
the German people were already predisposed to kill Jews, and thus became
willing and enthusiastic followers of the Nazi leadership in its successful
efforts to implement the Final Solution. While Goldhagen gained international celebrity, his book's simplistic argument was widely criticized by serious scholars and historians.[5]

In his new book, Goldhagen's historical understanding and interpretation
of anti-Semitism is, once again, remarkably simple and simplistic. It is irre-
sponsibly dishonest and misleading as well. In *A Moral Reckoning*, Goldhagen condemns Christianity, and specifically the Catholic Church, as the
preeminent source of anti-Semitism ancient, medieval, and modern.

Much like *Hitler's Willing Executioners*, Goldhagen's new book is full of
factual errors, historical misrepresentations, and suppression of overwhelming counterevidence to his argument. Thus, for example, several of
the dates he provides for the establishment of European ghettos are wrong.[6]
The establishment of the Jewish ghetto in Rome, one of the memorably
tragic milestones in the history of Catholic-Jewish relations, took place in
1556, not in 1555 as Goldhagen asserts. So, too, the Venice ghetto was erected
in 1517, rather than in 1516 as stated by Goldhagen, while the Frankfurt
ghetto was established in 1462, rather than in 1460. In dating the establishment of the Vienna ghetto in 1570, moreover, Goldhagen is wrong by more
than fifty years, as Viennese Jewry were not confined to a ghetto in their city
until 1626.

In *A Moral Reckoning*, Goldhagen focuses on Pius XII as the symbol of
Catholic evil and repeats almost every accusation, including the most discredited ones, that has ever been leveled against him. While condemning Pius
XII as an anti-Semite and a collaborator with Nazi Germany, however, Goldhagen doesn't limit his anti-Catholic diatribe to Pius alone. Goldhagen's irresponsible screed climaxes with an attack on Pope John Paul II and the
Catholic Church today, minimizing or virtually ignoring John Paul II's historic role as a friend of the Jewish people, a pope who did more than any
other to usher in a new and unprecedented era of Catholic-Jewish dialogue
and reconciliation.

Goldhagen also identifies Christianity itself with anti-Semitism. He declares, "the main responsibility for producing the all-time leading Western hatred lies with Christianity. More specifically, with the Catholic Church,"[7] conveniently ignoring the anti-Semitism of atheistic Soviet Russia and the fact that the Nazis who perpetrated the Holocaust were anti-Christian as well as anti-Semitic. For Goldhagen, as for Carroll and other papal critics, anti-Semitism is a core Catholic value that is the source of European anti-Semitism. Goldhagen, in fact, repudiates the New Testament and Catholic thought deriving therefrom as inherently anti-Semitic with an "obvious integral relationship to the genesis of the Holocaust."[8] Goldhagen sees Pius XII's alleged anti-Semitism as something to be expected, since he rose through "the profoundly anti-Semitic establishment of the Church, an institutional culture centrally animated by the notion that all Jews were Christ-killers and responsible for many of the perceived evils of modernity."[9]

As Jewish scholar Michael Berenbaum has noted, Goldhagen "omits all mention of the countervailing traditions of tolerance"[10] within Roman Catholic thought, past and present. He misrepresents the early Church leaders who advocated tolerance toward the Jews, and his skewed treatment of Saint Augustine's views of Jews and Judaism is especially appalling. Similarly, Goldhagen's unsubstantiated claim that "there is no difference in kind between the Church's 'anti-Judaism' and its offshoot European anti-Semitism" that led to the Holocaust is as unsophisticated and wrong a statement as someone claiming to be a historian could possibly make.

Goldhagen's book—despite its near utter lack of disinterested scholarship—has carved a permanent niche for itself in the list of anti-Catholic literature, alongside Paul Blanshard's 1949 scaremongering book *American Freedom and Catholic Power*. Blanshard was a much-reprinted staple for anti-Catholic Evangelical readers. Goldhagen has become one of many staples for secular leftists whose hatred of Catholicism derives from the Church's opposition to abortion, gay rights, the ordination of women, and the rest of the liberationist agenda. If, as Jewish theologian Will Herberg once put it, "anti-Catholicism is the anti-Semitism of secular Jewish intellectuals," then Goldhagen is the most anti-Semitic of Jewish papal critics.

Goldhagen's demand that the Catholic Church as we know it be abolished as a disgrace and a danger to us all should be a warning to all people of faith of the hatred that burns in secular hearts to abolish traditional religion. That the book has found its readership out in the fever swamps of anti-Catholicism isn't surprising. But that a mainstream publisher like Knopf—and a mainstream liberal magazine like the *New Republic*—would print it is an intellectual and publishing scandal.

But it is scandal made intelligible by the myth of Hitler's pope that the liberal mainstream media has been so eager to propound as truth. When Cornwell's *Hitler's Pope* was published in 1999, it became a bestselling international sensation. Cornwell denounced Pope Pius XII as "the most dangerous churchman in modern history" without whom "Hitler might never have . . . been able to press forward with the Holocaust." Readers of Cornwell's bestseller were led to believe that before assuming the papacy Pacelli had been a devoted follower and supporter of Hitler. In fact, as we will see, he was one of Hitler's earliest and most consistent critics.

Hitler's Pope was excerpted in *Vanity Fair* and London's *Sunday Times*. Most liberal reviewers and commentators uncritically endorsed Cornwell's allegations, apparently without investigating their veracity. Cornwell became a celebrity in demand on the lecture, talk-show, and book-signing circuit, and was given a flattering profile on television's *60 Minutes*.

Cornwell later backed away from his own claims, but it wasn't under pressure from the mainstream media, which happily endorsed his unverified (and strongly anti-religious) conclusions.[11] Author Eugene Fisher—who holds a doctorate in Hebrew culture and education—lamented, "It is a sad commentary on the secular media that this blatantly anti-Catholic screed was ever published, much less hyped into bestseller status."[12]

To be sure, there have been recent books published by Catholic scholars like Ronald J. Rychlak, Pierre Blet, Margherita Marchione, Ralph McInerny, Justus George Lawler, and Jose Sanchez defending Pope Pius XII. They offer well-documented accounts of papal efforts to save and shelter Jews during the Holocaust, and show how the pope's diplomacy and the Vatican's rescue operations saved hundreds of thousands of Jews and other innocent victims from Nazism. But these books—well documented as they are—have been virtually ignored by the liberal mainstream media, published not by mainstream presses but by small Catholic ones. They have not appeared on bestseller lists—in fact, they aren't easy to find in major chain bookstores.[13]

The best of these, Rychlak's *Hitler, the War, and the Pope*—the most thorough, well-researched, and elegant study to date—provides a devastating point-by-point refutation of Cornwell's allegations. *The Defamation of Pius XII* by Ralph McInerny, a distinguished professor of medieval Christian philosophy at the University of Notre Dame, has also been virtually ignored. Unlike the books by Cornwell, Wills, and Carroll, these scholarly defenses of Pius were never reviewed by the *New York Times Book Review*, the *New York Review of Books*, or the *New Republic*. The result is that the myth of Hitler's pope is falsely given the mantle of mainstream scholarship, while the truth about Pope Pius XII as a defender of the Jews at their time of greatest peril is written off as merely minority Catholic pleading.

This is the case even when the accusations against the pope seem self-evidently hysterical. For instance, in Cornwell's "sensationalist and unreliable" account in *Hitler's Pope*, as Eugene Fisher has noted, "Pacelli is not only solely responsible for the rise and triumph of Hitler in the 1930s, but is also responsible for the outbreak of World War I as well! . . . Nazi Germany is let off the hook and virtually all the woes of the twentieth century are laid at the feet of a lone Italian Catholic."[14]

Other reviewers have attacked Cornwell's sloppy scholarship, but without denting the myth. For example, Jewish historian William D. Rubenstein, a noted authority on the Holocaust, has characterized *Hitler's Pope* as "a malign exercise in defamation and character assassination."[15] One of the most devastating reviews came from *Newsweek* columnist and religion editor Kenneth L. Woodward, who described Cornwell's book as "a classic example of what happens when an ill-equipped journalist assumes the airs of sober scholarship. . . . Most of his sources are secondary and written by Pacelli's harshest critics. Errors of fact and ignorance of context appear on almost every page.

Cornwell questions [Pius's] every motive, but never doubts those who tell a different story. This is bogus scholarship."[16] This is true, but the myth of Hitler's pope is too convenient a tool for liberals who want to denigrate the papacy, Christianity, and traditional religion. Esteemed historian Philip Jenkins is right when he says that "*Hitler's Pope* cannot be understood except as a series of very low blows against the modern Catholic Church, and specifically the papacy of John Paul II."[17]

In *Papal Sin*, Garry Wills not only attacks Pope Pius XII over the Holocaust but also attacks Pope John Paul II as the inheritor and defender of the "structures of deceit" (stated in the subtitle) of the Church. In his follow-up book, *Why I Am a Catholic*, Wills condemns the entire papacy, medieval and modern. As Philip Jenkins notes, in Wills's view, the second Vatican Council represented "one brief shining moment of liberal enlightenment, but hellish darkness descended once more in the form of John Paul II, whom Wills depicts as a credulous megalomaniac" more sinful than Pius XII.[18] While attacking the papacy as "a deeply flawed institution,"[19] Wills, like Cornwell, considers himself to be part of a liberal but "loyal opposition" within the conservative pontificate of John Paul II. But one might reasonably question whether the "loyal opposition" of Wills and other recent papal critics can realistically be considered loyal. Wills condemns John Paul II for upholding traditional Church teachings on priestly celibacy, contraception, abortion, homosexuality, the ordination of women, papal infallibility, the doctrine of the Real Presence in the Eucharist, apostolic succession, the Immaculate Conception, the Assumption, and the Magisterium itself. Wills calls for an end to the priesthood "in anything like the sense it has been known for many centuries," while advocating the ordination of women, the abolition of priestly celibacy, and an end to papal supremacy, however defined.

As one critic of Wills has recently noted: "What we have in Wills is a Catholic [but] his attacks on the Church are so basic as to raise questions about just what this term means."[20] Indeed, Wills is so extreme in his attacks on the Church that even his ideological friends have called him to task. In a review for the *New York Times*, liberal philosopher Richard Rorty agreed with

Wills's recommendation to "overthrow papal tyranny," but, taking his reasoning to its logical conclusion, concluded that if what Wills says is true, "then it is not clear why we need a church of Christ" at all.[21]

In a sharp, scathing critique of Wills in *Commonweal*, Eamon Duffy of Cambridge University, perhaps the world's preeminent authority on the history of the papacy, wrote:

> There is something repellently illiberal about Wills's angry liberal certainties, his wholesale and unqualified conviction that every right-thinking Catholic must agree with him, and that the positions he rejects can be held together by nothing except rank tyranny and the intellectual equivalent of chewing gum. Every issue he discusses is open and shut, and he finds in the standard works of biblical commentary or popular history on his shelves unchallengeable proofs of his own views. The arguments made by the Church are not *prima facie* ridiculous in the way Wills characterizes them. He does little to present the arguments and reasoning offered by the Catholic Church and instead spends his time railing against the conclusions.[22]

Ralph McInerny, a distinguished University of Notre Dame philosopher and novelist, has argued that liberal Catholic critics of Pope Pius XII are motivated by hatred for Pope John Paul II—in particular, hatred for the latter's stand against the "culture of death" as represented above all by abortion-on-demand, which many of Pius XII's (and John Paul II's) liberal critics openly support. The irony of Pope Pius XII's detractors "attacking Pius for allegedly not doing more to oppose Hitler's 'Final Solution'—and yet simultaneously supporting what many consider the 'Final Solution' for today's unwanted pregnancies"—is not lost on McInerny, who ruthlessly exposes their moral inconsistency.[23]

For the liberal critics, the argument is that Pius XII and the Catholic Church must shoulder the blame for the Holocaust. Moreover, Catholicism's guilt is due to aspects of the Church represented by the late Pope John Paul II.

Pope John Paul II's reaffirmation of traditional Church teachings is of a piece with Pius's alleged anti-Semitism; the Vatican's current stand on papal authority is in a direct line with its complicity in the Nazi extermination of the Jews.

This is a monstrous moral equivalence and a misuse of the Holocaust to which Jews must object. The Holocaust cannot legitimately be used for partisan purposes in such a debate. This is true particularly when the attempt disparages the testimony of Holocaust survivors who praised Pope Pius XII for his efforts on their behalf. And it is an abominable slander to spread blame that belongs to Hitler and the Nazis to a pope who was a friend of the Jews and who opposed Hitler and the Nazis. Jews, whatever their feelings about Roman Catholicism, have a duty to reject arguments that usurp the Holocaust and use it for a liberal war against the Catholic Church that if successful would undermine the foundations of Christianity and Judaism alike, because of the liberal critics' overwhelming disregard for traditional religion and the truth.

The Defense of a Pope

That some popes, both medieval and modern, were anti-Jewish is a matter of historical fact. It is true that Pope Pius XII has had Jewish detractors in the past. In 1964, for example, Guenther Lewy published *The Catholic Church and Nazi Germany*; Saul Friedlander added *Pius XII and the Third Reich* in 1966. Both volumes claimed that Pius's anti-Communism led him to support Hitler as a bulwark against the Soviet Union. The scholarship—or historical analysis—of both books was seriously questioned, and Livia Rothkirchen, the respected historian of Slovakian Jewry at Yad Vashem, Israel's Holocaust memorial and museum in Jerusalem, wrote a memorable and excoriating review of Friedlander's book.

For every Jewish detractor, however, Pope Pius XII has been blessed with a Jewish defender. Foremost amongst these was Israeli historian and diplomat Pinchas Lapide, who had been the Israeli consul in Milan and had spoken with many Italian Jewish Holocaust survivors. In his meticulously researched and comprehensive 1967 book *Three Popes and the Jews*, Lapide persuasively argued that Pius XII "was instrumental in saving at least 700,000, but probably as many as 860,000 Jews from certain death at Nazi hands." Lapide's volume remains the definitive work by a Jewish scholar on the subject.

Joseph L. Lichten, the Anti-Defamation League's representative in Rome, wrote the influential and much quoted 1963 monograph *A Question of Judgment* to rebut the false and malicious allegations of Rolf Hochhuth's play *The Deputy* and to document for posterity the high opinion Jewish leaders had of Pius XII during and immediately after World War II.

Jeno Levai, the great Hungarian Jewish historian, was so angered by accusations of papal "silence" that he wrote *Hungarian Jewry and the Papacy: Pius XII Did Not Remain Silent* (published in English in 1968), with a powerful introduction and epilogue by Robert M. W. Kempner, the deputy chief U.S. prosecutor at Nuremberg. In 1938, Jeno Levai had been able to see Eugenio Pacelli when the then Vatican secretary of state delivered a number of searing addresses against Nazism and Communism in Budapest. Years later, when the charges against Pacelli first surfaced, Levai, who had become one of Europe's leading Holocaust scholars, leapt to Pacelli's defense.

Levai's magisterial work, sadly ignored by most papal critics, rebuts all the major accusations against Pius XII, concentrating on the Jewish experience in Hungary. Using Church and state archives in Hungary, Levai demonstrated how the papal nuncio and bishops "intervened again and again on the instructions of the pope," and that because of these directives "in the autumn and winter of 1944 there was practically no Catholic Church institution in Budapest where persecuted Jews did not find refuge."[24]

Robert M. W. Kempner's compelling introduction and epilogue to Levai's study are noteworthy in their own right. As deputy chief U.S. prosecutor at Nuremberg, Kempner did not hesitate to compare those who defamed Pius XII with revisionists who deny the full reality of the Holocaust:

In the last few years, there has been no lack of farfetched or malicious attempts to obscure or interpret perversely this historical fact. . . . We are concerned here with another deliberate, or at the very least negligently applied method which aims at reducing the guilt of those who were really responsible. This is done by focusing the guilt for the Holocaust not on Hitler as the central figure for the liquidation system but on Pope Pius XII; by propagating in print and in the theater a new theory which runs as follows: Pope Pius XII never made an energetic protest against Hitler's "Final Solution of the Jewish Problem," and that is how the catastrophe came to reach the proportions it did. Both the premise and the conclusion drawn from it are equally untenable. The archives of the Vatican, of the diocesan authorities and of Ribbentrop's Foreign Ministry contain a whole series of protests—direct and indirect, diplomatic and public, secret and open.[25]

In the book's epilogue, Kempner added:

I myself am thoroughly familiar with . . . the important role of the Catholic Church in the struggle against the "Final Solution in Hungary" and had always emphasized it—among other places, in my book, *Eichmann and His Accomplices*. Neither Rolf Hochhuth's play . . . nor the books by Guenther Lewy and Saul Friedlander provide any reason for changing this standpoint. The Church documents published for the first time in this book by Levai . . . strengthen my favorable view of the Vatican's attitude at the time and of Pope Pius XII, for whom I have had the greatest respect ever since the time he spent in Berlin.[26]

Several Jewish scholars have spoken out in Pius's defense in response to the new attacks since the publication of *Hitler's Pope*. Michael Tagliacozzo, the foremost authority on the Nazi roundup of Rome's Jews—and a survivor of that roundup himself—has strongly defended Pius's role during the Nazi occupation of Rome, documenting that Pius himself was instrumental in saving the lives of close to five thousand Roman Jews who, at the pope's instructions, were sheltered within the Vatican and in the numerous monasteries and convents in Rome. Having lived through the terror of the Nazi occupation of Rome and studied the primary documents relating to it, Tagliacozzo has had nothing but praise for Pius XII. "I know that many criticize Pope Pacelli," he said in a recent interview. "I have a folder on my table in Israel entitled 'Calumnies Against Pius XII,' but my judgment cannot but be positive. Pope Pacelli was the only one who intervened to impede the deportation of Jews on October 16, 1943, and he did very much to hide and save thousands of us."[27] The relevant Italian Holocaust archival documents clearly prove, Tagliacozzo says, that Pius XII's protests and actions were decisive in rescuing 80 percent of Rome's Jews.[28] Richard Breitman (the only historian authorized to study classified American espionage files from World War II) noted that secret documents prove the extent to which "Hitler distrusted the Holy See because it hid Jews."[29] Some of this, of course, is public, including Hitler's order to the SS to kidnap the pope. There are many recorded exchanges of Nazis sharing the view of high-ranking Nazi leader Reinhard Heydrich, who told his subordinates in late spring 1943: "We should not forget that in the long run the pope in Rome is a greater enemy of National Socialism than Churchill or Roosevelt."[30]

Sir Martin Gilbert is another outspoken Jewish defender of Pius XII. Gilbert, the highly acclaimed official biographer of Winston Churchill, is widely acknowledged as one of the most distinguished and respected historians and biographers of our time. He has written many acclaimed works on the Holocaust, including *The Holocaust: A History of the Jews of Europe During the Second World War*, *Auschwitz and the Allies*, and *Never Again: A History of the Holocaust*. These books are indispensable for anyone working in the field of Holocaust studies.

Gilbert documents how Pius XII was one of the first to publicly condemn Nazi atrocities (via Vatican Radio), and to speak out on behalf of Europe's

Jews. In Gilbert's most recent book, *The Righteous: The Unsung Heroes of the Holocaust*, he recounts the achievements of the extraordinary Catholics who, under the leadership of Pius XII, rescued Jews at great peril to themselves and to their Church throughout Nazi-occupied Europe. Overall, Gilbert estimates that the various Christian churches saved up to half a million Jewish lives during the Holocaust, and that the majority of these were saved by the clergy and laity of the Catholic Church—the dominant religion of the countries under Nazi occupation. When asked in a recent interview whether he would agree with an estimate (published by the Vatican in 1998) that Pius XII "personally or through his representatives" had a direct role in saving hundreds of thousands of Jewish lives, Gilbert answered: "Yes.... Hundreds of thousands of Jews [were] saved by the Catholic Church, under the leadership and with the support of Pope Pius XII.... [T]o my view [that estimate would] be absolutely correct."[31]

One of Gilbert's central points, ignored by papal critics, is that Pius XII not only provided guidelines and inspiration to Catholic diplomats, clergy, and lay rescuers, but directly engaged in rescue efforts himself. In a major address on Christians and the Holocaust, delivered at Church House in London, Gilbert declared: "The pope himself... gave his personal order on the eve of the German deportation of Jews from Rome to open the sanctuaries of Vatican City to all Jews who could reach it.... As a result of the pope's order and of the Catholic clergy's rapid response in Rome, of Rome's 6,800 Jews, only 1,015 were actually deported.... The papal action, which I do not find mentioned in the current 'J'accuse'-style debates, saved more than 4,000 lives."[32]

For Jewish leaders of a previous generation, the idea that Pope Pius XII could be smeared as "Hitler's pope" would have been shocking. At the end of World War II, and for decades thereafter, Pius XII was universally acclaimed by Jewish leaders, including renowned Noble Prize–winning physicist Albert Einstein; Chaim Weizmann, who would become Israel's first president; Israeli prime ministers Golda Meir and Moshe Sharett; Rabbi Isaac Herzog, the chief rabbi of Israel; and Dr. Alexander Safran, the chief rabbi of Romania. Jewish public figures showered Pius with praise for the actions he took in defense of the Jews during World War II.

Since 1962, Yad Vashem, Israel's Holocaust Memorial and Museum, has recognized and honored as "righteous gentiles" those non-Jews who saved Jewish lives during the Holocaust. Millions of people have seen Steven Spielberg's movie *Schindler's List*, about Oskar Schindler, the German Catholic industrialist who saved the lives of 1,200 Jews. Many have also heard of Raoul Wallenberg, the young Swedish diplomat who is credited with saving tens of thousands of Jews in Budapest during World War II, and of Monsignor Angelo Rotta, the Vatican's heroic ambassador to Hungary. Other Catholic priest rescuers, such as Cardinal Pietro Palazzini, have been similarly honored by Israel. Pope Pius XII, as I will argue in this book, deserves to be recognized as a "righteous gentile" as well; no other pope in history had ever before been so universally praised by Jews as Pius was for his role in saving Jews during the Holocaust.

This book will debunk the myth of Hitler's pope, and it will also remove the tarnish that liberal Catholics have smeared on their own Church, which is not the source of the anti-Semitism of the National Socialists. In fact, as I will document in some detail in the next chapter, there has been a tradition of papal support for the Jews of Europe since at least the fourteenth century, a philo-Semitic Catholic tradition that continues into our own time with Pope Benedict XVI. At his investiture, on April 24, 2005, Pope Benedict, the former Cardinal Ratzinger, specifically extended his greetings to his "brothers and sisters of the Jewish people, to whom we are joined by a great shared spiritual heritage, rooted in God's irrevocable promises."[33]

Pius XII and especially John Paul II were the heirs and exemplars of this long and venerable philo-Semitic tradition within papal-Jewish relations, a tradition that has been ignored or dismissed by recent papal critics, Catholic and Jewish alike. A historically accurate assessment of the role of Pius XII during the Holocaust leads to exactly the opposite of Cornwell's conclusion: Pius XII was not "Hitler's pope" but a protector and friend of the Jewish people at a moment in history when it mattered most.

And, as we'll see, Hitler did have one loyal cleric within his entourage. It was not the pope. It was Hajj Amin al-Husseini, the viciously anti-Semitic grand mufti of Jerusalem, the leader of the radical Islamic fundamentalists in Palestine, the leader of the 1929 mass murders of Jews in Hebron, and the mentor of and inspiration for Yasser Arafat and many other Arab leaders. Hajj Amin al-Husseini was an open ally of Hitler, met with Hitler several times, and repeatedly called for the destruction of European Jewry. It is radical Islam—Hitler's overt ally in World War II—not the Catholic Church, that threatens Jews today.

CHAPTER TWO

POPES IN DEFENSE
OF THE JEWS

═══════════════

T O PUT POPE PIUS XII into historical perspective, we need to do a little history on papal-Jewish relations, which have been far better than most people think.

Thanks to the efforts of many liberal ax-grinding writers, it is commonly assumed that most, if not all, medieval and modern popes were violently anti-Semitic. Writers like David Kertzer, James Carroll, Daniel Jonah Goldhagen, and other recent papal critics paint a gruesome picture of the papacy. In *Constantine's Sword*, Carroll argues that "Auschwitz, when seen in the links of causality, reveals that hatred of Jews has been no incidental anomaly but a central action of Christian history... that achieved its climax in the Holocaust."[1] In *A Moral Reckoning*, Goldhagen declares that "the main responsibility for producing the all-time leading Western hatred [of anti-Semitism] lies with Christianity. More specifically, with the Catholic Church."[2] These writers attribute anti-Semitism to the Catholic Church and its papal leadership throughout history, including Pope Pius XII in the line of shame.

But this is bad history and bad scholarship. The historical fact is that popes have often spoken out in defense of the Jews, have protected them during times of persecution and pogroms, and have protected their right to worship freely in their synagogues. Popes have traditionally defended Jews from wild anti-Semitic allegations. Popes regularly condemned anti-Semites who sought to incite violence against Jews. Popes employed Jewish physicians in the Vatican and counted Jews among their personal confidants and friends. You won't find these facts in the liberal attack books, but they are true.

As the great Cambridge University Jewish scholar Israel Abrahams noted in his monumental work, *Jewish Life in the Middle Ages*, first published in 1896, it "was a tradition with the popes of Rome to protect the Jews who were near at hand,"[3] especially those living in Italy and Spain. Moreover, notes historian Thomas Madden, "of all medieval institutions, the [Catholic] Church stood alone in Europe in its consistent condemnation of Jewish persecutions."[4] Throughout the Middle Ages, Rome and the papal states "were the only places in [western] Europe where the Jews were at all times free from attacks or expulsions."[5] The Jews were expelled from Crimea in 1016, Paris in 1182, England in 1290, France in 1306, Switzerland in 1348, Hungary in 1349, Provence in 1394, Austria in 1422, Spain in 1492, Lithuania in 1495, and Portugal in 1497. In Italy, however, the Jewish community was under papal protection and was never expelled. Indeed, by the beginning of the fifteenth century, "the only safe place in Europe to be a Jew was in the lands of the pope."[6]

More than that of any other historian, the monumental scholarship of Cecil Roth, who held Oxford University's prestigious chair in Jewish history from 1939 to 1964, refutes the false and misleading allegations of papal critics like Kertzer, Carroll, and Goldhagen. Roth "left a lasting mark on Jewish scholarship, with an immense literary output of some six hundred works, a distinguished tenure as reader in Jewish history at Oxford, and the culminating distinction of editor in chief of the *Encyclopedia Judaica*."[7] Over the years, Roth wrote the definitive scholarly books *The History of the Jews of Italy*, *History of the Jews in Venice*, and *The Jews in the Renaissance*, as well as popular surveys of the Jewish past such as *A History of the Jews*, *A Short History of the Jewish People*, and *The Jewish Contribution to Civilization*. By the time of his death in 1970, Roth had achieved international renown as the most prolific and widely read Jewish historian of his generation, and as the century's preeminent Jewish scholar of Italian Jewish history and the history of papal-Jewish relations. Time and again, throughout his many writings and lectures, Roth pointed out that during eras of rampant anti-Semitism, the popes in Rome were often the only world leaders to raise their voices in defense and support of the Jews. "Of all the dynasties in Europe," noted Roth, "the papacy not only refused to persecute the Jews... but through the ages popes were protectors of the Jews....The truth is that the popes and the Catholic Church from the earliest days of the Church were never responsible for physical persecution of Jews and only Rome, among the capitals of the world, is free from having been a place of Jewish tragedy. For this we Jews must have gratitude."[8]

The Beginnings of Papal Protection

Pope Gregory I (590–604), later known as Gregory the Great, began the tradition of protecting Jews. He issued a historic decree beginning with the words *Sicut Judaeis* ("As for the Jews"), which thereafter introduced all subsequent papal edicts defending the Jews. He affirmed that the Jews "should have no infringement of their rights.... We forbid to vilify the Jews. We allow them to live as Romans and to have full authority over their possessions." During his pontificate, Pope Gregory put these words into practice, forbidding forced conversions of Jews, intervening to protect Jews from violence, and insisting that Jewish religious rituals and practices be tolerated. In Naples, for example, where the local citizenry "had been exhorted to disturb the Jewish Sabbath service," Gregory came to the defense of the Jews and "quieted down the militant spirits." When the bishop of Palermo, "in an excessive act of religious zeal," confiscated several synagogues, Jewish poor houses, and Jewish schools, Pope Gregory again "intervened and righted the wrongs."[9] When the Jews of Terracina, in central Italy, complained "that

Bishop Peter had seized their synagogue, ejecting them because their singing had been audible at a nearby church," Gregory ordered that a synagogue elsewhere be given to them for worship services.[10] The Jews of Italy and other countries frequently appealed to Pope Gregory for protection because of his reputation for benevolence and were greatly appreciative of his interventions on their behalf. Indeed, Gregory came to be admired in Jewish history as the first great papal friend of the Jews and was widely praised by medieval Jewish communal leaders and scholars. Judah Mosconi, an important fourteenth-century Jewish philosopher and scholar, praised Gregory as "a great sage and complete philosopher" who delved into Hebrew books "and loved Jews very much and made for them great deliverances [from harm] in his days."[11]

Gregory's decree *Sicut Judaeis* gave its name to a second landmark papal edict, this one from Pope Calixtus II (1119–1124), who promised to defend European Jews from persecution by their Christian neighbors or at the hands of Crusaders. "Setting an iron precedent," Calixtus promised Jews "the shield of our protection."[12] Calixtus II condemned physical attacks on the Jews, opposed their forced baptism, and forbade the destruction of their synagogues and cemeteries.[13] These prohibitions were, as James Carroll has noted, "a strengthening" of those enunciated by Gregory "in recognition that, after the events of [the First Crusade in] 1096, the tradition of papal protection of the Jews had to be urgently reinforced."[14] Calixtus's defense of the Jews, with its promise of continuing papal protection, was reissued at least twenty-two times by successive popes between the twelfth and fifteenth centuries.

Pope Gregory X (1271–1276) was another philo-Semitic pope. He renewed *Sicut Judaeis* in 1272 and added an important clause: "An accusation against Jews based solely on the testimony of Christians was invalid; Jewish witnesses must also appear."[15]

During the fourteenth century, when Jews were blamed for the Black Death, Pope Clement VI (1342–1352) came to their defense—the only European leader to do so. The Black Death devastated Europe, killing one-third of the population. Jews were accused of causing and spreading the plague, which led to a firestorm of anti-Semitism that engulfed more than three hundred Jewish communities. Thousands of Jews were killed, especially in Germany, Austria, France, and Spain.[16] On September 26, 1348, Pope Clement VI issued a bull that refuted Jewish blame for the plague, saying that such charges had "no plausibility."[17] In refuting the allegation of Jewish blame, he pointed out "the obvious fact that the supposed instigators of the plague were dying like everyone else."[18] He urged priests, bishops, and monks "to take Jews under their protection as he himself offered to do." Edward A. Synan, one of the preeminent historians of papal-Jewish relations during the Middle Ages, has noted that Pope Clement VI was the Jews' "principal defender," his bull a significant addition "to the papal tradition of protecting the Jews."[19]

Boniface IX, Martin V, and the Jews

The papacy's pro-Jewish policies continued with Pope Boniface IX (1389–1403), who expanded papal protections of the Jews, including recognizing Roman Jews as full citizens of the city in 1402. He was the first of many popes to employ Jews as physicians in the Vatican. In 1392, Boniface promoted his friend Angel ben Manuel to be his personal physician and "familiaris" (member of the household) "under the protection of the holy Peter and Paul, so that under the patronage of the Holy See you can profit more and shall benefit from all honors."[20]

Pope Martin V (1417–1431) reaffirmed papal protections of the Jews. He reiterated the papal prohibition against forced baptism and expanded the civil rights and privileges of Jews in Rome, Germany, and Savoy. In 1419, 1422, and 1429, he issued papal edicts protecting Jews.[21] Wishing that "every Christian treat the Jews with a humane kindness,"[22] and seeking to encourage "the fullest possible intercourse between Jews and Christians,"[23] Pope Martin took the Jews "under his paternal protection against unjust vexations on the part of the Christians and against false accusations resulting from hypocritical religious zeal."[24] The Jews of Italy were especially grateful when Martin V proclaimed: "Jews are created like other men in the image of God, and in order to protect their future, they must not be molested in their synagogues, nor hindered in their commercial relations with Christians." In 1417, he affirmed: "The laws of the Jews should not be impaired. They should not be obliged to undergo forced baptism, nor to keep Christian holidays."[25] In Martin V's Papal Edict of Protection of 1422, the pope specifically warned Franciscan friars led by Giovanni da Capistrano, the infamous "scourge of the Jews," to stop inciting Italians against the Jews.[26] In his papal edict of 1429, Pope Martin went even further, categorically forbidding the friars "to preach against the Jews, to attempt to interrupt their normal relations with their neighbors, to infringe upon their religious rights, or to exclude them from normal activities (including attendance at universities)."[27] Cecil Roth credits Martin with offering Jews a "sweeping...measure of protection,"[28] and Italian Jews were grateful. Indeed, there is a celebrated drawing of the pope being welcomed by the Jews of Constance.[29] Wherever he traveled in Italy, the pope was greeted enthusiastically by Jews.

The Jews of Rome and the Papal States appreciated that Martin V employed Elijah ben Shabbetai Be'er as his personal physician. He served as physician to both Martin and his successor, Pope Eugene IV (1431–1437), and also lectured in medicine at the University of Pavia, becoming the first Jew on the faculty of a European university.[30] He was also awarded Roman citizenship. Pope Martin V encouraged Jewish physicians to practice their profession in the Papal States and urged Jews to enroll in European medical schools. Thanks to such papal patronage, for at least two centuries thereafter Jewish physicians were prominent in Italy and southern Europe and served as the court physicians to popes and prelates, princes and nobles.[31] Papal physicians were also often rabbis and became the Jewish community's representatives and spokesmen at the papal court. These papal physicians ensured that Jews in Rome and the Papal States always had the ear of the popes.

Renaissance Popes and the Jews

Pope Sixtus IV (1471–1484) is best known as the pontiff who transformed Rome from a medieval to a Renaissance city, built the Sistine Chapel, and established the Vatican library and archives.[32] He was also one of the most philo-Semitic Renaissance popes during a period that continued the tradition of papal support for the Jews.

Deeply interested in Hebrew literature—and with many Jewish friends—Sixtus was the first pope to employ Hebrew copyists at the Vatican Library. An important collection of 116 Hebrew books and manuscripts—probably, as Cecil Roth has concluded, the best collection of its kind in any European library—was assembled at the Vatican at the beginning of the fifteenth century. One of Sixtus's predecessors, Pope Nicholas V (1447–1455), had added significantly to the Vatican's Hebrew library in his quest for the original copy of the Gospel according to Saint Matthew.[33]

Sixtus himself was a celebrated patron of scholarship; he bought many old Hebrew manuscripts so that new copies could be made by a recognized Hebrew scholar working in the Vatican.[34] In thus encouraging Hebrew manuscript collection and preservation, Sixtus IV set a precedent—both in assembling Jewish works and in employing Hebrew scholars—that his papal successors continued.

Prominent members of Rome's Jewish community were welcome guests in the Vatican of Sixtus IV. They were grateful that the pope had vehemently denied the vile rumor that Jews had drained the blood of a Christian child, Simon of Trent, to prepare their unleavened Passover bread. In 1475, to the delight of Italian Jewry, Sixtus refused to canonize Simon of Trent as a holy martyr, facing down Simon's militant supporters among the Dominican friars.

The Renaissance pope many historians judge as one of the worst pontiffs in history was, for Italy's Jews, one of the best. Alexander VI (1492–1503), the scandalously corrupt Borgia pope who fathered four children, including the notorious siblings Cesare and Lucretia, was one of the most pro-Jewish popes in history. He created the first chair in Hebrew at the University of Rome, frequently entertained Rome's chief rabbi at the Vatican, and provided a safe haven for persecuted Jews. During Alexander's tenure, the Jewish population of Rome almost doubled as Jews fled the Spanish and Portuguese Inquisitions perpetrated by the royal courts. The Borgia pope welcomed them and gave them his official protection.[35]

One eminent Jew serving as physician to Pope Alexander was Bonet de Lattes, a native of Provence. A renowned rabbi and astronomer as well as a physician and papal confidant, Lattes served as chief rabbi of Rome's principal synagogue while also publishing an annual astronomical calendar that foretold the events of the coming year. Lattes invented an astronomical ring-dial—"a sort of miniature astrolabe worn on the finger"—with which one could calculate the position of the sun and tell time.[36] He dedicated his book on his invention, *The Astronomical Ring*, to his friend and patron Pope Alexander VI.[37]

Alexander VI's successor, Pope Julius II (1503–1513), is best known as the patron of such great artists as Michelangelo, Raphael, and Bramante, and as the pope who commissioned plans for the new Basilica of Saint Peter and other enduring works of Renaissance architecture. Among the works inspired and funded by Julius were Michelangelo's statue of Moses, Michelangelo's paintings in the Sistine Chapel, Raphael's frescoes in the Vatican, and other works touching on Old Testament themes. Julius's physician was another Jew, Samuel Sarfatti,[38] and Julius included encouragement and funding of Jewish learning and scholarship as part of his patronage of the arts. From the perspective of the Jewish community of Rome, Pope Julius II was a friend.

The most favorable relations between the papacy and the Jews, however, occurred during the pontificate of the House of Medici. As Cecil Roth has noted: "No Italian rulers showed themselves better disposed toward the Jews than the popes of the Renaissance period—particularly those of the House of Medici, Leo X and Clement VII. Enlightened beyond their time and tolerant to a degree, they regarded even Jewish scholarship as an integral part of that intellectual life of which they were such passionate devotees."[39] The reign of the first Medici pope, Leo X (1513–1521), was an especially happy time for the Jews. Indeed, as Roth has pointed out, Leo X was so well regarded by the Jews of his day that it was said that the Jews of Rome considered his pontificate a presage of messianic times.[40]

One especially benevolent edict from Leo X repealed the onerous obligation on Jews to wear distinctive (and degrading) Jewish badges. The badges had been imposed by the Fourth Lateran Council (1215) to prevent Christians from mistakenly marrying Jews. It was enforced in the papal dominions of France but had fallen into disuse in Italy. So in 1514, Leo affirmed the civil rights of Jews in the French papal territory of Comtat Venaissin, despite protests from the area's anti-Semitic bishop.

Leo took a lively interest in Jewish literature, fostered Jewish learning, authorized the first Hebrew press in Rome, approved the printing of the Talmud, and in a letter to the bishops of Speyer and Worms, showed that his patronage of Jewish learning was not just the patronage of a Renaissance pope interested in the arts, but of a pope with a sympathetic understanding of the Talmud and of Jewish literature in general.

Moreover, during his papacy, a lingering dispute over the Talmud came to a head. The controversy began in Germany, where a Jewish apostate named Johann Pfefferkorn declared that Talmudic literature blasphemed Jesus and Christianity. The Dominican friars of Cologne promoted Pfefferkorn as an expert on the wickedness of Judaism. In several ghostwritten pamphlets published under his name, Pfefferkorn purported to describe the dangers of Judaism and praised the holiness that would result from the destruction of the Talmud. As a result, the Holy Roman Emperor Maximilian I considered confiscating and burning the Talmud and other Jewish books.

Johann Reuchlin, the foremost Christian scholar of Hebrew in Germany, refuted Pfefferkorn. Reuchlin, a German jurist and one of Europe's greatest humanists, was the first Christian to compile a Hebrew grammar and had performed a detailed study of Jewish literature, including the Kabbalah, the great work of Jewish mysticism on which he wrote several learned treatises. Reuchlin begged the emperor and all intelligent Christians not to permit the destruction of Jewish books. When the controversy continued, Reuchlin approached Rome's chief rabbi and papal physician, Bonet de Lattes. Could the rabbi ask Pope Leo X to intervene on behalf of the Jews? Lattes passed on Reuchlin's request, and Pope Leo X acted by encouraging a Christian printer in Rome to publish the Talmud's entire text, uncensored. Pope Leo was hailed by Rome's Jews as "an example of the just and humane attitude of the pope,"[41] a great friend and protector of the Jewish people.

The second Medici pope, Clement VII (1523–1534), was so philo-Semitic that contemporary Jewish writers praised him as a "favorer of Israel,"[42] and he was so well respected that when disputes split the Jewish community in Rome, the city's Jewish leadership appealed to him to intervene and mediate the disputes. In response, Clement VII asked his friend Rabbi Daniel ben Isaac Donzeille of Pisa, a wealthy banker and Jewish communal leader held in high esteem by both Christians and Jews, to revamp the system by which Rome's Jewish community governed itself. At the pope's behest, Rabbi Donzeille appointed three *fattori*, or administrators, who "would be respon-sible to the Papal Court for everything connected with life inside the Jewish community."[43] They were to be assisted by a governing council of sixty mem-bers, "to be chosen half and half from among the poor and the rich" of Rome's Jewish community. In 1524, these new rules, which became the basis of Roman Jewish communal administration and decision-making for decades to come, were confirmed by the pope, who decreed that they "should be observed by all for all times."[44] Throughout this period, Rabbi Donzeille acted as the pope's adviser and trusted confidant.

Clement VII played a central role in another dramatic episode in papal-Jewish relations. It involved a "romantic adventurer" named David Reubeni, a Jewish traveler from Jerusalem welcomed in Italy by the Jews and the pope. In fact, Reubeni was, for a while, a favorite of Clement VII and his papal court. Claiming to be the brother of Joseph, king of the tribe of Reuben, he appeared in Venice in late 1523, asking Venetian Jews "to aid him on an important mission to the pope."[45] He arrived in February 1524 riding a white horse and accompanied by a jubilant escort. He was greeted by throngs of cheering Roman Jews as well as by Cardinal Egidio da Viterbo, a friend of the pope renowned as a Hebrew scholar well versed in rabbinics and Jewish mys-ticism. In keeping with his reputation as "a great friend of the Jews," Cardi-nal Egidio arranged for Reubeni to meet Clement VII.[46]

During his audience with the pope, Reubeni proposed a treaty between his "state"—the 300,000 members of the dispersed tribe of Reuben—and the states of Christian Europe against the Muslims. Reubeni proposed a Jewish

Crusade to take back the Holy Land from the Muslim Turks, for which he wanted the active support and blessing of the pope as well as weapons from Christian countries.[47] To facilitate his plan, Reubeni requested that the pope give him letters of introduction to some of the leading monarchs of Europe—including the Holy Roman Emperor Charles V, John III of Portugal, and Francis I of France. Clement eagerly supported Reubeni and provided the requested papal letters of introduction.

At Clement VII's invitation, Reubeni remained in Rome for more than a year—with a papally arranged tourist agenda and even permission to enter the Basilica of Saint Peter on horseback. He became a fixture at the papal court, lived near the papal palace, and conferred with the pope on a regular basis.[48] Although, in due time, David Reubeni's negotiations with the king of Portugal broke down, and his utopian scheme for a Jewish crusade to reconquer the Holy Land never materialized, his brief sojourn in Rome was a historically memorable one. That Reubeni could enjoy the popularity and hospitality that he did at the papal court is indicative of the especially cordial relations that existed between the Jews of Rome and the Medici popes, especially Clement VII.

Clement VII's personal physician and medical adviser was Joseph Sarfati, one of Rome's most successful physicians, a prominent leader of the Jewish community, and a continuing presence at the papal court, where he was able to converse with some of the most influential cardinals.[49] In addition to his medical work, Sarfati was renowned as a philosopher, mathematician, and Hebrew poet. He translated the Spanish comedy *Celestina* into Hebrew and composed a Hebrew epitaph for one of Clement VII's cardinals at the Vatican.[50]

Jacob Mantino, another Jewish physician, was highly esteemed at the Vatican. In 1529 he was appointed as a lecturer on medicine at the University of Bologna, "through an ingenious device of his patron, Pope Clement VII, to secure him a regular source of income without cost to the papal treasury."[51]

Pope Clement VII's patronage of Jewish literature included commissioning a new translation of the Old Testament from the original Hebrew into

Latin, to be carried out by six Jewish and six Christian scholars working together. This historically remarkable project was informed, says Cecil Roth, by "a superbly tolerant attitude on the part of the Supreme Pontiff."[52] Roth also affirms that "it was at the [papal] court of Clement VII, that the friendly relations between Jews and Christians in Renaissance Italy reach their climax."[53]

Papal-Jewish relations remained friendly during the pontificate of Paul III (1534–1549), a "magnificently pro-Jewish pope"[54] who encouraged Jews expelled from other countries to settle in Italy and later accepted *marranos* (Jews who had feigned conversion to Christianity in order to avoid persecution), promising them protection from the Spanish Inquisition.[55] His successor, Pope Julius III, renewed these protective guarantees.

The Blood Libel

In his book *The Popes Against the Jews*, David Kertzer devotes three chapters to the horrific allegation that Jews engaged in the ritual murder of Christian children during the Passover holiday. Jews were accused of using the children's blood in the unleavened bread eaten at the Passover meal. Yet he makes little mention of the relevant and indisputable historical fact that a succession of popes since the twelfth century (when the accusation of ritual murder was first made) condemned this libel.

The first alleged case of ritual murder was reported in 1144 in Norwich, England. The body of a Christian child was found on Good Friday, and the rumor spread that the boy had been murdered by the town's Jews, who partook of his blood during the Passover holiday. As Leon Poliakov, a distinguished historian of anti-Semitism, has pointed out, such rumors of Jewish ritual murder emerged "almost simultaneously" in England, France, and Germany in the 1140s and 1150s, and soon swept through Europe,[56] finding "especially fertile soil" in England.[57] When, in 1255, the body of Hugh of Lincoln, a Christian child of eight, was found in a well, suspicion once again fell on the Jews. After a trial, ninety Jews were sent to the Tower of London, and eighteen were executed. Little Hugh of Lincoln became the object of a cult and a pilgrimage, and the tale of his ritual murder "became so much a part of the nation's traditions"[58] that it shaped the popular image of the Jew in England for centuries. Indeed, this blood libel became part of English literature, becoming deeply embedded in the popular imagination, as evidenced in the well-known story told by the Prioress in *The Canterbury Tales* of a child martyr murdered by Jews.[59] So, too, as Jewish scholar Marc Saperstein has pointed out, the "Ballad of Sir Hugh or the Jew's Daughter," about Hugh of Lincoln, "would be sung by Stephen Daedalus to Leopold Bloom near the end of James Joyce's *Ulysses*."[60]

In France, as in England, the ritual murder accusation was the basis on which hundreds of Jews were charged, tried, and burned at the stake. In May 1171, the same charge (unsubstantiated on this occasion even by the discovery of a body) led to the execution by burning of almost the entire Jewish community of Blois, France, including seventeen women.[61] During the next hundred years, there was a virtual epidemic of ritual murder accusations throughout continental Europe. As a result, hundreds of Jewish men and women were imprisoned and put to death.

Despite the fact that Jews are prohibited by Jewish law from consuming animal blood in any shape or form, and despite "its affinity with one of the calumnies leveled against Christians by pagan Roman persecutors, the implausible claim that Jewish ritual demands human sacrifice, and that, in order to provide victims, Jews kidnapped and slaughtered Christian children,"[62] has had a history that has extended more than eight hundred years, into the twentieth century. From the beginning, popes raised their voices in protest against this anti-Semitic libel. Indeed, as Saperstein has pointed out, whenever "charges of ritual murder were brought to the attention of medieval popes, they regularly condemned them as baseless and inconsistent with Jewish religious teaching."[63] In 1247, Pope Innocent IV promulgated the first of several papal bulls devoted to refuting the Jewish ritual murder libel, a historic papal decree that goes completely unmentioned in the anti-papal diatribes of writers like Kertzer, Goldhagen, and Carroll. Innocent IV's "most important contribution to the long list of papal texts in defense of the Jews,"[64] which was addressed to the archbishops and bishops of Germany and France, read in part:

> Although the Holy Scriptures enjoin the Jews: "Thou shalt not kill" and forbid them to touch any dead body at Passover, they are wrongly accused of partaking of the heart of a murdered child at the Passover, with the charge that this is prescribed by their laws, since the truth is completely the opposite. Whenever a corpse is found somewhere, it is to the Jews that the murder is wickedly imputed. They are persecuted on the pretext of such fables or of others quite similar; and contrary to the privileges that have been granted them by the apostolic Holy See, they are deprived of trial and of regular judgment; in mockery of all justice, they are stripped of their belongings, starved, imprisoned and tortured, so that their fate is perhaps worse than that of their fathers in Egypt.[65]

Perceiving an underlying motive for the blood libel, he vigorously denounced those Christians who devise "pretexts so as to rob [the Jews] unjustly and seize their property."[66] Furthermore, in confirming the *Sicut Judaeis*, Innocent IV added the following important clause, which not only condemned the blood libel, but also forbade faithful Catholics to participate in its propagation:

> Nor shall anyone accuse them [the Jews] of using human blood in their religious rites, since in the Old Testament they are instructed not to use blood of any kind, let alone human blood. But since ... many Jews were killed on the ground of such a suspicion, we ... strictly forbid that this should be repeated in the future. If anyone knowing the tenor of this decree should, God forbid, dare to oppose it, he shall be punished by loss of his rank and office, or be placed under a sentence of excommunication, unless he makes proper amends for his presumption.

This historic edict set an important precedent that subsequent popes followed in defending Jews against the accusation of ritual murder. In 1272, for
example, Gregory X, in reissuing and confirming the *Sicut Judaeis*, similarly
added a lengthy discussion of the blood libel, which he condemned in
unequivocal terms:

> It sometimes happens that certain Christians lose their Christian
> children. The charge is then made against the Jews by their enemies
> that they have stolen and slain these children in secret, and have sac-
> rificed the heart and blood. The fathers of the said children, or other
> Christians who are envious of the Jews, even hide their children in
> order to have a pretext to molest the Jews, and to extort money from
> them so as to pay their dues. They assert thereupon, most falsely, that
> the Jews have taken away these children and slain them, and have sac-
> rificed the heart and blood. Yet their law expressly forbids the Jews
> to sacrifice or to eat or drink blood.... This has been confirmed in
> our *curia* on many occasions by Jews converted to the Christian faith.
> None the less, on this pretext many Jews have frequently been seized
> and detained, against all justice. We accordingly have determined
> that no Christian shall be allowed to make any allegations against the
> Jews on such a pretext. We command, moreover, that the Jews
> imprisoned on this account shall be released from prison, and that
> they shall not be arrested again on such groundless charge unless
> (which we think impossible) they are captured in flagrant crime.[67]

So, too, in 1422, when a delegation of Jews asked Pope Martin V for his
protection from the ritual murder libel, "which had again raised its head," he
proceeded in accordance with the precedent set by his predecessors, and "stig-
matized the accusation that the Jews mingle blood with their unleavened
bread as being 'a charge brought unjustly against them.'"[68] When, in 1540,
the charge was once more brought up against Jewish communities in Central Europe, Jews appealed to Pope Paul III. He responded in his bull *Licet*

Judaei ("Let it be permitted for the Jews"), addressed to the bishops of Hungary, Bohemia, and Poland, and repudiated the "bitter and mortal enemies of the Jews," who "pretend, in order to despoil them of their goods, that the Jews kill little children and drink their blood."[69] The pope decried that Jews "were unjustly deprived, not only of their possessions, but in many cases also of their lives" because of the blood libel. Pope Paul unequivocally condemned the ritual murder libel and declared himself the Jews' supporter and protector. The pronouncements of Popes Innocent IV, Gregory X, Martin V, and Paul III, rejecting and condemning the ritual murder libel, expressed "as plainly as words could do, the official attitude of the papacy and the Catholic Church."[70] Sadly, the popes were often the only European leaders condemning the libel.

In seventeenth- and eighteenth-century Poland, accusations of Jewish ritual murder and outbreaks of popular violence against the Jews eventually reached epidemic proportions. In 1650, Giovanni Battista de Marini, vicar general of the Dominican order, brought "instructions from Rome to the Polish members of his order to fight against the libel from their pulpits."[71] Nevertheless, anti-Semitic peasant violence worsened, leading to the imprisonment, torture, and execution of many innocent Jews and to the expulsion of entire Jewish communities from several Polish towns.

In 1758, Jewish leaders in Poland sent a special representative, Jacob Zelig, to Rome for an audience with the pope. Zelig gave Pope Benedict XIV a poignant account of the suffering and persecution endured by Polish Jews. In response, the pope appointed a Franciscan "of vast learning and high reputation," Lorenzo Ganganelli, to investigate the matter. Ganganelli had been an influential and distinguished professor of theology and rector of the College of Saint Bonaventura in Rome and would soon be named a cardinal by Pope Benedict's successor, Clement XIII, in 1759.[72] He would be elevated to the papacy as Pope Clement XIV ten years later. After a thorough year-long investigation, Ganganelli produced his official report, "one of the most remarkable, broad-minded and humane documents in the history of the

Catholic Church—a document which will always cause his memory to be cherished in gratitude and affection by the Jewish people."[73] The comprehensive report was both scholarly and investigative, analyzing sources and texts and reviewing all reported cases of Jewish ritual murder in history. With the exception of two cases of dubious veracity (which have been rejected by most historians), he established the complete lack of any basis for the accusation.[74]

Ganganelli's historic refutation of the blood libel was cheered by the Jews of eastern Europe. When Ganganelli became pope, Jews already regarded him as their friend and protector, a feeling that intensified during his five-year pontificate. As Pope Clement XIV, he endorsed the rights of Jews to travel freely and manage shops outside of their ghetto, to practice medicine, to work as artisans, and to open small silk and hat factories. From the perspective of the Jews, he was one of history's best popes.

In the nineteenth and twentieth centuries, Pope Leo XIII (whose twenty-five-year pontificate, from 1878 to 1903, was at that time the second longest in history after that of Pius IX, his predecessor),[75] spoke out in defense of the Jews, and especially in defense of Captain Alfred Dreyfus, the French Jewish military officer falsely accused of treason in 1894. This striking historical fact often goes unmentioned in accounts of the Dreyfus Affair and histories of Catholic-Jewish relations. Papal critics like Kertzer, Carroll, and Goldhagen, for instance, don't mention it, but it can be found in the work of the distinguished—and non-politicized—British church historian Owen Chadwick. Chadwick points out in his authoritative volume *A History of the Popes, 1830–1914* that "Protestants everywhere condemned the papacy for the Dreyfus Affair, though the papacy had nothing to do with the matter. So far as he expressed an opinion publicly, Leo XIII was on the side of Dreyfus."[76] Also unmentioned by papal critics is the important historical fact that in 1892—two full years before the Dreyfus Affair began—Leo XIII strongly defended Jews in a widely circulated interview published in the French daily newspaper *Figaro*.

Popes and Jews in the Twentieth Century

Leo XIII's successor, Pope Pius X (1903–1914), "was the first pope in centuries to come from peasant stock, and to rise all the way from the lowliest of
ecclesiastical positions to Saint Peter's throne,"[77] which seems to have influenced his friendly feelings toward the Jews.[78] Born Giuseppe Sarto, following
his ordination he spent nine years as an assistant pastor and eight more as a
simple parish priest prior to being named bishop of Mantua and subsequently patriarch of Venice. Sarto was a friend to the Jews throughout his
ecclesiastical career, defended the Jewish people against defamation and violence, and was instrumental in halting a twenty-year-old anti-Semitic political campaign in Italy.[79]

When he was a young parish priest in the early 1870s, Sarto met Romanin
Jacur, a Jewish engineer from Padua who was an influential politician. Their
friendship lasted forty years.[80] Jacur was a conservative member of the Italian parliament for thirty-nine years (1880–1919) and a senator from 1920
until his death in 1928. After Sarto became pope, his longtime friend was a
frequent dinner guest at the Vatican and served as a papal confidant and
adviser on a host of Jewish issues, from anti-Semitism in Czarist Russia to
Zionist aspirations for a Jewish state in Palestine. The pope endorsed his
friend's reelection campaigns, and after the general election of 1913, Pius X
personally wrote to Jacur congratulating him on his "peaceful and triumphant reelection."[81]

While bishop of Mantua (1884–1893), Sarto enjoyed the philanthropy of
prominent Jewish families with which he was friendly. Indeed, when asked
by Pope Leo XIII who the best Christians in the city were, the bishop is said
to have replied: "To tell the truth, as far as charity is concerned, the best Christians are the Jews."[82]

As pope, he met with the Zionist leader Theodore Herzl, who was trying
to mobilize support for a Jewish homeland in Palestine, on January 26, 1904.
As even critics of Pius X have admitted, the very fact that he would receive
Herzl was historically significant. As Herzl would later recall, during their
conversation, the pope spoke (among other topics) about the temple in

Jerusalem and asked whether any thought had been given to rebuilding it and renewing the ancient sacrificial services.[83] Pius also told Herzl that he was pleased to have had many Jewish friends since his days in Mantua. "Only the other evening," Pius added, "two Jews were here to see me. There are more bonds than religion: social intercourse, for example, and philanthropy."[84]

In 1905, in the aftermath of a new wave of anti-Semitic pogroms, Pius X sent a strongly worded letter to the Polish bishops reminding them that the Church condemned anti-Semitic violence. During the most famous ritual murder trial of the twentieth century—the 1913 trial of the Russian Jew Mendel Beilis—Pius X not only reiterated the papacy's refutation and denunciation of the blood libel, but offered evidence and testimony in a letter he sent to Lord Leopold Rothschild of England.

The context for the letter was that a Catholic priest was a key prosecution witness. He intended to testify that "murdering Christian children and consuming their blood was a religious duty for Jews." The priest also asserted that papal documents defending the Jews from charges of ritual murder were forgeries. So Pius X had his secretary of state, Rafael Merry del Val, write Rothschild to verify the accuracy and authenticity of both Innocent IV's papal bull of protection for the Jews and Lorenzo Ganganelli's eighteenth-century report refuting the blood libel. The Russian embassy in London certified the letter as authentic and forwarded it to Mendel Beilis's attorneys in Kiev, where it helped win Beilis's acquittal. (There is evidence that Czar Nicholas himself read del Val's letter and had Russian officials pressure the jury to reach a verdict of not guilty.)

Pope Benedict XV (1914–1922) suppressed the last vestiges of anti-Semitism in Italy's "papally linked press"[85] and condemned anti-Semitism in a widely circulated 1916 statement, issued at the request of the American Jewish Committee, which pleaded for the pope to protest another anti-Semitic outburst in Poland. This historic papal denunciation of anti-Semitism is another fact that goes unmentioned in the books of Kertzer, Carroll, and Goldhagen.

On May 10, 1917, in an effort to win papal support for the Balfour Declaration, which called for the creation of a Jewish state in Palestine, the great

European Zionist leader Nahum Sokolow met with Benedict XV at the Vatican. Prior to his meeting with Pope Benedict, Sokolow had several preliminary meetings with Eugenio Pacelli, then the Vatican undersecretary of state, who is credited with engineering Sokolow's historic private audience on May 10, which lasted well beyond the scheduled half hour. Pope Benedict asked Sokolow to explain the Zionist program, listened attentively, and then described it in accordance with divine will.[86] "How much history has changed," the pope said to Sokolow. "Nineteen hundred years have passed since Rome destroyed your country, and now Your Excellency comes to Rome in order to revive that land!"

Even when the controversial issue of the Christian holy places in Palestine came up in conversation, goodwill prevailed. "I have no doubt," said the pope, "that a satisfactory agreement will be reached." The audience concluded with Pope Benedict saying: "*Si, si, io credo che saremo buoni vicini!*" ("Yes, yes, I believe we shall be good neighbors!") For emphasis, he repeated the last sentence several times.[87]

Four months later, papal goodwill was put to the test and, according to Sokolow's son, resulted in saving the city of Tel Aviv:

> In the autumn of 1917, when the British Army under General Allenby launched its victorious onslaught on Palestine, the Turkish commander in chief, Djemal Pasha, ordered a reckless evacuation of Tel Aviv, which would have meant the looting, if not the complete destruction of the town.... Who would help? Sokolow thought that the Vatican was the most suitable neutral medium to influence the Turkish government; the more so since he had heard that the apostolic delegate in Constantinople, Monsignor Dolce, was on good terms with official circles there. He appealed to [the Vatican secretary of state] Cardinal Gasparri, who, with the consent of the pope, sent instructions to this effect to Monsignor Dolce. The Vatican's intervention had the desired result and the order of evacuation was cancelled, thus saving Tel Aviv from certain ruin.[88]

"A Great Pope and Peacemaker": Pius XI and the Jews

One of the most scholarly of modern pontiffs, Pope Pius XI (1922–1939), spent much of his early career as the director of two of the world's great church archives, the Ambrosian Library in Milan and the Vatican Library in Rome. After his 1918 appointment by Benedict XV as papal nuncio in War-saw, Poland, where he served for three years, he was named archbishop of Milan and made a cardinal in June 1921. Less than a year later, in February 1922, he was elected pope. While he also achieved some minor distinction as the first pope to use the radio as a means of communication and "the first pope with a serious avocation for mountain climbing,"[89] one of the great (and today forgotten) legacies of his pontificate was his historic role as an oppo-nent of anti-Semitism and as a papal defender of the Jews.

Pius XI had enjoyed friendships with Italian rabbis and other Jewish lead-ers since his days as the director of Milan's Ambrosian Library, when he often discussed Hebrew manuscripts with the chief rabbi of Milan and other nota-bles from the city's Jewish community. As a young priest in Milan, he had studied Hebrew with a local rabbi and on one occasion Milan's chief rabbi specifically asked for his prayers on behalf of himself and his people. It was during his tenure as papal nuncio in Poland that Pius confronted for the first time the anti-Semitism, persecution, and suffering experienced by Europe's Jews. Shortly after his arrival in Warsaw in 1918, pogroms erupted, killing many Jews and destroying Jewish homes, synagogues, and businesses. The future pope was shocked by Polish anti-Semitism and fought bitterly against it, as is amply documented in Sir William Clonmore's definitive biography *Pope Pius XI and World Peace*. As papal nuncio, he looked to the welfare of Polish Jewry, notes Clonmore, and "made it quite clear that any anti-Semitic outburst would be severely condemned by the Holy See."[90] He also person-ally helped Jewish victims in a more tangible way. Instructed by Pope Bene-dict to direct the administration and distribution of Catholic relief in post–World War I Poland, he distributed funds not only to Catholics, but also to impoverished Jews who had lost their homes and businesses in the pogroms.[91]

In 1928, as pope, he issued a decree condemning anti-Semitism. "Moved by this Christian charity, the Holy See has always protected this people [the Jews] against unjust vexations, and just as it reprobates all rancour and con-flicts between peoples, it particularly condemns unreservedly hatred against the people once chosen by God; the hatred that commonly goes by the name of anti-Semitism."[92]

In a pastoral letter of February 10, 1931, prepared at the behest of the Vat-ican and addressed to the Catholic clergy of Germany, the bishops of eight Bavarian dioceses stated that the rising National Socialist party of Adolf Hitler rejects "the basic premises" of Catholic teaching. Moreover, the Bavar-ian bishops "recognized the fact that the ideology proclaiming superiority of race and the anti-Semitism deriving from that ideology were contrary to Christian teaching."[93] In November 1931, the chief rabbi of Milan—on a per-sonal visit to the Vatican—thanked the pope for his appeals against religious persecution and his continuing support for Italy's Jews.[94]

As the 1930s progressed, Pius came to regard Hitler as "the greatest enemy of Christ and of the Church in modern times," and compared Hitler to an Antichrist. "The persecution against the Catholic Church in Germany," he declared, was Hitler's work, "wholly and solely his."[95] In one of his annual Christmas addresses to the College of Cardinals, he vigorously denounced both Italian and German Fascism and described the Nazi swastika as "a cross hostile to the cross of Christ."[96] On March 12, 1937, Pius XI issued his famous anti-Nazi encyclical *Mit brennender Sorge* ("With Burning Anxiety"). Addressed to the German bishops and read in its entirety from the pulpits of all of Germany's Catholic churches, Pope Pius's encyclical produced an angry response from the Nazi government in Berlin.

Mit brennender Sorge did not specifically mention Nazi anti-Semitism—it focused instead on how "aggressive paganism" was persecuting the Catholic Church in Germany—but it certainly struck close in stating: "Whoever wishes to see banished from church and school the Biblical history and the wise doctrines of the Old Testament, blasphemes the name of God, blas-phemes the Almighty's plan of salvation, and makes limited and narrow human thought the judge of God's designs over the history of the world: he denies his faith in the true Christ." The papal document also states that "'Revelation' in its Christian sense, means the word of God addressed to man. The use of this word for the 'suggestions' of race and blood, for the irradiations of a people's history, is mere equivocation. False coins of this sort do not deserve Christian currency." The Nazis certainly regarded *Mit brennender Sorge* as a decidedly pro-Jewish document, and they launched a vitriolic counterattack on the papacy. The Nazi propaganda ministry went so far as to circulate rumors that Pius XI was a half-Jew whose mother had been a Dutch Jewess.

In 1938, at the very time that British prime minister Neville Chamberlain was appeasing Hitler at Munich, Pius XI emerged as one of the few European leaders to unequivocally condemn anti-Semitism. In March 1938, he suspended the "Society of the Friends of Israel" (Amici Israel), a Catholic organization that for many years had tried to convert Jews and that had begun to publish pamphlets "manifesting sentiments of hate" against the Jewish people. "Inasmuch as the Holy See disapproves of all hatred and all animosity between people," the papal order of suppression read, "it most categorically condemns the hatred against the people who once were chosen by God, a hatred which nowadays is commonly indicated by the word anti-Semitism."[97]

Later that spring, when Hitler made a triumphant entry into Vienna during the *Anschluss*, Pius XI was furious that the prelate of Austria, Cardinal Theodore Innitzer, rang the bells of the city's churches and flew the Nazi flag. In response, Pius summoned Innitzer to Rome to chastise him and had this fact "communicated through diplomatic channels to the United States so that world governments would know where the Vatican stood regarding Hitler's Germany."[98] When Benito Mussolini "decked out Rome's streets with Nazi swastikas on the occasion of Hitler's state visit in May," the pope snubbed Hitler by leaving the city. While Hitler was still in Rome, the Vatican newspaper *L'Osservatore Romano*, at the pope's behest, carried a front-page article condemning Nazi racism and forbidding Catholics from teaching such racist ideas.[99]

Pius was appalled when fascist professors, at Mussolini's direction, issued a Racial Declaration on July 14, 1938, stating that "Jews do not belong to the Italian race," which was "a pure Aryan race."[100] In September 1938, Mussolini's government announced its first wave of anti-Jewish laws (more would come two months later). These so-called racial laws, modeled on the infamous Nuremberg laws enacted by the Nazis, dismissed Jewish teachers from the public schools and expelled Jewish children from the secondary schools. Jews were also dismissed from the civil service and the armed forces and banned from other realms of public life, including the universities. Marriage between Jews and Catholics was forbidden, and Jews could no longer employ Christians in their homes. On more than one occasion, Pius publicly denounced Mussolini's anti-Jewish legislation.

On September 6, 1938, ailing and with only months to live, Pius XI received a group of Belgian pilgrims. He accepted an ancient prayer book and read from one of the prayers. Then he said, "I cannot help being deeply moved. Anti-Semitism is not compatible with the thinking and the sublime reality that are expressed in this text. It is a hateful movement, a movement that we cannot, as Christians, take any part in." With tears in his eyes he concluded, "Anti-Semitism is inadmissible; spiritually, we are all Semites."

As scholars have pointed out, "this last phrase may well be the most famous words ever uttered by Pius XI."[101] The Vatican's 1998 Commission on the Shoah correctly cites them as evidence of the pope's continuous opposition to anti-Semitism and his benevolent attitude toward the Jewish people. David Kertzer notes that the pope's words were not reported in the Vatican's own newspaper, *L'Osservatore Romano*, because they were "informal and spontaneous . . . they were not recorded in any official papal document."[102] Other Catholic newspapers in Europe, however, carried the story, and his words provided "inspiration for Catholic rescuers during the Holocaust."[103]

During the last months of his life, Pope Pius XI continued to condemn the Nazi regime and its anti-Semitic policies. In November 1938, after the infamous Nazi "Kristallnacht" pogrom destroyed hundreds of German synagogues and businesses, Pius denounced the Nazi atrocities, instructed

Cardinal Michael Faulhaber of Munich to do so as well, and directed his cardinal to help the chief rabbi of Munich save the Torah scrolls before his synagogue was thoroughly vandalized.[104] He directed *L'Osservatore Romano* to declare the Italian fascists' banning of Jews from theatres and other public places as "acts of un-Christian persecution." He asked Catholic cardinals of the United States and Canada to help Jewish scholars and professors expelled from their positions in Germany find places in North American universities. On January 14, 1939, Pius spoke to the diplomatic corps at the Vatican and told the assembled ambassadors to obtain as many entry visas as possible "for the victims of racial persecution in Germany and Italy."[105]

Since June 1938, Pius XI had been preoccupied with preparing a papal encyclical that would directly condemn anti-Semitism. It was written with the utmost secrecy after Pius met with an American Jesuit priest, Father John LaFarge, at Castel Gandolfo (the pope's summer residence). LaFarge was the editor of the Jesuit magazine *America* and an early and prominent opponent of Southern segregation laws, as seen in his 1937 book attacking racism and segregation. Pius had read and admired the book and asked LaFarge to draft an encyclical for him. LaFarge accepted the pope's commission and asked for the help of Father Wladimir Ledochowski, who had assisted Pius in writing his earlier encyclicals. LaFarge completed his first draft in September 1938 and delivered it to Father Ledochowski in Rome, with the expectation that the pope would receive it immediately. Instead, Ledochowski held on to the draft for months. It did not reach Pius XI until the pope was on his deathbed. Pius died suddenly on February 10, 1939, and the secret encyclical died with him. It was never released as an official papal document, but remained in the Vatican archives.[106]

The Jews mourned Pius XI's death. On February 11, 1939, the chief rabbi of Paris, Julien Weil, addressed the following public homage to the pope's memory:

> The death of his Holiness Pius XI moves me deeply and painfully. Judaism wholeheartedly joins the universal veneration that surrounded

the august Pontiff, admiring and honoring him as a servant of God, a true apostle of social justice, peace, and the human fraternity. On numerous occasions, Pius XI denounced with luminous firmness and clarity the pernicious errors of racist paganism, and he condemned anti-Semitism as irreconcilable with the Christian faith and as an instigator of iniquities and odious violence. I am sure that I express the feelings of my fellow Jews in saluting with respect the great figure of Pius XI and in giving in our prayers a religious expression to our homage of regret and gratitude toward this great servant of the God of justice and love.[107]

The following day, Leon Blum, the former prime minister of France and one of its preeminent Jewish citizens, joined Rabbi Weil in mourning: "A great pope and peacemaker...has considered it his duty towards Peace to fight against the racist powers and against the propagation of racist theories throughout the world.... More than the respect due to his great office and undaunted courage makes us bow our heads before his coffin." The leaders of the Alliance Israelite Universelle, the central communal organization of the French Jewish community, wrote to Rome: "Never shall we forget the kindness and courage with which the late pope has defended all victims of persecution, irrespective of race and religion, in the name of those eternal principles whose noblest spokesman he has been on earth.... He has truly earned our eternal gratitude and everlasting admiration."[108]

Bernard Joseph, on behalf of the Jewish Agency, the future government of the State of Israel, wrote to the Latin patriarch in Jerusalem: "In common with the whole of civilized humanity, the Jewish people mourns the loss of one of the greatest exponents of the cause of international peace and goodwill.... More than once did we have occasion to be deeply grateful for the attitude which he took up against the persecution of racial minorities and, in particular, for the deep concern which he expressed for the fate of the persecuted Jews of Central Europe. His noble efforts on their behalf will ensure for him for all time a warm place in the memories of the Jewish people wherever they live."[109]

The February 1939 issue of the *National Jewish Monthly*, a leading American Jewish periodical published by B'nai B'rith, featured a picture of Pope Pius XI on its cover and devoted an editorial to praising his courageous opposition to fascism and anti-Semitism. "Regardless of their personal religious beliefs," wrote the magazine's editors, "men and women everywhere who believe in democracy and the rights of man have hailed the firm and uncompromising stand of Pope Pius XI against Fascist brutality, paganism, and racial theories." The editors quoted a statement made by Bishop Bernard J. Sheil of Chicago: "I glory in the fact that the first international voice in the world to be raised in stern condemnation of the ghastly injustice perpetrated upon the Jewish people by brutal tyrannies was Pope Pius XI. I am proud and happy to unite my feeble voice with the powerful voice of this illustrious pontiff in denouncing these ruthless tyrannies which lay the cruel lash of persecution upon the defenseless backs of God's children—whatever may be their race, religion, or nationality."[110]

This was the tradition of the papacy, and the tradition of the next pope, Pius XII. Far from being Hitler's pope, he became a great defender of the Jewish people, as so many popes before him had been. But the circumstances that confronted Pope Pius XII were far more horrific than previous popes could have imagined: the biggest war in the history of the world and a powerful regime dedicated to exterminating the Jewish people.

CHAPTER THREE

THE FUTURE POPE

EUGENIO PACELLI WAS BORN IN ROME on March 2, 1876, the scion of a distinguished and aristocratic Roman family. The Pacelli family had been serving the Holy See since 1819, when Eugenio's grandfather, Marcantonio Pacelli, arrived in Rome to study canon law. He rose to prominence during the pontificate of Pius IX, and by 1848, had become one of the pope's most trusted advisers.[1] In 1851, Pius IX appointed him undersecretary of the interior in the papal state, a position he held until 1870.[2] Pacelli also helped establish the Vatican newspaper, *L'Osservatore Romano*, the most influential Catholic newspaper in the world and the "moral and political" voice of the Holy See.[3] He remained its editor until his death in 1902, at the age of 102.[4]

Eugenio's father, Filippo Pacelli, was another distinguished Vatican lawyer, serving as a trusted financial adviser to Pius IX and Leo XIII. In addition, he was a prominent member of Rome's "Black Nobility," Roman aristocrats and civic leaders who sided with the popes against Italy's monarchy in the bitter struggle over a unified Italian state. The unification of Italy (including Rome) under the liberal monarchy in 1870 brought political emancipation and religious freedom to Jews to a greater degree than they had ever known.

The first two Jews were elected to Rome's city council in 1870, the same year the city's Jewish ghetto was dissolved.[5] The old barriers to Jewish and Catholic social integration broke down, and Jews became "fully integrated into Italian society and politics and had access to careers . . . generally closed to them elsewhere in the West."[6] Filippo Pacelli's involvement in local politics (he twice won election to the city council) brought him into close contact with Rome's Jews and also allowed him to forge a friendship with his two Jewish colleagues on the council. In 1872, when the violently anti-Catholic liberals of the municipal council proposed the removal of the cross from the entrance to the Camp Verano cemetery, Jewish council member (and longtime president of the Jewish community) Samuel Altari joined Filippo Pacelli in fighting the resolution.[7] The pope, with whom Altari had always been friendly, remarked: "I always knew that Sor Samuele was the most Catholic of all city councilors."[8]

Eugenio Pacelli's parents socialized with some of Rome's leading Jewish families, including the Altaris. In addition, his parents sent him to one of Rome's most liberal ("free-thinking") state-supported high schools, where Eugenio had several Jewish classmates. This was unprecedented personal experience for a future pope. No previous pontiff had grown up in a city in which Jewish social and political equality and religious freedom were taken for granted. All of this would help shape Eugenio Pacelli's antipathy to anti-Semitism.

Eugenio's older brother, Francesco Pacelli, followed the family tradition and became a prominent lay canon lawyer. He assisted the Vatican secretary of state, Cardinal Pietro Gasparri, during the cardinal's negotiations with Benito Mussolini that led to the Lateran Treaty of 1929.[9] The treaty created a sovereign, independent Vatican City state and recognized Roman Catholicism as the official religion of Italy—historic concessions to the Church after nearly sixty years of Church/state hostility.

Initially, it was thought that Eugenio would follow the Pacelli family tradition and become a lay canon lawyer. Instead, at the age of eighteen, he chose the priesthood and entered Rome's prestigious Almo Capranica College to begin his seminary training. A gifted linguist—and one of the best students in his seminary class—he eventually became fluent in Latin, Greek, English, French, German, Spanish, Portuguese, Hebrew, and Aramaic. After further studies at Rome's Pontifical Gregorian University, Pacelli was ordained on Easter Sunday, April 2, 1899. He was named assistant to the pastor of Chiesa Nuova, the parish church of his family, where he had once served as an altar boy. He also continued his studies, earning a doctorate in theology in 1902, and subsequently a second doctorate in canon and civil law.

With such a background, Eugenio Pacelli, as the historian Jose Sanchez notes, "was born to be pope and was on the papal fast track even before he was ordained."[10] He was talent-spotted immediately. Pope Leo XIII had created a program under the auspices of the Vatican's Department of Extraordinary Ecclesiastical Affairs that trained promising young clerics for service in the Vatican diplomatic ranks. Two years after Pacelli was ordained, Cardinal Gasparri, the Department of Extraordinary Ecclesiastical Affairs' newly appointed secretary (and future Vatican secretary of state), invited him to join the program. At first, Pacelli demurred, saying that he preferred to serve "as a pastor of souls,"[11] but Cardinal Gasparri reassured the young priest that serving the church as a Vatican diplomat was also serving souls.[12]

A few weeks later, Pope Leo XIII chose Pacelli to deliver the Vatican's condolences to King Edward VII of England after the death of Queen Victoria. This was further proof that the twenty-five-year-old was already well on his way to greatness within the Holy See.[13] In 1908, Pacelli returned to England as a Vatican representative at the International Eucharistic Congress in London. On this visit he met Winston Churchill, who was then a young member of Parliament eager to stamp out anti-Catholic bigotry in English public life.[14] Pacelli and Churchill, a year apart in age, struck up a friendship, and their careers would parallel one another; as Churchill rose in Britain's parliament, Pacelli rose as a Vatican diplomat and statesman.

In 1904, Pope Pius X named Pacelli a monsignor and assigned him to assist a team of scholars under the supervision of Cardinal Gasparri, who were revising and codifying canon law. Pacelli would spend twelve years on the project. He also served as the pope's *minutante*, editing the pope's speeches and minutes, and as a personal envoy from the pope to Emperor Franz Josef of Austria.[15]

As a scholar, Pacelli was offered professorships in canon law at a Roman university in 1908 and at the Catholic University of America in 1911. In both instances, Cardinal Gasparri convinced Pacelli to turn the offers down and remain a diplomat. In 1914, Pacelli succeeded Gasparri (who was promoted to Vatican secretary of state) as secretary of the Department of Extraordinary Ecclesiastical Affairs. In his new position, Pacelli concluded a concordat with Serbia, the first of many such treaties that he would negotiate. The Serbian concordat was signed only four days before Archduke Franz Ferdinand of Austria was assassinated at Sarajevo.[16] At the outbreak of World War I, Pacelli was charged with maintaining a registry of prisoners of war and arranging their exchanges, one of the humanitarian tasks taken on by the Vatican.[17]

During the next three years, Pacelli was Gasparri's right-hand man, helping to formulate and draft all official documents prepared by the secretary of state for Pope Benedict XV's signature. Many important papal documents, including the Vatican's February 1916 condemnation of anti-Semitism, were first drafted and often proposed by Eugenio Pacelli.

Eugenio Pacelli and the Jews

By the time Eugenio Pacelli became Cardinal Gasparri's chief Vatican deputy in 1914, Jews were well represented in both the government of Italy and that of Rome. In 1907, Ernesto Nathan—a personal friend of Pius X—became the first Jewish mayor of Rome. On the national level, as early as 1874, nine Jewish deputies had been elected to the new Italian parliament convened after Italy's unification in 1870. By 1894, that number had risen to fifteen. Before the turn of the century, several Jews were elder statesmen in the royally nominated Italian senate, including Giuseppe Ottolenghi, Italy's first Jewish general, who became minister of war in 1902,[18] and Isaac Artom, Italy's first Jewish undersecretary of state for foreign affairs (from 1870 to 1876) and the first European Jew to serve in a high diplomatic post outside his home country, when he was named Italy's ambassador to Denmark.[19]

The most successful Italian Jewish politician was Luigi Luzzatti. Regarded as a financial genius, he was an economist and professor of constitutional law before he was elected to parliament in 1870. He had an illustrious political career, serving as minister of finance in three separate terms: 1891–1892, 1896–1898, and 1904–1906. During his career, he also served as minister of agriculture, minister of commerce and industry, minister of the interior, and secretary of state. In 1910, he became Italy's (and Europe's) first Jewish prime minister—twenty-six years before the first Jew would serve as prime minister of France.[20] A political moderate, Luzzatti did not share the harsh anticlericalism of many Italian politicians.

Eugenio Pacelli regarded Jewish politicians as social equals and as social and political friends. After World War I, and with the advent of Mussolini's Fascist government in the 1920s, the Italian parliament had twenty-four Jewish deputies and eleven Jewish senators.[21] But Pacelli saw anti-Semitism first not in Italy, but in Germany.

A Future Pope in Germany

In 1917, with World War I raging, Pacelli was named papal nuncio to Bavaria. Before he departed, the pope made him a bishop and then immediately elevated him to archbishop. The appointment to such a key country, combined with his speedy elevation (he was forty-one years old), offers further proof that Pacelli's contemporaries regarded him as "the outstanding papal diplomat" of his day.[22] As papal nuncio to the kingdom of Bavaria, he was for all practical purposes the ambassador to the entire German Empire, as there was no nuncio to Prussia.[23] It was Pacelli's responsibility to develop a new concordat with Bavaria and work to establish diplomatic relations with the rest of Germany.[24] To these ends, in June 1917, Pacelli went to Berlin to introduce himself to the German government, including Kaiser Wilhelm II.[25] For the remaining years of World War I, Pacelli lived in Munich working as a papal diplomat, devoted especially to the welfare of prisoners of war and civilian victims of the war.[26] As Benedict XV's (and subsequently Pope Pius XI's) papal ambassador to Bavaria, Pacelli remained in Germany for twelve years, finally returning to Rome in 1929 to prepare for his next assignment, as Vatican secretary of state.

One of the first Jews whom Pacelli met and befriended on his arrival in Munich in 1917 was another newcomer to the city, Bruno Walter, the brilliant conductor of the Munich Opera. Walter was a protégé of Gustav Mahler, and as Pacelli was an opera lover and devotee of Mahler, the two men had much in common. Later in life, Walter (like Mahler) converted to Catholicism, and one can safely assume that Pacelli was a spiritual mentor as well as a friend.

Incredibly, the Pacelli-Walter friendship is never mentioned by Pope Pius XII's critics—or even by his defenders, who have missed this significant portion of Pacelli's life. But in Walter's memoir, *Theme and Variations*, Walter reveals how Pacelli helped free his wrongly imprisoned Jewish friend and fellow musician Ossip Gabrilowitsch during an anti-Semitic pogrom in Bavaria. After fruitless attempts to secure his friend's release through the German authorities, Walter writes, "we called on Nuncio Pacelli, of whose noble personality and love of music, I knew a great deal. The nuncio listened to us with sympathy and promised us his help. Ossip was a free man the next day."[27]

Through the good offices of his friend, the "sympathetic and helpful Nuncio Eugenio Pacelli," Walter wrote, Ossip Gabrilowitsch was able to go with his family to Zurich and then America, where he became the founding musical director of the Detroit Symphony Orchestra. Ossip Gabrilowitsch is, amazingly, mentioned in no previous book on Pope Pius XII. But he is the first of many Jews whom Eugenio Pacelli would help rescue as a Vatican diplomat, secretary of state, and eventually as pope.

Also unmentioned in previous books is how Pacelli tried to prevent the assassination of Walter Rathenau, Germany's Jewish foreign minister, in June 1922. The assassination of Rathenau by anti-Semitic German extremists changed the course of German politics, contributing immeasurably to the decline and instability of the Weimar Republic.

Walter Rathenau was the son of a wealthy Jewish industrialist. He built his father's company into one of the world's largest industrial conglomerates.[28] Rathenau then had a long career in the German government as an economic adviser and later as director of the Raw Materials Supply Department for the German war ministry.

Joseph Wirth, a leading member of Germany's Catholic Center Party and a former foreign minister, became chancellor of the new Weimar government in May 1921,[29] and he named Rathenau minister of reconstruction. In February 1922, he appointed Rathenau to the post of foreign minister—an appointment greeted by open threats on Rathenau's life. In May 1922, Pacelli confided to Wirth that a priest had told him about a plot against Rathenau.[30] Wirth gave Rathenau's friend and biographer, Count Harry Kessler, this account of his conversation with Pacelli:

> Pacelli informed me simply and soberly in a few sentences that Rathenau's life was in danger. I could not question him: the interview took place in absolute privacy. . . . Then Rathenau himself was called in. I implored him . . . to give up his resistance to increased police protection . . . [but] he stubbornly refused. . . . With a calm such as I have never witnessed in my life . . . he stepped up to me, and putting both his hands on my shoulders, said: "Dear friend, it is nothing. Who would do me any harm?"[31]

He got his answer on June 24, when an assassin pulled up beside his open limousine—he had refused a police escort—and killed him with a quick succession of shots at close range.[32]

The Munich Letter

One of the prime exhibits Pacelli's critics often use against him is a letter he wrote in 1919. But their use of this letter is both false and misleading, and their subsequent portrayal of Pacelli's behavior in Munich has no basis in historical fact.

Munich, when Pacelli arrived, was a hotbed of political ferment owing to its branch of the militant, pro-Soviet German Communist Party led by Eugene Levine. The German Communist Party, which had been co-founded by Rosa Luxembourg, included many highly assimilated, secular Jews amongst its growing membership.

On November 7, 1918, Levine and Kurt Eisner (another secular Jew) led a revolution in Munich and established the short-lived Soviet Republic of Bavaria. Most foreign diplomats left Munich, but Pacelli remained in his post, becoming a target of Bolshevik hostility and violence. As John Cornwell acknowledges, on one occasion a car sprayed Pacelli's official residence with machine-gun fire. Another time, a small group of Bolsheviks broke into the nunciature, threatened Pacelli with revolvers, and tried to rob him. On yet another occasion, an angry mob of Bolshevik revolutionaries attacked Pacelli's car, screaming and threatening to turn the car over.[33] In the last two episodes, Pacelli faced the revolutionaries down, convincing them to abandon their assaults. The Bolsheviks, however, did manage to take over the royal palace in Munich, which became the headquarters of their government.

Diplomats were at risk under the new Bolshevik regime. Two embassies were invaded, and the Austro-Hungarian consul general was arrested without being charged and was held for several hours.[34] Concerned for the safety of people under his protection, Pacelli sent Monsignor Lorenzo Schioppa to meet with Eugene Levine, now chairman of the Council of People's Commissars in the new Bavarian Soviet Republic.[35] The meeting did not go well. Levine warned Monsignor Schioppa that if Pacelli did anything to oppose the Communist government, he would be expelled—the Communists "had no need" of the nunciature.[36]

Pacelli wrote a letter to Rome recounting Schioppa's meeting with Levine. In *Hitler's Pope*, John Cornwell translates a few carefully selected sentences from this letter, attempting to prove that Pacelli was anti-Semitic. The carefully selected passage, as translated by Cornwell (and accepted uncritically by his fellow critic of Pius XII, Daniel Jonah Goldhagen), is as follows:

> A gang of young women, of dubious appearance, Jews like all the rest of them, hanging around in all the offices with lecherous demeanor and suggestive smiles. The boss of this rabble was a young Russian woman, a Jew and a divorcee (while their chief) is a young man of about 30 or 35, also Russian and a Jew. Pale, dirty, with vacant eyes, hoarse voice, vulgar, repulsive, with a face that is both intelligent and sly.[37]

To Cornwell, these words (reflecting Schioppa's observations) prove that Pacelli was an anti-Semite. The use of the words "Jew" and "Jews," together with unflattering descriptions of the revolutionaries, Cornwell suggests, gives an impression of "stereotypical anti-Semitic contempt."[38]

In truth, however, as the scholar Ronald J. Rychlak has pointed out, this translation "is grossly tendentious," using pejorative words that imply anti-Semitism, instead of neutral ones that are more true to the original Italian. For example, the most damning phrase in the translation, "Jews like all the rest of them," is a distorted, unquestionably inaccurate translation of the Italian phrase *i primi*. The literal translation would be "the first ones" or "the ones just mentioned." Similarly, the Italian word *schiera* is translated by Cornwell as "gang" instead of "group," which would be both more accurate and appropriate. Furthermore, the Italian *gruppo* should likewise be translated as "group," not "rabble."[39]

Pacelli's letter, it should be noted, is six pages long, but Cornwell quotes only two paragraphs describing "a chaotic incident at a former royal palace taken over by revolutionaries."[40] While these paragraphs might lead one to assume that everyone at the palace is being described as a Jew, that is clearly not the case when the entire letter is read. Indeed, read in its entirety, the letter is not anti-Semitic. Rychlak, in my view, is correct in saying that the tone of anti-Semitism is introduced "deliberately... by Cornwell's dubious trans-lation."[41]

Many of Munich's Bolshevik leaders—like Kurt Eisner, Eugene Levine, and Gustav Landauer[42]—were Jews, and it is not anti-Semitic to note that fact. But they were secularized Jews, alienated from their Jewish religious faith and very often from their own families. Pacelli and Schioppa were well aware of this. They recognized that the Church was threatened by militantly atheistic Communism. They had no fear of or hatred for Judaism; their animosity was to Bolsheviks, not to Jews.[43] Pacelli, in relating Schioppa's description of what happened at the Munich palace, was not writing about persecuted Jews, but about the leaders of an oppressive revolutionary government that had threatened the Church.[44]

Pacelli and the Jews

More revealing than that 1919 Munich letter is Eugenio Pacelli's lifelong friendship with Guido Mendes, a Jewish friend from his school days who would become one of Rome's most distinguished physicians and professors of medicine. Mendes, a descendant of an illustrious line of Jewish physicians that traced its lineage back to Fernando Mendes, the court physician to King Charles II of England, was the scion of Roman Jewry's most eminent fami-lies, at whose home young Eugenio was a welcome guest.[45] Pacelli was the first pope to have, in his youth, shared a Sabbath dinner at a Jewish home and to have discussed Jewish theology on an informal basis with prominent mem-bers of Rome's Jewish community. Mendes remembered that Pacelli forged close friendships with his Jewish classmates at the prestigious Collegio Romano Gymnasium,[46] spoke favorably of Jewish faith and culture, and was a frequent guest at the Mendes home. He even borrowed books on Jewish philosophy and theology from the Mendes family library,[47] including *Apolo-getica* and *Dogmatica* by nineteenth-century Italian rabbi Elijah ben Hamozeg.[48] Mendes recalled Pacelli's desire to learn Hebrew so that he could read the Hebrew Scriptures.

It is curious that no previous book about Pius XII has mentioned Guido Mendes. This is especially striking in the case of John Cornwell, who devotes considerable space to what he alleges were anti-Semitic influences on Pacelli by one of his schoolteachers. According to Cornwell, the headmaster of Pacelli's school "was in the habit of making speeches from his high desk about the 'hard-heartedness' or obstinacy of the Jews."[49] The headmaster, we are told, "knew that the impressions gained by small children are never lost,"[50] and Pacelli, Cornwell claims, "was surely influenced in the classroom by the headmaster's remarks about Jewish obstinacy"[51] with "its potential to reinforce the conviction, amongst impressionable young schoolchildren, widely held by Catholics innocent of anti-Judaism, let alone anti-Semitism, that the Jews were responsible for their own misfortunes."[52] This view, says Cornwell, "was to encourage Catholic Church officials in the 1930s to look the other way as Nazi anti-Semitism raged in Germany."[53]

The problem with Cornwell's argument and analysis is that it is based on an erroneous translation of what Pacelli's Italian schoolmaster said about Jews. Cornwell relies on the English translation of a biography of Pius XII by Nazzareno Padellaro. The original Italian version of this work, however, reveals that Pacelli's schoolmaster warned his students "not against hard-headed Jews, but against block-head pupils."[54]

More important than mistranslations of what Pacelli's schoolmaster said is Pacelli's role in the drafting of Pope Benedict's 1916 condemnation of anti-Semitism.[55]

On December 30, 1915, the American Jewish Committee had appealed to Pope Benedict to use his moral and spiritual influence to condemn the anti-Semitic pogroms that had erupted throughout Poland, killing hundreds of Jews and wounding thousands. Written in response to the worsening plight of the Jews of Poland, the papal statement said, in part:

> The Supreme Pontiff ... as Head of the Catholic Church, which faithful to its divine doctrine and to its most glorious traditions, considers all men as brothers and teaches them to love one another, he never ceases to inculcate among individuals, as well as among peoples, the observance of the principles of natural law and to condemn everything

which violates them. This law must be observed and respected in the case of the children of Israel, as well as of all others, because it would not be conformable to justice or to religion itself to derogate from it solely on account of religious confessions. The Supreme Pontiff at this moment feels in his fatherly heart... the necessity for all men of remembering that they are brothers and that their salvation lies in the return to the law of love which is the law of the Gospel.[56]

Benedict XV's 1915 statement on behalf of the Jews of Poland is now generally recognized as the twentieth century's first important expression of papal opposition to anti-Semitism. The "dramatic appeal to His Holiness, Pope Benedict XV," noted the Jewish historian Abraham A. Neuman, "drew worldwide comment and approval and... aided in mitigating the postwar suffering of the Jews of Poland."[57] Jewish leaders regarded the pope, Cardinal Gasparri, and Pacelli as advocates, not enemies.

Pope Benedict's condemnation of anti-Semitism was published in the *New York Times* on April 17, 1916, under the headline: "Papal Bull Urges Equality for Jews." It was reprinted in *La Civiltà Cattolica* on April 28, 1916, and in the *Tablet* (London) on the following day.[58] And yet this remarkable and historic papal condemnation of anti-Semitism—one of the most important twentieth-century official Vatican documents on Jews and Judaism—is never mentioned by Cornwell, Goldhagen, or any of the other recent critics of Pius XII. Nor is it ever once mentioned or examined by other critics of the modern papacy such as David Kertzer.

Also ignored or forgotten by these papal critics is Cyrus Adler, the American Jewish leader who drafted the American Jewish Committee's appeal to Pope Benedict XV. For close to fifty years, Cyrus Adler occupied a unique place in American Jewish public life, serving as president of the American Jewish Historical Society, the Jewish Theological Seminary, and other major Jewish institutions.[59] On a visit to Rome in 1917, Adler met with Pacelli and was impressed by his "great knowledge and experience."[60] It was the first time that Pacelli, in his role as a Vatican diplomat, had met with a major American Jewish communal, and the meeting was an immense success. Adler thanked Pacelli for the Vatican's statement condemning anti-Semitism. Pacelli, he said, shared his opposition to religious persecution and discrimination. As Adler recounted in his memoirs, he and Pacelli were "striving for the same things"[61]—religious freedom and civil rights for all religious minorities, Catholics and Jews alike

The Adler-Pacelli dialogue initiated during World War I would continue in the years ahead. In 1936, when Pacelli (then Vatican secretary of state) visited the United States, he would once again meet with Adler and also privately with two other Jewish leaders, Judge Joseph Proskauer and Lewis S. Strauss, to discuss issues of mutual Catholic-Jewish concern.

Pacelli and Father Coughlin

Pacelli's 1936 visit to the United States was the first by a Vatican secretary of state. During his thirty-day tour, he traveled 16,000 miles by airplane. He visited countless Catholic colleges, seminaries, convent schools, monasteries, parish churches, and hospitals across the country. He walked to the top of the Empire State Building, watched the filming of a Hollywood movie, and saw the Grand Canyon, San Francisco's Fisherman's Wharf, and Niagara Falls. Dubbed "The Flying Cardinal" by the press, Pacelli was said "to have been moved by the aerial view of the country's mountains, plains, deserts, and forests."[62] He remembered his visit to America as leaving "on me the deepest impression of my whole life."[63] The highlight of his visit was his private meeting with President Franklin Roosevelt at the president's Hyde Park estate on November 6, 1936. Their meeting, two days after Roosevelt's reelection to a second term, was the first meeting between a Vatican secretary of state and an American president on American soil. Most important to American Jews during Pacelli's visit was his behind-the-scenes role in silencing the notorious anti-Semitic "radio priest" Father Charles Coughlin—a subject that came up in his meeting with President Roosevelt.

Roosevelt's objective in requesting this meeting was simple: He wanted Detroit's Father Coughlin and his anti–New Deal radio program off the air.

Coughlin's Sunday afternoon radio broadcasts, in which he often gave anti-Roosevelt diatribes laced with anti-Semitism, had become immensely popular throughout America, and had a nationwide audience of thirty million people.[64] The demagogic priest, who had supported Roosevelt in 1932, was now feared by FDR and his administration. Politically, Coughlin aligned himself with Democrat Huey Long, the Louisiana governor and rabid Roosevelt critic. By one Democrat's estimate, "an independent ticket put together by Long and Coughlin could steal away as many as six million votes from Roosevelt, assuring victory for the Republicans."[65] Even after Long's assassination in 1935, Roosevelt viewed Coughlin as a threat and thought that the priest's broadcasts, which attacked him as a "liar," as "anti-God," and as a Communist, would cost him thousands of Catholic votes, which made up a crucial part of the New Deal's base of support.[66]

The first objective of Roosevelt's meeting with Pacelli—the silencing of Father Coughlin—was immediately achieved. Although Pacelli never revealed what he had said to his fellow priest, Father Coughlin announced on November 8 that he was making his final broadcast.[67] Coughlin attributed his decision to Roosevelt's huge electoral victory—he had carried every state but Maine and Vermont in the 1936 election—rather than to a directive from Vatican officials. But years later, Coughlin admitted that he'd been "silenced." When Pacelli visited America, he "had conversations with our high government officials, which conversations could be regarded as a type of informal pact," Coughlin wrote in a 1954 letter. "Small as I was, it was necessary to silence my voice."[68]

Aside from stopping Coughlin, Pacelli achieved his own political objective: securing Roosevelt's promise to appoint an official United States representative to the Holy See. This diplomatic tradition had been broken in 1870 when the pope had lost his temporal power and, in the opinion of the U.S. government, the basis for official diplomatic ties between Washington and the Vatican.[69] Roosevelt assured Pacelli that he would appoint a personal envoy to the Holy See, a diplomat who would serve informally by presidential appointment and would not require Senate confirmation. Roosevelt made good on his promise in December 1939, when just before Christmas he appointed Myron C. Taylor as his personal representative to Pope Pius XII.[70] Taylor, reappointed by President Truman, served in the post until 1950.

A Cardinal Faces the Nazis

Pacelli's meeting with Jewish leaders in the United States and his silencing of Father Coughlin is especially important in the context of what happened three years before: the Holy See's 1933 concordat with Germany. This is yet another issue critics of Pius XII have used to attack him. Concordats, or diplomatic treaties, had been a major instrument of papal diplomacy for more than a century, at least since Pope Pius VII had entered into the controversial concordats with Napoleon Bonaparte in 1801.[71] Indeed, as Cambridge University historian Eamon Duffy has noted in his history of the modern papacy: "The nineteenth century was to be the age of concordats, as the popes bargained with the monarchies of Europe and beyond . . . with Bavaria and Sardinia in 1817, with Prussia and with the Upper Rhine Provinces in 1821, with Hanover in 1824, with Belgium in 1827, with Switzerland in 1828 and again in 1845, with the two Sicilies in 1834, and so on into the rest of the century, more than two dozen such agreements."[72] And the making of concordats would remain a hallmark of Vatican diplomacy in the early twentieth century as well: Between 1919 and 1933, approximately thirty-eight concordats, treaties, and agreements were signed by the Vatican with foreign states.[73]

The Reich Concordat, as the Vatican's 1933 concordat with Nazi Germany has come to be known, is considered one of the most controversial of the twentieth-century Vatican treaties.[74] Critics of the Reich Concordat claim that it silenced German Catholics who otherwise might have openly opposed Hitler and held him in check. On the contrary, as Jose Sanchez convincingly points out, the concordat was a pragmatic and morally defensible diplomatic measure to protect German Catholics and the relative freedom of the Catholic Church in Germany. "The Germans had proposed the concordat," Sanchez reminds us, and for the Vatican "to have rejected it out of hand would have been prejudicial to the rights of Catholics in Germany."[75] It was morally defensible from the vantage point of German Jews as well, as it had been signed in July 1933, well before Hitler had enacted any of his anti-Semitic legislation or decrees.

Contrary to what Pacelli's critics have alleged, the concordat did not precipitate the collapse of Germany's Catholic Center Party. The Vatican wanted the concordat "primarily to protect German Catholics in political situations in which their traditional protector, the Catholic Center Party, no longer existed."[76] The Catholic Center Party had been founded during the pontificate of Pius IX to defend Catholics at the time of Chancellor Otto von Bismarck's campaign against them: the *Kulturkampf*. The Center Party's influence, however, had steadily declined during the last years of the Weimar Republic. By 1933, it was hardly a political factor at all. In fact, on July 5, 1933, two weeks before the concordat was signed, the party membership decided to dissolve.[77] As James Carroll reluctantly concedes, "even before the concordat was formally signed, the Center Party had ceased to exist."[78]

Nonetheless, the Vatican's—and Pacelli's—alleged role in the demise of the Center Party is still hotly debated. Cornwell claims that Pacelli torpedoed the Center Party in order to forge an unholy alliance with Hitler, and that the Vatican hastened to sign the concordat as a means of consolidating its control over the Catholic Church in Germany, part of Pacelli's lifelong effort to centralize authority in the Vatican. Contrary to Cornwell's assertions, the concordat did not end the German Catholic clergy's opposition to the Nazi regime. In fact, in making this case, Cornwell and other critics virtually ignore the overwhelming evidence to the contrary supplied by the historical record.[79]

Critics of Pacelli argue that Hitler pressed for the concordat in order to give his regime moral legitimacy. As Sanchez points out, however, the concordat gave no moral approval to Hitler's regime. Indeed, when Hitler tried to make this claim, hailing the Vatican's "recognition of the present government," Pacelli specifically denied it in two articles in the Vatican newspaper *L'Osservatore Romano*. "All the Church had done was to negotiate a treaty, and nothing more," Pacelli argued.[80] The concordat did not imply a moral endorsement of Hitler or Nazism; that was not the purpose of such treaties. When Pius VII signed his concordat with Napoleon in July 1801, it conferred no moral endorsement; the pope, in fact, became one of Napoleon's leading opponents. Vatican diplomats negotiated agreements with constitutional monarchies and revolutionary dictatorships alike for more than a century, with the goal of trying to protect Catholic rights, not of endorsing tyrannical regimes.

On August 11, 1933, in a private conversation with Ivone Kirkpatrick, the British ambassador to the Vatican, Pacelli expressed his "disgust and abhorrence" at Hitler's reign of terror. "He had to choose [between] an agreement on [Nazi] lines," Kirkpatrick said, "and the virtual elimination of the Catholic Church in the Reich."[81] During the negotiations for the concordat, Hitler had arrested ninety-two Catholic priests, searched the premises of sixteen Catholic youth clubs, and closed down nine Catholic publications—all within the space of three weeks.[82] On August 19, 1933, Ambassador Kirkpatrick reported to the British Foreign Office: "His Eminence, the cardinal secretary of state, was extremely frank and made no effort to conceal his disgust at the proceedings of Hitler's government." He underlined an important point:

> The Vatican usually professes to see both sides of any political question, but on this occasion there was no word of palliation or excuse.... [Cardinal Pacelli] deplored the action of the German government at home, their persecution of Jews... their reign of terror to which the whole nation was subjected.... These reflections on the iniquity of Germany led the cardinal to explain apologetically how it was that he had signed a concordat with such people. A pistol, he said, had been pointed at his head and he had no alternative... not only that, but he was given no more than one week to make up his mind.... If the German government violated the concordat—and they were certain to do that—the Vatican would have at least a treaty on which to base a protest.[83]

Recent scholarship has confirmed the contention of Pius's defenders that in signing the Reich Concordat the Vatican did not intend to confer moral legitimacy upon the Nazi regime. Professor John Conway of the University of British Columbia, while not uncritical of Pius XII, says: "The conclusion of the Reich Concordat with the new Nazi regime in 1933 is . . . not to be seen as a sign of the Vatican's approval . . . but rather as an attempt to control [the regime's] unpredictable revolutionary fervor within some legally binding framework."[84] German historian Konrad Repgen agrees that for the Catholic Church, the concordat "was not an alliance but an instrument of defense."[85]

Surely there is another factor to consider when it comes to the myth of Hitler's pope. Why did Pacelli never meet with Hitler? Neither in negotiating the Reich Concordat nor as a papal nuncio nor as pope nor in any other role did Pacelli ever speak with or meet with Adolf Hitler. During Hitler's much-publicized visit to Rome in 1938, Pacelli (with Pope Pius XI) very publicly snubbed the Nazi by refusing to meet with him and by leaving Rome for the papal summer residence of Castel Gandolfo. No one accuses Neville Chamberlain of being "Hitler's prime minister" because of the Munich Agreement, and no one can fairly call Eugenio Pacelli "Hitler's pope" for trying to secure the rights of Catholics against a dangerous regime that he despised.

"Fairly" might be the key word. The malicious title *Hitler's Pope* is reinforced by the book's misleading jacket, which has a picture of Pacelli, then the papal nuncio in Berlin, leaving a reception given for the constitutionally elected president of Germany, Paul von Hindenburg, in 1927. This photograph, a favorite of those who wish to portray Pius XII in an unfavorable light, shows him dressed in formal diplomatic regalia (which could easily be confused with papal garments), being saluted by two German soldiers of the Weimar Republic as he leaves a German government building. The distinctive helmets of the German soldiers could easily mislead viewers to think these soldiers of the Weimar Republic were soldiers of the Third Reich. The use of this photograph under the title *Hitler's Pope* gives the impression that Pope Pius XII has just left a friendly diplomatic meeting with Adolf Hitler. "The casual reader," suggests historian Philip Jenkins, "is meant to infer that

Pacelli is emerging from a cozy tete-a-tete with Hitler—perhaps they have been chatting about plans for a new extermination camp?"[86] "Perhaps photographs do not lie," concludes Jenkins, "but this particular book cover—offered in the context it was, and under the title *Hitler's Pope*—comes close."[87] Making matters even worse is the caption inside the British edition of the book, which reads: "Cover photograph shows Cardinal Pacelli, the future Pope Pius XII, leaving the presidential palace in Berlin, March 1939," which is patently false.

The American edition of *Hitler's Pope* does not bear the faulty caption, but it does use the same photograph, though with an apparently intentional blurring effect: Pacelli is in focus, but the picture of the soldier to his left is badly blurred, perhaps to make the uniform of the German soldier even more ambiguous. Because the British cover photo is not blurred, and because Pacelli is in focus on the cover of the American edition, some have concluded that "Viking Press intentionally altered the photograph to support the author's thesis."[88] The selection of the photo was no publisher's error; Cornwell himself admitted in an interview that he personally approved the photograph that Viking Press selected.

Pius XI's "Jew-Loving" Cardinal

It is especially ironic that Pacelli should be slandered with the title of "Hitler's pope" when the Nazis considered him a "Jew-loving" cardinal. In fact, from 1933 to 1945, both before and after he became pope, Pacelli was almost universally recognized, especially by the Nazis themselves, as an unrelenting opponent of the Nazi regime. Pacelli's criticism of National Socialism predated Hitler's regime. As early as November 14, 1923, just five days after Adolf Hitler's failed attempt to take over the local government in Munich, Pacelli wrote to Cardinal Gasparri denouncing Hitler's National Socialist movement and favorably noting Munich archbishop Michael Faulhaber's vocal defense of Bavaria's Jews.[89] Of the forty-four speeches Pacelli gave in Germany as papal nuncio between 1917 and 1929, forty denounced some aspect of the emerging Nazi ideology.

On April 4, 1933, then Vatican secretary of state Cardinal Pacelli told the nuncio in Berlin to warn Hitler's regime against persecuting Germany's Jews.[90] Pacelli's letter was sent in response to appeals from Jewish leaders. These Jewish leaders, writes Pacelli, "have appealed to the Holy Father to ask for his intervention against the danger of anti-Semitic excesses in Germany... the Holy Father asks your Excellency" (papal nuncio Monsignor Cesare Orsenigo in Berlin) to become actively "involved" on behalf of the Jews of Germany.[91] This letter is another document never cited by Pacelli's critics.

In 1962, Father Robert Leiber, who served as an assistant to Pacelli both before and after he became pope, wrote an article on the background of *Mit brennender Sorge* (Pius XI's anti-Nazi papal encyclical of 1937, which Pacelli had helped draft). "It is significant," Lieber wrote, "that the *first* initiative of the Holy See toward the government in Berlin concerned the Jews. As early as April 4, 1933, ten days after the Enabling Act, the Apostolic Nuncio in Berlin [Orsenigo] was ordered by Pius XI and Cardinal Pacelli to intervene with the government of the Reich on behalf of the Jews and point out all the dangers involved in an anti-Semitic policy."[92] Past skeptics have questioned Lieber's testimony because he was a close friend of Pacelli, but the authenticity of the Pacelli letter, which has been made available to researchers, is now beyond question. It has been confirmed by historians, archivists, and Vatican officials.[93] The timing of Pacelli's letter is important, because on April 1, 1933, the newly formed Hitler government announced a major boycott of Jewish businesses. Three days later, Pacelli sent his orders to the papal nuncio in Berlin. Pacelli's critics, typically, ignore the letter.

They also ignore the fact that throughout the 1930s, the Nazi press lampooned Pacelli as Pius XI's "Jew-loving" cardinal because of the more than fifty-five protests he sent the Nazi regime while serving as Vatican secretary of state. His outspoken opposition to Nazism led Hitler's regime to lobby against him as a successor to Pius XI.[94] The day after his election, the Berlin *Morgenpost* lamented: "The election of Cardinal Pacelli is not accepted with favor in Germany because he was always opposed to Nazism and practically determined the [pro-Jewish] policies of the Vatican under his predecessor."[95]

In March 1935, in an open letter to the bishop of Cologne, Pacelli called the Nazis "false prophets with the pride of Lucifer."[96] That same year, speaking to an enormous crowd of pilgrims at Lourdes, he assailed ideologies "possessed by the superstition of race and blood."[97] At the Cathedral of Notre Dame two years later, he named Germany "that noble and powerful nation whom bad shepherds would lead astray into an ideology of race."[98] The Nazis were "diabolical," he told friends. Hitler "is completely obsessed," he said to his longtime secretary, Sister Pascalina. "All that is not of use to him, he destroys; . . . this man is capable of trampling on corpses."[99] Meeting with the heroic anti-Nazi Dietrich von Hildebrand, he declared: "There can be no possible reconciliation" between Christianity and Nazi racism; they were like "fire and water."[100]

Pacelli also expressed his strong anti-Nazi views in private talks with two U.S. diplomats in 1937 and 1938. Alfred W. Klieforth, the U.S. consul general in Berlin, has described a memorable three-hour meeting that he had with the future pope in 1937, during which it became clear that Pacelli "regarded Hitler not only as an untrustworthy scoundrel but as a fundamentally wicked person."[101] In an official report that he later filed with the State Department about his 1937 meeting with Pacelli, Klieforth further noted that the cardinal "did not believe Hitler capable of moderation, in spite of appearances, and "that he opposed unalterably every compromise with National Socialism."[102]

Pacelli was friends with Joseph P. Kennedy. In a private meeting at the Vatican in April 1938, Pacelli gave Kennedy—who was then serving as the United States ambassador to Great Britain—a copy of a confidential memorandum. The memorandum was written by Pacelli and discussed in detail why he opposed National Socialism (one of the reasons was because it attacked "the fundamental principle of the freedom of the practice of religion"). Most of the memorandum, which Pacelli discussed with Kennedy, was devoted to denouncing the Austrian bishops who had issued a statement supporting the Nazi occupation of Austria. Pacelli believed the Austrian bishops had been coerced, and told Kennedy that the Church felt "at times powerless and isolated in its daily struggle against all sorts of political excesses from the Bolsheviks to the new pagans arising from the 'Aryan' generations." Pacelli told Kennedy that "evidence of good faith" by the Nazi regime was "completely lacking," and that "the possibility of an agreement" or a "political compromise" with the Nazis should be "out of the question."[103] Pacelli wrote that the memorandum reflected his "personal views," but that the ambassador had his permission to share them with "your friend at home," which, presumably, meant President Roosevelt.[104]

These contacts between Pacelli and American diplomats were recently brought to light by Charles R. Gallagher, S.J., Ph.D., a historian at St. Louis University, in an article in the September 1, 2003, issue of the Jesuit journal *America*. Scholars who have seen these two historically significant diplomatic documents, which were unknown to earlier papal critics, say that "they bolster the view [of Pacelli's defenders] that the man who became Pope Pius XII was *not* a Nazi sympathizer," and was in fact convinced that the Nazis were a threat to the Catholic Church and the stability of Europe.[105] The Reverend Gerald P. Fogarty, a professor of history at the University of Virginia and an authority on Vatican diplomacy, has stated that these documents "make clear that from the 1930s, Pacelli was opposed to National Socialism." Other historians share Fogarty's assessment, believing that these diplomatic documents conclusively "indicate that while serving as a Vatican diplomat" during the 1930s, "the future pope expressed strong antipathy to the Nazi regime in private communication with American officials."[106]

During his last two years as Vatican secretary of state, Pacelli's "strong antipathy to the Nazi regime" was expressed in other ways as well. In 1938, Pope Pius XI told a group of Belgian pilgrims that "it is impossible for a Christian to take part in anti-Semitism. Anti-Semitism is inadmissible; spiritually, we are all Semites." Secretary of State Pacelli had not only endorsed these words, he publicly repeated them.[107] Jacques Maritain, perhaps the preeminent Catholic philosopher of the era, paid tribute to Pius XI and Pacelli the following year when he wrote: "Spiritually we are all Semites—no stronger word has been uttered by a Christian against anti-Semitism, and this Christian was the successor to the Apostle Peter."[108]

In 1937, of course, the successor to the Apostle Peter issued the encyclical *Mit brennender Sorge*, a condemnation of National Socialism drafted by Pacelli that stated, in part:

> Whoever exalts race, or the people, or the State, or a particular form of State, or the depositories of power, or any other fundamental value of the human community—however necessary and honorable be their function in worldly things—whoever raises these notions above their standard value and divinizes them to an idolatrous level, distorts and perverts an order of the world planned and created by God; he is far from the true faith in God and from the concept of life which that faith upholds.

In 1939, Pacelli's confrontation with Nazi Germany became even more dramatic when he ascended to Saint Peter's chair in Rome.

CHAPTER FOUR

A RIGHTEOUS GENTILE: POPE PIUS XII AND THE HOLOCAUST

P IUS XI HAD LONG THOUGHT THAT Cardinal Pacelli would be an excellent pope,[1] and once said that if he were sure Pacelli would be elected as his successor, he would retire.[2] Pacelli was elected in March 1939, just months before the beginning of World War II.[3] His experience as a skilled and seasoned diplomat made him, in Father Richard P. McBrien's words, "the inevitable candidate."[4]

The Election of Pope Pius XII

The Vatican debate over whether the Church needed a "spiritual" or "diplomatic" pope was settled in favor of "the most experienced and brilliant diplomat available."[5] Pacelli was known for his "cool and critical thinking" and as "a veritable prince of diplomats."[6] He had met with Franklin Roosevelt and Winston Churchill, and was better known among the world's leading politicians and statesmen than previous men who had been elevated to the papacy.[7] He was so obvious a choice that the College of Cardinals deliberated only one day, even though he was the first Vatican secretary of state elected pope since 1667.[8]

He was a pope of "firsts." He was the first native Roman and citizen of Rome to claim the throne of Saint Peter in two hundred years.[9] He was the first pope to have his initial papal blessing broadcast over radio; the first to have the entire coronation ceremony captured on film; and he would later be the first pope to use television as "a means of pastoral communication."[10] Almost every nation of the world sent delegates to the coronation. The American ambassador to Great Britain, Joseph P. Kennedy, accompanied by his son John F. Kennedy, was the first official representative of the United States to attend a coronation of a pope, and his son was the first future U.S. president to be present at a papal coronation.

Germany alone among the nations of Europe did not send a representative to Eugenio Pacelli's coronation as Pope Pius XII on March 12, 1939. Indeed, Pius XII's election had been enthusiastically welcomed by every country in Europe and the Western Hemisphere—except for Nazi Germany. The morning after his election, the *Frankfurter Zeitung* wrote: "Many of [Pacelli's] speeches have made it clear that he does not fully grasp the political and ideological motives which have begun their victorious march in Germany."[11]

Pacelli was elected pope on March 2, 1939. According to the March 4, 1939, entry in Joseph Goebbels's diary, Hitler considered abrogating the 1933 concordat in light of Pacelli's election as pope.[12] The Nazi leadership believed that as pope, Pacelli would continue the "pro-Jewish" policy he had followed as Vatican secretary of state.

The Pope Saves Jewish Scholars

On July 15, 1938, the Fascist government of Benito Mussolini published its "Manifesto of the Race," in which Italian Jews were referred to as unassimilable aliens.[13] The manifesto was followed by a spate of anti-Jewish laws and regulations that, in the words of Cecil Roth, "reduced the position of the Italian Jews to that of pariahs."[14] The first of these laws forbade Jews to study or teach in any Italian school or university and banned from university libraries books written by Jewish authors.

After the enactment of these anti-Semitic regulations, hundreds of Jews were dismissed from their jobs in government, the universities, and other professions. The decree forbidding the employment of Jews in the nation's universities hit Italian Jewry particularly hard, because Jews had made notable contributions to Italian intellectual life for decades. In 1930, 8 percent of all university professors were Jewish.[15] A preliminary list of nearly one hundred dismissed Jewish university professors, compiled soon after the new racial laws were first enacted, included some of the most honored names in Italian scholarship.[16]

The newly elevated Pope Pius XII responded to the anti-Semitic decree by appointing several displaced Jewish scholars to posts in the Vatican Library. Pius XII's appointment of the eminent Jewish cartographer Roberto Almagia was especially noteworthy. Professor Almagia was a leader in Italian geographical scholarship, noted in particular for his seminal monograph on the Holy Land's topography and geology. The Italian foreign ministry had even assigned him to write a history of Italian explorers.[17] A day after Almagia was dismissed from his position—which he had held since 1915—at the University of Rome, he was named director of the geography section of the Vatican Library and appointed to restore and catalogue its maps.[18]

After Mussolini introduced his anti-Semitic legislation, all Almagia's contributions to Italian scholarship and public life counted for nothing—except to the Vatican. Almagia's books disappeared from Italian libraries and classrooms. Deprived of his university chair and his membership in the Italian Royal Academy, Almagia was faced with a choice between exile from Italy or a life of financial woe.[19] But the personal intervention of Pius XII saved him from this fate. The pope commissioned him to prepare an artistic reproduction of a map of the Danubian States originally drawn in 1546. The papal nuncio in Berlin presented a copy of Almagia's map to Nazi foreign minister

Joachim von Ribbentrop in February 1940 on behalf of the pope. On January 25, 1940, Pius received Almagia in a private audience, thanking the Jewish scholar in writing for "his splendid work."[20]

Another victim of Mussolini's anti-Semitic legislation was Professor Giorgio del Vecchio, a noted authority on civil and international law. He, too, through the personal intervention of Pius, was employed by the Vatican. Descended from one of Italy's oldest and most venerable Jewish families, del Vecchio had been the first rector of the University of Rome under the Fascist regime and for fifteen years had been the popular dean of the university's law faculty. A member of the Fascist Party since its founding, he had been one of Mussolini's strongest supporters. Nonetheless, with the adoption of Italy's anti-Semitic laws, del Vecchio was immediately ousted from his university post—and hired by Pius XII, who appointed him to the Vatican Library staff and made him a member of the Pontifical Academy of Sciences, entrusting him with research in the field of Roman jurisprudence.[21]

Another prominent Jewish scholar employed by Pius XII at the Vatican Library was Professor Giorgio Levi della Vida, one of the world's greatest Jewish authorities on Islam. After his dismissal from the University of Rome, he was given a job cataloguing Arabic manuscripts in the Vatican Library.[22]

Both Pius XI and Pius XII valued science and scholarship above political differences. Pope Pius XII showed his determination to uphold this difficult doctrine when he made Professor Tullio Levi-Civita, Italy's greatest living physicist, a member of the Pontifical Academy of Sciences, after Mussolini barred Jews from the newly created Fascist Academy of Sciences.[23] Levi-Civita, at Pius XII's personal invitation, reported over Vatican Radio about the latest developments in the field of physics. It was, as one contemporary Jewish observer noted, "the first time in history that a Jew broadcast from the center of Catholicism."[24]

Beginning in November 1938, Eugenio Pacelli, first as Vatican secretary of state and then as pope, personally intervened to secure the necessary immigration documents for other displaced Jewish professors to escape Fascist Italy and to emigrate to Palestine and America. For instance, with the pope's active support, Vito Volterra, one of twentieth-century Italy's preeminent mathematicians and physicists (who had found temporary employment on the Vatican Library staff), escaped Italy. He emigrated to America and became a professor at the University of Pennsylvania.

Pacelli also intervened on behalf of his childhood friend Guido Mendes. In November 1938, when Mendes lost his professorship at the University of Rome Medical School, Pacelli arranged for a Catholic university in South America to offer him an important post.[25] When Mendes let it be known that he wanted to move with his family to Palestine, Pacelli helped the Mendes family escape to Switzerland, where they waited for the necessary immigration certificates.[26] In 1939, Pacelli's Vatican secretary of state, Giovanni Battista Montini, obtained immigration certificates for the Mendes family, even though it was outside the regular immigration quotas.[27] Guido Mendes eventually established a successful medical practice in the Tel Aviv suburb of Ramat Gan.

The "Not Silent" Pope

Upon ascending to the papacy, Pius XII was a persistent, vocal critic of Hitler and Nazism. His first encyclical, *Summi Pontificatus*, begged for peace, expressly rejected Nazism, and expressly mentioned Jews—all of which his modern critics have missed. Released just weeks after the outbreak of World War II, *Summi Pontificatus* states that in the Catholic Church there is "neither Gentile nor Jew, circumcision nor uncircumcision"—a clear rejection of Nazi anti-Semitism. It was widely recognized as such, especially within Nazi Germany. "This encyclical," wrote Heinrich Mueller, head of the Gestapo, "is directed exclusively against Germany, both in ideology and in regard to the German–Polish dispute. How dangerous it is for our foreign relations as well as our domestic affairs is beyond dispute."[28] The *New York Times* greeted the encyclical with a front-page headline on October 28, 1939: "Pope Condemns Dictators, Treaty Violators, Racism." Allied aircraft dropped 88,000 copies of the encyclical over parts of Germany in an effort to raise anti-Nazi sentiment.[29]

Throughout World War II, Pius XII spoke out on behalf of Europe's Jews. When he learned of Nazi atrocities in Poland, he urged the bishops of Europe to do all they could to save the Jews and other victims of Nazi persecution. On January 19, 1940, at the pope's instruction, Vatican Radio and the Vatican newspaper *L'Osservatore Romano* revealed to the world "the dreadful cruelties of uncivilized tyranny" the Nazis were inflicting on Jewish and Catholic Poles.[30] The following week, the *Jewish Advocate* of Boston reported on the Vatican radio broadcast, praising its "outspoken denunciation of German atrocities in Nazi Poland, declaring they affronted the moral conscience of mankind."[31] The *New York Times* editorialized: "Now the Vatican has spoken, with authority that cannot be questioned, and has confirmed the worst intimations of terror which have come out of the Polish darkness."[32] In England, the *Manchester Guardian* hailed Vatican Radio as "tortured Poland's most powerful advocate."[33]

In March 1940, Pius granted an audience to Joachim von Ribbentrop, the German foreign minister and the only high-ranking Nazi to visit the Vatican. The German's understanding of Pius's position was clear: Ribbentrop chastised the pope for siding with the Allies, whereupon Pius began reading from a long list of German atrocities. "In the burning words he spoke to Herr Ribbentrop," the *New York Times* reported on March 14, Pius "came to the defense of Jews in Germany and Poland."[34]

In his 1940 Easter homily, Pius XII condemned the Nazi bombardment of defenseless citizens. On May 11, 1940, he publicly condemned the Nazi invasions of Belgium, Holland, and Luxembourg, and lamented "a world poisoned by lies and disloyalty and wounded by excesses of violence." In June 1942, he spoke out against the mass deportation of Jews from Nazi-occupied France. Moreover, he ordered the papal nuncio in Paris to protest to Vichy France's chief of state, Marshal Henri Petain, against "the inhuman arrests and deportations of Jews from the French occupied zone to Silesia and parts of Russia."[35]

The *London Times* of October 1, 1942, explicitly praised Pius for his condemnation of Nazism and his public support for the Jewish victims of Nazi terror. "A study of the words which Pope Pius XII has addressed since his accession," noted the *Times*, "leaves no room for doubt. He condemns the worship of force and its concrete manifestations in the suppression of national liberties and in the persecution of the Jewish race."[36]

Pius XII's Christmas addresses of 1941 and 1942, broadcast over Vatican Radio to millions throughout the world, addressed the same themes. Critics of Pius argue that the pope's 1941 Christmas address was not forceful enough. But contemporary observers thought it was quite explicit. Indeed, the editors of the *New York Times* wrote:

> The voice of Pius XII is a lonely voice in the silence and darkness enveloping Europe this Christmas.... In calling for a "real new order" based on "liberty, justice and love"... the pope put himself squarely against Hitlerism. Recognizing that there is no road open to agreement between belligerents "whose reciprocal war aims and programs seem to be irreconcilable," Pius XII left no doubt that the Nazi aims are also irreconcilable with his own conception of a Christian peace.[37]

To listeners in 1941, the pope's Christmas message was understood as a clear condemnation of Nazi attacks on Europe's Jews.

So, too, was the pope's Christmas message of December 24, 1942, in which he expressed his passionate concern "for those hundreds of thousands who, without any fault of their own, sometimes only by reason of their nationality or race, are marked down for death or progressive extinction." This statement was widely understood to be a very public denunciation of the Nazi extermination of the Jews. Indeed, the Nazis themselves interpreted this as a clear condemnation of Nazism, and as a plea on behalf of Europe's Jews: "His speech is one long attack on everything we stand for," stated an internal Nazi analysis of the speech prepared by the German foreign office. "He is clearly speaking on behalf of the Jews... he is virtually accusing the German people of injustice toward the Jews, and makes himself the mouthpiece of the Jewish war criminals."[38]

"Both Mussolini and Ambassador Ribbentrop were angered by this speech," notes Professor Eamon Duffy of Cambridge University in his recent history of the modern papacy, "and Germany considered that the pope had abandoned any pretence of neutrality. They felt that Pius had unequivocally condemned Nazi action against the Jews."[39] Critics of Pius minimize the significance of the pope's 1942 Christmas message and fail to note the Nazi reaction to it.

At the time, however, there was speculation that the pope's condemnation of the Nazis would lead to retaliatory violence. Even the virulent papal critic Rolf Hochhuth admitted that Hitler considered invading the Vatican.[40] And there was ample historical precedent for that possibility. Napoleon had besieged the Vatican in 1809, captured Pius VII at bayonet point, forcibly removed him from Rome, and for five years (until Napoleon's defeat and abdication in 1814) was a prisoner "placed in virtual solitary confinement," guarded by almost 1,400 soldiers.[41] This happened despite a concordat between Pope Pius VII and Napoleon in 1801. But the pope had opposed Napoleon's blockade of England in 1808 and had excommunicated the French dictator the following year, causing Napoleon's quest for revenge.

So, too, in November 1848, had Pope Pius IX fled Rome for his life after revolutionary followers of Giuseppe Mazzini assassinated his chancellor. Besieged by the revolutionaries in Vatican City, he remained in exile for fourteen months until after the restoration of papal rule in Rome.[42] Leo XIII (1878–1903) had also been driven into temporary exile during the late nineteenth century.

Despite such precedents, Pius XII was "ready to let himself be deported to a concentration camp, rather than do anything against his conscience," Mussolini's foreign minister railed. In fact, Hitler spoke publicly of wanting to enter the Vatican and "pack up that whole whoring rabble,"[43] and Pius was aware of the various Nazi plans to kidnap him.

It has long been known that at one point Hitler planned to kidnap the pope and imprison him in Upper Saxony. We have minutes from a meeting on July 26, 1943, at which Hitler openly discussed invading the Vatican. Ernst von Weizsacker, the German ambassador to the Vatican, wrote that he heard of Hitler's plan to kidnap Pius XII and that he regularly warned Vatican officials against provoking Berlin. The Nazi ambassador to Italy, Rudolf Rahn, also described one of Hitler's kidnapping plots and his attempts, along with those of other Nazi diplomats, to prevent it. So, too, General Karl Otto Wolff, the SS chief in Italy at the end of the war, testified to having received orders from Hitler in 1943 to "occupy as soon as possible the Vatican and Vatican City, secure the archives and the art treasures, which have a unique value, and transfer the pope, together with the Curia, for their protection, so that they cannot fall into the hands of the Allies and exert a political influence." Wolff managed to talk Hitler out of the plan in December 1943.[44]

Excommunicating Hitler

Pius XII's critics often point to his "failure" to excommunicate Hitler and other Nazi Party leaders. Indeed, even many of the pope's defenders believe he should have done this. Such sentiments notwithstanding, the weight of evidence suggests that excommunicating Hitler would have been a purely symbolic gesture—and would likely have led to more persecution, not less.

Hitler, Heinrich Himmler, and other Nazi leaders were baptized—if apostate—Catholics never formally excommunicated by papal decree. But history shows that excommunication "is a papal weapon which has to be used with considerable care."[45] It has been at least temporarily effective on a few occasions, as when Pope Gregory VII's pronouncement brought Henry IV to Canossa in 1077. More often, however, papal excommunication has not resulted in what the papacy intended. In 1324, for example, Pope John XXII excommunicated the elected emperor of Germany, Louis IV of Bavaria. The pope called on princes and nobles to rebel against Louis. "In a few words," notes Pinchas Lapide, "he did everything that Hochhuth would have wanted Pius XII to have done against Hitler." The unintended result was that Louis marched on Rome with an army and crowned himself Holy Roman Emperor. An anti-pope was elected, and John XXII died in exile. That happened almost seven hundred years ago, when—as all historians agree—the prestige and power of the papacy were ten times greater than they were in Pius XII's day. Moreover, Louis IV of Bavaria had only a fraction of the immense military power that Hitler commanded.[46]

Pius V's excommunication of Queen Elizabeth I of England in 1570 was disastrous for the Catholic Church. It resulted in the final secession of the Anglican Church, the execution of hundreds of English Catholics, and the consolidation of English power under the monarchy, as the vast majority of English Catholics remained faithful to their queen.

Excommunication was equally ineffective against Napoleon; it led only to the pope's exile. Nor did papal excommunication have any effect on Napoleon's *Grande Armee*, whose Catholic soldiers cheerfully accompanied their emperor into battle after battle.[47] It was a lesson of history that papal excommunication of a ruler could backfire, inspiring people to rally round their national leader.

Moreover, many at the time feared that papal excommunication of Hitler would incite the Führer to lash out at the Church and the Jews in even more violent ways. Aryeh Leon Kubovy, an official of the World Jewish Congress during the Holocaust era, asked Don Luigi Sturzo, the founder of the Christian Democratic Movement in wartime Italy, why the Vatican did not excommunicate Hitler. Sturzo replied that the papacy feared that if Hitler felt threatened by excommunication, he would have killed even more Jews than he did.[48] Writers and scholars familiar with Hitler's psychology share Sturzo's fear, believing that any provocation by the pope would have resulted in violent retaliation, the loss of many more Jewish lives (especially those then under the protection of the Church), and an intensification of Nazi persecution of Catholics. This is a compelling argument supported by the testimony of Jewish Holocaust survivors such as Marcus Melchior, the former chief rabbi of Denmark, who argued that "it is an error to think that Pius XII could have had any influence whatsoever on the brain of a madman. If the pope had spoken out, Hitler would probably have massacred more than six million Jews and perhaps ten times ten million Catholics, if he had the power to do so."[49] Robert M. W. Kempner called upon his experience as a prosecutor at the Nuremberg trials. He said, "every propaganda move of the Catholic Church against Hitler's Reich would have been not only 'provoking suicide,'... but would have hastened the execution of still more Jews and priests."[50]

An example frequently cited by defenders of the Vatican is the public protest of Dutch bishops in July 1942 against the deportation of Jews from the Netherlands. The Dutch bishops, who credited Pope Pius XII for their inspiration, distributed a pastoral letter that was read in every Catholic church in the Netherlands denouncing "the unmerciful and unjust treatment meted out to Jews by those in power in our country." In no other Nazi-occupied country did local Catholic bishops more furiously resist Nazism than in Holland. But their well-intentioned pastoral letter backfired. As Pinchas Lapide notes: "The saddest and most thought-provoking conclusion is that whilst the Catholic clergy in Holland protested more loudly, expressly, and frequently against Jewish persecutions than the religious hierarchy of any other Nazi-occupied country, more Jews—some 110,000, or 79 percent of the total— were deported from Holland to death camps."[51] The protest of the Dutch bishops thus provoked the most savage of Nazi reprisals. The vast majority of Holland's Jews—and the highest percentage of Jews of any Nazi-occupied nation in western Europe—were deported and killed.

When Pius XII's revisionist critics attack the pope's "silence," they do so while ignoring the fact that Jewish leaders and Catholic bishops in Nazi-occupied countries strongly advised him not to incite the Nazis to further atrocities. When Clemens August von Galen, the bishop of Munster, wanted to speak out against the persecution of the Jews in Germany, the Jewish leaders of his diocese begged him not to, fearing that even greater persecution would result. Pinchas Lapide quotes an Italian Jew helped by the Vatican who escaped the Nazi deportation of Rome's Jews in October 1943. He stated unequivocally twenty years later: "None of us wanted the pope to speak out openly. We were all fugitives and we did not want to be pointed out as such. The Gestapo would only have increased and intensified its inquisition.... It was much better the pope kept silent. We all felt the same, and today we still believe that." Bishop Jean Bernard of Luxembourg, an inmate of Dachau from February

1941 to August 1942, notified the Vatican that "whenever protests were made, treatment of prisoners worsened immediately."[52]

The pope had to weigh his words so that he did not jeopardize the lives of the thousands of Jews hidden in the Vatican; in Rome's many churches, convents, and monasteries; and in Catholic churches and institutions throughout Italy. He had to speak without endangering the lives of Catholic clergy, religious, and laypeople who were trying to save Jews. And, of course, he had to speak without provoking the Nazis into sending even more priests to concentration camps. In Poland, for instance, one-fifth of all priests were sent to Auschwitz or other concentration camps and killed.[53]

Many Italian Jewish Holocaust survivors have agreed with Michael Tagliacozzo, a Roman Jew hidden for several months at the Seminario Romano, the pontifical seminary, near the Basilica of San Giovanni in Laterano. A clearer public denunciation of the Nazis, they believe, would have jeopardized the lives of the priests and Catholic laity who were sheltering and protecting them. Indeed, as even Susan Zuccotti admits in her recent critique of Pius XII, "the pope's inclination to silence might well have been influenced by a concern for Jews in hiding and for their Catholic protectors."[54]

One might ask what could have been worse than the mass murder of six million Jews. The answer is the slaughter of hundreds of thousands more. Pope Pius XII knew that his words would not stop the Holocaust. He measured his words so as not to risk the lives he could save. And, as we'll see, when he thought his words might have influence—as with the governments of Admiral Miklós Horthy in Hungary and President Jozef Tiso (himself a priest) in Slovakia—he used them mightily in stern protests that saved more lives.

The Nazi Occupation of Rome

From a Jewish perspective, Pinchas Lapide is one of the best sources for documenting the extraordinary relief and rescue efforts conducted by Pius XII and his diplomats during the Holocaust. Through his country-by-country analysis of papal efforts to rescue Jews throughout Nazi Europe, Lapide proves that the efforts of the Catholic Church saved more Jews than all other churches, religious institutions, and rescue organizations combined.

While approximately 80 percent of the Jews in Europe perished during World War II, 85 percent of Italy's 40,000 Jews were saved.[55] The Nazi deportations of Italy's Jews began on October 16, 1943, just over five weeks after the German army occupied Rome and entrusted internal security matters to the SS. The infamous Nazi roundup of Rome's Jews has been most vividly described by Susan Zuccotti:

> At 5:30 a.m. on the rainy morning of Saturday, October 16, 1943, German SS police in Rome launched what would be the greatest single roundup of Jews in occupied Italy. In thousands of moldering apartment buildings in Rome's former ghetto and in hundreds of others scattered throughout the Holy City, police pounded on doors and roused sleeping people from their beds. Waiting trucks sped victims, often still in their night clothes, to a temporary detention center at the Italian Military College, only six hundred feet from the Vatican. Within nine hours, 1,259 Jews from a community of about 12,000 had been arrested and confined. These included 896 women and children.
>
> Two days later, before dawn on Monday, October 18, trucks again gathered up the arrested Jews and carried them to the cargo-loading platform of Rome's Tiburtina Station. As the prisoners arrived, guards quickly packed them into about twenty freight cars and bolted the doors from outside. Fifty to sixty people in each car waited in darkness, stifling heat, and terror until the loading process was completed. At about 2:00 p.m, the dreadful journey began.[56]

Thus, within forty-eight hours of the October 16 Nazi roundup, more than 1,200 Roman Jews were packed into a Nazi "death train" and deported to Auschwitz, where they were murdered a week later. From October 1943 until the Allied capture of the city in June 1944, the deportations continued, with 2,091 Roman Jews eventually meeting their deaths in Nazi concentration camps.

What Pius XII did or did not do on behalf of Roman Jews during and immediately after the October 1943 roundup, and throughout the Nazi occupation of the city that followed, remains a source of contention. There has been a tendency among Holocaust scholars to uncritically accept the argument of Pius's detractors that the pope knew beforehand of the impending Nazi roundup of Rome's Jews. Pius had the opportunity and obligation, Zuccotti and others argue, to inform the Jews and give them time to escape. But this line of indictment is drawn from Robert Katz's book *Black Sabbath*, a highly polemical work published in 1969. Katz was the first to argue—without reliable documentation—that Pius XII had foreknowledge of the October 16 roundup. Katz cites German diplomat Eitel Mollhausen, who passed information about the planned roundup to Germany's Vatican ambassador Ernst von Weizsacker. Mollhausen assumed that Weizsacker would inform the Vatican. But no historian has ever validated this assumption.

In fact, in his memoirs and throughout his life, Weizsacker never claimed to have alerted anyone at the Vatican, much less Pius XII himself, about the roundup before it occurred. No Vatican official has ever said that Weizsacker warned them, nor has anyone said that they passed such information to Pius XII. On the contrary, we have the firsthand testimony of Princess Enza Pignatelli Aragona, who visited the Vatican on the morning of October 16 and personally told the pope what was happening. She asserts that Pius XII was shocked and angry—and then took action. He immediately protested personally to Weizsacker, demanding that the Nazis stop the arrests.

Austrian bishop Alois Hudal also wrote a letter protesting the Nazi roundup of Rome's Jews. Some writers have alleged that Pius was ignorant of this letter, but Hudal's own memoirs recount that it was Carlo Pacelli—a nephew of the pope—who told him to write the letter on the direct instructions of his uncle.

Beginning in October 1943, Pope Pius XII asked the churches and convents throughout Italy to shelter Jews. In Rome, 155 convents and monasteries sheltered some five thousand Jews during the German occupation, in defiance of the Nazis and Mussolini's Fascists. No fewer than three thousand Jews found refuge at Castel Gandolfo, the pope's summer residence. Sixty Jews lived for nine months at the Jesuit Gregorian University, and many were sheltered in the cellar of the Pontifical Bible Institute. Pope Pius himself granted sanctuary within the walls of the Vatican in Rome to hundreds of homeless Jews.

The foremost authority on the October 1943 Nazi roundup of Rome's Jews—and a survivor of the raid himself—is Michael Tagliacozzo, an Italian Jewish Holocaust scholar now living in Israel. His monographs on the subject document the role of Pius XII and the Vatican in saving Roman Jews.[57] According to Tagliacozzo, 477 Roman Jews were sheltered in the Vatican and its enclaves, "while another 4,238 found refuge in the numerous monasteries and convents in Rome."[58] Tagliacozzo, who lived through the Nazi occupation of Rome and has studied all the primary documents relating to it, has nothing but praise for Pope Pius XII. "I know that many criticize Pope Pacelli," he said in a recent interview. "I have a folder on my table in Israel entitled 'Calumnies Against Pius XII,' but my judgment cannot but be positive. Pope Pacelli was the only one who intervened to impede the deportation of Jews on October 16, 1943, and he did very much to hide and save thousands of us."[59]

Tagliacozzo says that Pius XII's actions were decisive in rescuing 80 percent of Roman Jewry. He dismisses the notion (now fashionable amongst Pacelli's critics) that the pope was not behind the rescue effort. "There was much confusion in those days, but all knew that the pope and the Church would have helped us. After the Nazis' action, the pontiff, who had already ordered the opening of convents, schools, and churches to rescue the persecuted, opened cloistered convents to allow the persecuted to hide. Monsignor Giovanni Butinelli, of the parish of the Transfiguration, told me that the pontiff had recommended that parish priests be told to shelter Jews. I personally knew a Jewish family that, after the Nazis' request for fifty kilos of gold, decided to hide the women and children in a cloistered convent on Via

Garibaldi. The nuns said they were happy to take the mother and girl but they could not care for a little boy. However, under the pope's order, which dispensed the convent from cloister, they also hid the boy."[60]

Tagliacozzo, it should be noted, was rescued from starvation and death by Pius XII's assistants, led by Cardinal Pietro Palazzini. "I remember they treated me wonderfully," recalls Tagliacozzo. "After not having eaten for two days, Father Palazzini gave me a meal with all God's goods: a bowl of vegetable soup, bread, cheese, fruit. I had never eaten so well."

The diaries of other contemporary witnesses document the rescue efforts of Pius XII and the Vatican. So do the recently released memoirs of Adolf Eichmann, in which he notes that the Vatican "vigorously protested the arrest of Jews, requesting the interruption of such action."[61] At Eichmann's trial in Jerusalem, Israeli attorney general Gideon Hausner stated unequivocally that "the pope himself intervened personally in support of the Jews of Rome." Documents introduced at the trial provide further evidence of papal efforts to halt the arrest and deportation of Roman Jews.[62]

We know the names of some of the individual Italian priests, monks, cardinals, and bishops who were instrumental in saving hundreds of Jewish lives. Cardinal Boetto of Genova saved at least eight hundred. The bishop of Assisi hid three hundred Jews for more than two years. Many other prominent Church leaders, including several cardinals and two future popes, rescued and sheltered Jews. They later testified that they acted on the direct orders of Pius XII. In 1955, a delegation from Israel approached Archbishop Giovanni Montini (the future Pope Paul VI) to ask whether he would accept an award for his rescue work on behalf of Jews during the Holocaust. Montini declined, saying, "All I did was my duty. And besides I only acted upon orders from the Holy Father. Nobody deserves a medal for that."[63] In 1957, as I shall discuss in more detail below, Cardinal Angelo Roncalli (the future Pope John XXIII) made a very similar statement when he was offered thanks by an Israeli diplomat for his successful efforts to save thousands of Jewish lives in the early 1940s in Istanbul.

It was also on Pius XII's direct instructions that Cardinal Palazzini hid Michael Tagliacozzo and other Italian Jews for several months in 1943 and 1944. In 1985, Yad Vashem, Israel's Holocaust Memorial, honored Cardinal Palazzini as a "righteous gentile"—one of many Italian Catholic clergy who risked their lives to help Jews during the Holocaust. In accepting this honor, Cardinal Palazzini stressed that "the merit is entirely Pius XII's, who ordered us to do whatever we could to save the Jews from persecution."[64]

The Clergy Rallies to the Jews' Aid

The poignant story of how twenty-two-year-old Michael Tagliacozzo came to be sheltered at the Seminario Romano is worth retelling. Tagliacozzo had been living with relatives in Rome since the end of September 1943. He escaped from the German police when they knocked on the door of his relatives' home in the early morning of October 16. Still in his sleeping clothes, he slipped out a window and into the apartment of a Catholic family that he did not even know. Unable to return to his own home and desperate to find refuge, he remembered Maria Amendola, a former teacher, who sheltered him for a few days and subsequently put him in touch with a young assistant parish priest, Don Vincenzo Fagiolo. "It was he," Tagliacozzo has written, "who warmly defended my cause with the rector of the seminary, Monsignor Roberto Ronca."[65] The prestigious Pontificio Seminario Romano Maggiore was situated on the Piazza di Porta San Giovanni, in a vast complex that included the Basilica of Saint John Lateran and the Lateran Palace. Today it houses the offices of the vicariate of Rome.

As Susan Zuccotti has noted, "Tagliacozzo's place of refuge was not an ordinary Church institution."[66] The Seminario Romano was a Vatican property, "a remnant of the centuries of glory when the Papal States comprised not only all of Rome but a good portion of central Italy."[67] Together with the pope's summer residence at Castel Gandolfo, the seminary was one of the Vatican properties under direct papal jurisdiction that served as a safe haven and refuge for Italian Jews during the Nazi occupation. Of the approximately two hundred refugees who were sheltered at the Seminario Romano, at least fifty-five were Jews.[68] Michael Tagliacozzo, who knew all of the Jews sheltered at the Seminario Romano, has "nothing but good memories" about the way he and his fellow Jewish refugees were treated at the seminary. Jewish rituals and the observance of the Jewish dietary laws was not only permitted but encouraged. As he has reminisced:

> There was absolutely no pressure for conversion to Christianity. The respect shown to those being helped was exemplary. I remember fondly that Don Palazzini turned to me, knowing that among the refugees I was the closest to the Jewish traditions. He begged me to instruct him in the Jewish dietary laws, so that the sentiments of the refugees would not be offended. He gave me a Bible in Hebrew that inspired me with faith and hope in the future.[69]

Italian Catholics—from cardinals to policemen—tried to save Jewish lives by providing shelter, false identity cards, food ration cards, and other papers. Many of these Catholics were arrested by the Nazis and more than a few were killed. Giovanni Palatucci, police chief of Fiume, perished in Dachau for aiding Jews. The seven children of Edoardo Focherini, editor of the Bologna Catholic daily *Avvenire d'Italia*, died in a concentration camp because of their father's efforts on behalf of Bologna's Jews.

All this is indisputable, but the critics dispute whether these rescuers acted on their own or at Pius XII's request.[70] Thus, for instance, Susan Zuccotti devotes most of her study to denying the pope's role, because she was unable to find any written documentation of it. But there is much firsthand evidence testifying to Pius's explicit instructions to save Jews, including that of Monsignor John Patrick Carroll-Abbing. Carroll-Abbing was the founder of Boys' Towns of Italy and a confidant of Pius XII. He also, on explicit instructions from the pope, fed and sheltered Jews during the Nazi occupation of Rome. In his two memoirs, *A Chance to Live* and *But for the Grace of God*, published in 1952 and 1965, respectively, he provides extensive details about Pius XII's rescue efforts on behalf of the Jews—efforts with which he was directly involved.[71]

In a remarkable interview given to *Inside the Vatican* (August/September 2001) Carroll-Abbing recounted how the pope directly ordered him to save the Jews.[72] He stressed that the idea that he and others like him acted in spite of the pope's silence "is a blatant lie! I spoke to Pope Pius XII many times during the war, in person, face to face, and he told me not once but many times to assist the Jews. . . . I can personally testify that the pope gave me direct face-to-face verbal orders to rescue Jews."[73]

The Testimony of Tibor Baranski

The pope also ordered Catholic clergy in other countries to help Jews threatened by the Nazis. The personal testimony of Tibor Baranski, who has been honored by Yad Vashem as a "righteous gentile" for his rescue work, is especially compelling. Baranski was executive secretary of the Jewish Protection Movement of the Holy See in Hungary during World War II. He worked closely with Angelo Rotta, the papal nuncio in Budapest during the Holocaust, to help rescue more than three thousand Hungarian Jews. Baranski says unequivocally that he and Nuncio Rotta acted at the pope's behest.

In October 1944, Baranski was studying to enter the priesthood. His aunt was active in an underground movement that assisted Hungarian Jews in finding hiding places and acquiring false immigration documents. She asked him to help some Jewish family friends who were facing deportation.[74] Baranski went to the papal nuncio, who provided baptism and immigration certificates. Rotta also issued letters of protection for other family members so that they could be led to a safe house, and escape deportation and certain death. Young Baranski personally escorted his friends to safety. So began the successful efforts of Baranski and Rotta to aid and shelter thousands of Hungarian Jews. In his capacity as executive director of the Vatican's Jewish Protection Movement, Baranski also worked in Budapest with the anti-Nazi underground, which strived to rescue and hide as many Jews as possible. Under his direction, many Jews were hidden in the homes of Catholic families in Budapest, while others were concealed inside factories, in secret rooms constructed by the workers.[75]

With the assistance of his aunt, who worked in a pharmaceutical company, Baranski was able to obtain medicine, extra food, and other needed supplies for the Budapest Jews sheltered in the Vatican safe houses under papal protection. The papal nuncio also sent Baranski to the Austro-Hungarian border to rescue Jews who had been taken away on death marches in spite of the fact that they carried protection papers.[76] While doing so, he distributed food and medicine to the bedraggled marchers.

Baranski's rescue work ended on December 30, 1944, when the advancing Russians arrested him, assuming he was a Hungarian supporter of the Nazis. Baranski eventually left his native Hungary after the Hungarian Revolution of 1956 and emigrated to the United States. In 1979, he was honored by Yad Vashem as a "righteous gentile" to commemorate his rescue of Hungarian Jews during the Holocaust. In 1980, he was appointed by President Carter to the U.S. Holocaust Memorial Council.[77] "I was really acting in accordance with the orders of Pope Pius XII," Baranski has testified recently. "I did the work for the papal embassy."[78] Charges that Pius was uninvolved in their rescue activities are "simple lies; nothing else."[79]

As Ronald J. Rychlak has pointed out, Baranski "personally saw at least two letters from Pius XII instructing Rotta to do his very best to protect Jews but to refrain from making statements that might provoke the Nazis."[80] These two letters, notes Baranski, "were handwritten ones by Pope Pius himself."[81] Moreover, Baranski has personally testified that "all other nuncios of the Nazi-occupied countries received similar letters," handwritten by the pope, instructing them to rescue and shelter Jews.[82] "It is a disservice and distortion of history," he maintains, "to say that the pope did nothing. Plays like *The Deputy* are untruthful. . . . What Angelo Rotta did and what I [did] to save Jews is to the credit of the pope."[83]

Another interesting aspect of Baranski and Rotta's rescue work was that it was undertaken in close collaboration with the celebrated Swedish diplomat and rescuer Raoul Wallenberg. Baranski maintains that if Wallenberg—one

of the most famous of those Yad Vashem has declared a "righteous gentile"—
were alive today, he would defend Pius XII.[84] In fact, Baranski says that the
Catholic Church collaborated with Wallenberg in his rescue efforts. "There
was no problem or disagreement whatsoever between the Catholic Church
and Wallenberg. I personally arranged unofficial, private meetings between
Wallenberg and Nuncio Rotta."[85] Baranski reports that Wallenberg "knew
Pius was on his side."[86] Because Rotta, Baranski, Wallenberg, and—yes—Pius
XII worked together as a team, Baranski argues that Yad Vashem should rec-
ognize Pope Pius XII as a "righteous gentile" as well.[87]

Catholic Heroes

Catholic rescuers in France also risked their lives to save and shelter Jews. In
his important memoir, *Christian Resistance to Anti-Semitism*, French Jesuit
priest and theologian Henri de Lubac, a great defender of Pius XII, recounts
his efforts to rescue and aid the Jews of Vichy France.[88] Even as vocal a papal
critic as Susan Zuccotti, in *The Holocaust, the French and the Jews*, has high
praise for Lubac's efforts on behalf of French Jews. Those efforts, Lubac
makes clear in his memoir, were directly inspired by Pius XII.

So, too, were the heroic efforts of Italian bishop Giuseppe Palatucci, the
bishop of Campagna in southern Italy. Palatucci was instrumental in saving
the lives of several thousand Jews in the Italian port city of Fiume, which the
Nazis occupied until the final months of World War II.[89] Bishop Palatucci's
nephew, Giovanni Palatucci, was the chief of police of Fiume. Together they
were able to distribute false identity papers to five thousand Croatian Jews,
granting them refuge outside of the internment camps in Fiume and in the
safety of the bishop's southern Italian diocese.[90] For his own role in rescuing
these Jewish refugees from Croatia, Giovanni Palatucci was arrested by the
Nazis and sent to Dachau, where he was executed.

Newly released Vatican papers document that Giuseppe Palatucci acted
on the direct instructions of Pius XII. A letter signed by the pope in October 1940 instructed him to give money "in aid to interned Jews"[91] who were
being sheltered by the bishop in Campagna. A second letter, sent by Pius in

November 1940, contained a check, instructing him to use the enclosed money for the "support of Jews interned in your diocese."[92]

These papal letters, notes William Doino, Jr., an authority on Pius XII, "appear to give compelling proof that will testify to Pius's attitude toward the Jews. Given the dangers then existing and the reluctance of the Church to put such matters in writing, these letters are remarkable. They establish beyond question that Pius XII took a direct, personal interest in helping Jews [and] did so very early on in the war. Numerous authors have maintained that there is no credible written evidence that Pius XII himself ever gave direct orders to assist persecuted Jews. Now, we have that evidence."[93]

Of the many other Catholic rescuers who similarly acted on the direct instructions of Pius XII, one of the best known was the heroic French Capuchin monk Father Pierre-Marie Benoit, whose exploits on behalf of Rome's Jews are "one of the most celebrated rescue stories to come out of the Holocaust"[94] and which earned him the praise of Jewish survivors of the Holocaust, who called him the "father of the Jews." Prior to World War II, Benoit had been a professor of theology and Hebrew at the Capuchin monastery in Marseilles. With the German occupation of Vichy France in 1942, and the beginning of the deportation of thousands of Jews, his Capuchin monastery in Marseilles became the nerve center of a far-flung rescue network that assisted thousands of French Jews in escaping the country. Utilizing his ties with border guides, the French underground, and Catholic and Jewish religious organizations, Father Benoit helped provide food, shelter, and new identities for thousands of French Jews secretly smuggled into Spain and Switzerland. A printing press in the monastery's basement printed thousands of false baptismal certificates and asylum documents that enabled Jews fleeing Vichy France to travel freely under assumed names.

In November 1942, southern France fell under Nazi occupation and the escape routes into Switzerland and Spain were temporarily sealed. Benoit then smuggled French Jews into the city of Nice, in the nearby Italian zone of occupation, which had become the principal destination for escaping Jews.[95] The Gestapo soon discovered Benoit's activities, and he was forced to move to Rome, which became the new base of his rescue operations. In Rome, Benoit was elected to the board of directors of DELASEM (Delegazione Assistenza Emigranti Ebrei), the main Jewish welfare organization in Italy. When its Jewish president was arrested by the Nazis, Benoit was named the acting president, and chaired the organization's meetings at the Capuchin college in Rome.[96] His ingenuity and devotion to the cause of Jewish rescue knew no bounds. Father Benoit even contacted the Swiss, Romanian, Hungarian, and Spanish embassies, from which he obtained letters of protection and other important documents that enabled Jews to travel freely in Italy under assumed names. He also succeeded in acquiring numerous ration cards from the police in Rome under the pretext of obtaining them for non-Jewish homeless refugees.[97]

Contrary to what Susan Zuccotti and other critics of Pius XII have alleged, Father Benoit's Jewish rescue work (for which he would later be honored as a "righteous gentile" by Yad Vashem), was carried out with the full moral support and financial assistance of the pope. On July 16, 1943, Benoit met with Pius XII, and, according to Benoit's own personal testimony preserved at Yad Vashem, praised Pius for his direct encouragement and support of his rescue efforts. In 1976, on the occasion of the centenary of the pope's birth, Benoit publicly reiterated his praise for Pius XII's efforts on the Jews' behalf and most especially for the pope's direct financial support of his own rescue operations. Zuccotti's misleading discussion of Father Benoit completely ignores the priest's own testimony on the pope's behalf, just as she ignores the testimony of Monsignor Carroll-Abbing, who attests that the pope gave him and Benoit "direct face-to-face verbal orders to rescue Jews."[98]

Zuccotti also ignores the important personal testimony of Father Benoit's chief assistant and collaborator in rescuing Jews, Fernande Leboucher, who in her book *The Incredible Mission of Father Benoit* underlines the direct support they received from Pius XII. Zuccotti alleges that Pius XII's assistance "must be regarded as exceedingly sparse" and that Father Benoit "received no money from the Vatican."[99] But Leboucher states unequivocally that "the Vatican offered to supply whatever funds would be needed for Father Benoit's

work. It is estimated that a total of some four million dollars was thus chan-
neled from the Vatican to…Benoit's rescue organization—much of which
came from the American Catholic Refugees Committee, an official Catholic
collection and distribution agency whose funds were at the disposal of Pope
Pius XII."[100] Her memoir, published in 1969, is never mentioned by Zuccotti.

Castel Gandolfo and the Rescue of Roman Jewry

During the Nazi occupation of Rome, three thousand Jews found refuge at one
time at the pope's summer residence at Castel Gandolfo. Amazingly, Castel
Gandolfo is never once mentioned or discussed in the anti-Pius volumes of
Cornwell and Zuccotti. Yet at no other site in Nazi-occupied Europe were as
many Jews saved and sheltered for as long a period as at Castel Gandolfo during the Nazi occupation of Rome. Kosher food was provided for the Jews hidden there, where, as George Weigel has noted, Jewish children were born in the
private apartments of Pius XII, which became a temporary obstetrical ward.[101]

The tiny town of Castel Gandolfo, approximately seventeen miles outside
of Rome, has been a second home to popes, a summer residence and occasional retreat, for four hundred years. The Roman emperor Domitian
ordered the building of Castel Gandolfo as his summer residence more than
1,900 years ago. After several centuries as the imperial residence, Castel Gandolfo became the summer home of the Roman pontiffs in 1596.[102] The present papal palace, built in the sixteenth century, is "a rather large Italian
country house," with a lovely chapel and numerous apartments for guests. It
was said that Pius XII loved Castel Gandolfo "more than any other pope."[103]
And it was he who personally approved the transformation of his beloved
summer residence into a temporary refuge and shelter for Roman Jews.

Pius's critics who do mention Castel Gandolfo argue—ludicrously—that
the Jews were sheltered at the pope's summer residence without direct papal
knowledge or involvement. But the fact is that Castel Gandolfo is under the
official jurisdiction of the pope and no one but he has the authority to open
its doors. According to several eyewitnesses, including Monsignor Carroll-
Abbing, that is precisely what Pius XII did.

The Jews of Rome were (and would remain) profoundly grateful to Pius XII for sheltering and protecting them at Castel Gandolfo and elsewhere. In the summer of 1944, after the liberation of Rome but before the war's end, Pius told a group of Roman Jews who had come to thank him for his protection: "For centuries, Jews have been unjustly treated and despised. It is time they were treated with justice and humanity, God wills it and the Church wills it. Saint Paul tells us that the Jews are our brothers. They should also be welcomed as our friends."[104]

The Deportation of Hungarian and Romanian Jews

The survival rate of Jews in Catholic countries such as Italy and Belgium was much higher than in non-Catholic countries occupied by the Nazis. The indisputable fact is that in those Catholic countries where Pius XII and his Vatican diplomatic representatives had some political leverage—including Hungary, Romania, Slovakia, and Croatia—Pius was able to halt the deportation and mass murder of Jews by the Nazi puppet governments.

The examples of Hungary, Romania, and Slovakia are especially noteworthy. In 1944, the 750,000 Jews of Hungary were "the largest European Jewish community still surviving outside the German sphere of influence."[105] In March 1944, Germany invaded Hungary and immediately enacted anti-Jewish decrees. Monsignor Angelo Rotta promptly protested the decrees and then, as papal nuncio in Budapest, was the first foreign envoy to submit a formal note expressing Pope Pius XII's protest. At the pope's urging, within twenty-four hours after the anti-Jewish regulations came into effect, Rotta met with the Hungarian deputy minister of foreign affairs to denounce the new anti-Jewish measures.

Rotta repeatedly intervened against the mistreatment of Hungarian Jews and demanded an end to their deportation. As the great Hungarian Jewish historian Jeno Levai has noted: "Acting in accordance with the instructions of the Holy See and always in the name of Pius XII, the nuncio [Angelo Rotta] never ceased from intervening in against the dispositions concerning Jews, and the inhuman character of the [anti-Jewish] legislation."[106]

The Vatican's efforts on behalf of Hungarian Jewry were not limited to formal protests alone. Nuncio Rotta also issued baptismal certificates and passports that enabled thousands of Jews to leave Hungary and escape Nazi deportation. In his monumental work, *The Destruction of the European Jews*, Raul Hilberg estimates that Rotta issued twenty thousand passports that enabled several thousand Jews to leave Hungary before the end of 1944, and enabled many others to escape deportation to Auschwitz.[107]

Angelo Roncalli and the Jews

Archbishop Angelo Roncalli, the Vatican's apostolic delegate in Istanbul and the future Pope John XXIII, played an especially decisive role in helping Rotta save tens of thousands of Hungarian Jews from deportation. Carrying out the explicit verbal directives of Pius XII, he sent tens of thousands of immigration certificates, including Palestinian immigration papers that he had obtained from the British, to the papal nuncio in Budapest. Many Hungarian Jews were thus able to escape to Palestine. In addition, Roncalli saved thousands of Slovakian Jews who were detained in Hungary or Bulgaria by signing their transit visas to Palestine.[108] How effective Roncalli and Rotta's efforts were in rescuing innumerable Jews, who without their intervention would surely have perished at the hands of the Nazis, is attested to by the fact that Hajj Amin al-Husseini, the violently anti-Semitic grand mufti of Jerusalem (and a close ally of Hitler) complained to German foreign minister Joachim von Ribbentrop about the arrival of four thousand Jewish children, accompanied by five hundred adults. Al-Husseini pleaded with von Ribbentrop to prevent further emigrations of Jews.

Roncalli worked closely with such Jewish leaders as Isaac Herzog (the chief rabbi of Palestine) and Chaim Barlas (the Jewish Agency for Palestine's representative in Istanbul). In February 1944, Roncalli and Rabbi Herzog met twice to discuss the fate of the fifty-five thousand Jews of Transnistria, a Romanian-administered province made up of territories seized from the Soviet Union in 1941. "A bleak and inhospitable region," Transnistria became "a kind of penal colony for deported Jews. As the German eastern front began to crumble, the Jews were shunted westwards toward the extermination camps."[109] But the Vatican interceded with the Romanian government.[110] Roncalli brought the Jews' plight to the attention of Pius XII, who immediately authorized sending money to the Jews in Transnistria.[111] As Theodore Lavi has noted in his authoritative study *The Vatican's Endeavours on Behalf of Roumanian Jewry during World War II*: "This interest manifested by the Vatican at this grave juncture in the spring of 1944 was an important factor which greatly contributed to the rescue of Roumanian Jews. Their moral power of resistance grew when they saw that they were not abandoned to their fate."[112] On February 28, 1944, Rabbi Isaac Herzog wrote Roncalli from Jerusalem to express his gratitude "for the energetic steps you have taken and will undertake to save our unfortunate people. You follow in the tradition, so profoundly humanitarian, of the Holy See, and you follow the noble feelings of your own heart."[113] "Cardinal Roncalli," Rabbi Herzog would later say, "is a man who really loves the People of the Book, and through him thousands of Jews were rescued."[114] And Chaim Barlas, who directed the Jewish Agency's rescue committee in Turkey, added, "Much blood and ink have been spilled in the Jewish tragedy of those years, but to the few heroic deeds which were performed to rescue Jews belong the activities of the apostolic delegate, Monsignor Roncalli, who worked indefatigably on their behalf."[115]

On April 7, 1944, Alexander Safran, the chief rabbi of Romania, joined Herzog and Barlas in paying tribute to the Catholic Church's rescue efforts on behalf of Romanian Jews in a letter to the papal apostolic delegate:

> In these harsh times our thoughts turn more than ever with respectful gratitude for what has been accomplished by the Sovereign Pontiff on behalf of Jews in general and by your Excellency on behalf of the Jews of Romania and Transnistria.
>
> In the most difficult hours of which we Jews of Romania have passed through, the generous assistance of the Holy See, carried out by the intermediary of your high person was decisive and salutary. It is not easy for us to find the right words to express the warmth and

consolation we experienced because of the concern of the supreme
pontiff, who offered a large sum to relieve the sufferings of deported
Jews, sufferings which had been pointed out to him by you after your
visit to Transnistria. The Jews of Romania will never forget these
facts of historic importance.[116]

In 1957, Israeli consul general Pinchas Lapide paid his respects to Cardinal Roncalli to express on behalf of the Israeli government the profound gratitude for Roncalli's invaluable help in saving thousands of Jews. The future
Pope John XXIII would not let him finish. "In all those painful matters," he
said, raising his hand in deprecation, "I referred to the Holy See and afterwards I simply carried out the pope's orders: first and foremost to save
human lives."[117]

In his book *Pius XII and the Third Reich*, which is highly critical of Pius's role
during the Holocaust, Saul Friedlander points out: "The Zionist archives contain numerous documents concerning the unceasing activities of Nuncio Roncalli in favour of Jews. Let us underline that Monsignor Roncalli had declared
that all he did in this field was upon papal urging."[118] Cardinal Roncalli's biographer Lawrence Elliot has concluded that, in all Roncalli's rescue activities on
behalf of European Jewry during the 1940s, he "acted with the consistent
encouragement of the pope."[119] A great friend of the Jewish people, as well as a
devoted protégé of Pius XII, whom he would succeed as pope in 1958, Angelo
Roncalli was perhaps the most eminent of the many Catholic rescuers who
credited Pius XII for their efforts to save Jews from the Holocaust.

Despite the Vatican's efforts, by midsummer 1944, 437,000 Jews had been
deported from Hungary. On June 25, Pius XII sent an open telegram to the
regent of Hungary, Admiral Miklós Horthy, urging him "to use all possible
influence in order to cease the pains and torments which innumerable persons must undergo for the sole reason of their nationality or their race. Our
paternal heart cannot rest unmoved in the face of their appeals and the
demands of charity which embraces all men without distinction. I therefore
appeal to Your Excellency personally… in the hope that Your Excellency will

do everything in order to spare these poor people further sorrow and suffering."[120] Within twenty-four hours of receiving the pope's cable, Horthy convened the Hungarian Crown Council, informing its members of the papal intervention and demanding that "the cruelties of the deportations" be stopped immediately.[121] Days later, Horthy went further and ordered that all deportations of Hungarian Jews should cease. In Hungary, the Nazi plan for exterminating the Jews was terminated. Because of Admiral Horthy's action in response to Pope Pius XII's telegram, 170,000 Hungarian Jews were saved from imminent deportation to Auschwitz. "The appeals from the pope," concludes Holocaust scholar David S. Wyman, "had been especially important in stopping the deportations." By December 1944, when the German occupation of Hungary ended, most of the Jews of Budapest had been saved from the Nazi crematoria.

The Deportation of the Jews of Slovakia

Legal scholar and diplomat Dr. Joseph L. Lichten, in his book *A Question of Judgment*, showed that "Pius XII intervened directly—and contrary to the allegations of his accusers—in unambiguous terms"[122] to help the Jews of Slovakia. Through persistent diplomatic protests, Pius XII and other Church officials were able to save tens of thousands of Slovak Jews from deportation and eventual extermination in Nazi death camps. When it became known in March 1942 that 80,000 Jews were to be forcibly removed from their homes in Slovakia, the Vatican's response was instantaneous. The Vatican secretary of state immediately filed a protest with the Slovak government. Acting in the name of Pope Pius XII, formal protests also came from the papal representatives in Bratislava and from the papal nuncio in Hungary. The Vatican official in Slovakia protested on March 9 that "the deportation of 80,000 persons to Poland, at the mercy of the Germans, is equivalent to condemning them to certain death."[123] On March 21, 1942, a pastoral letter was read by episcopal orders in all Slovak churches. This letter, inspired by the Vatican, spoke of the "lamentable fate of thousands of innocent fellow citizens, due to no guilt of their own, as a result of their descent or nationality."[124]

When a second round of deportations was scheduled for 1943, the Vatican again denounced the proposal. On April 7, 1943, Pope Pius himself wrote a strongly worded letter of protest to the Slovak government "deploring" the planned deportations:

> The Holy See has always entertained the firm hope that the Slovak government ... would never proceed with the forcible removal of persons belonging to the Jewish race. It is, therefore, with great pain that the Holy See has learned of the continued transfers of such a nature from the territory of the republic. The pain is aggravated further now that it appears ... that the Slovak government intends to proceed with the total removal of the Jewish residents of Slovakia, not even sparing women and children. The Holy See would fail in its Divine Mandate if it did not deplore these measures, which gravely damage man in his natural right, mainly for the reason that these people belong to a certain race.[125]

The following day, Pius XII instructed the Vatican's representative in Bulgaria to take all steps necessary in support of Jewish residents facing deportation.

Subsequently, when it appeared that yet more deportations were to take place, Pope Pius instructed the Vatican's representative in Slovakia to approach President Tiso (himself a Catholic priest) in the pontiff's name. The papal representative's instructions were to make clear "that the Holy See anxiously implores the Slovak government ... to assume an attitude consonant with the Catholic principles and sentiments of the people of Slovakia."[126] President Tiso relaxed pressure on Slovakia's Jews and curtailed planned deportations after the pope's intervention.

The six official papal protests by Pius XII and the numerous oral intercessions undertaken on behalf of Slovak Jews in his name were significant factors in stopping the Nazi deportation of Slovakia's Jews. Pius's persistent pleas were finally heeded. Although seventy thousand Jews had been deported from the new pro-Nazi Slovak Republic, the papal nuncio in Bratislava secured a promise from the new regime that planned deportations would be abandoned.[127] As distinguished French Jewish scholar Leon Poliakov has concluded, "the cessation of the deportations of Jews from Slovakia in the summer of 1942—and consequently the survival of nearly 25 percent of the Slovakian Jews—must be attributed to Vatican pressure exerted on Monsignor Tiso, chief of the Slovakian puppet state."[128] In short, Pope Pius XII played an instrumental role in saving the lives of approximately twenty thousand Slovak Jews.

In Tribute to Pius XII:
Praise from the Jewish Community

During his lifetime, Pope Pius XII was widely praised for having saved hundreds of thousands of Jewish lives during the Holocaust. As early as 1940, Albert Einstein, himself a Jewish refugee from Nazi Germany, paid tribute to the moral "courage" of Pope Pius and the Catholic Church in opposing "the Hitlerian onslaught" on liberty.

> Being a lover of freedom, when the Nazi revolution came in Germany, I looked to the universities to defend it, knowing that they had always boasted of their devotion to the cause of truth; but, no, the universities immediately were silenced. Then I looked to the great editors of the newspapers, whose flaming editorials in days gone by had proclaimed their love of freedom; but they, like the universities, were silenced in a few short weeks. Only the Catholic Church stood squarely across the path of Hitler's campaign for suppressing the truth. I never had any special interest in the Church before, but now I feel a great affection and admiration because the Church alone has had the courage and persistence to stand for intellectual truth and moral freedom. I am forced thus to confess that what I once despised, I now praise unreservedly.[129]

Throughout the 1940s and 1950s, Jews praised Pope Pius XII for saving Jewish lives.[130] In 1943, Chaim Weizmann, who would become Israel's first president, wrote that "the Holy See is lending its powerful help wherever it can, to mitigate the fate of my persecuted co-religionists."[131] The following year, Rabbi Maurice Perlzweig, representing the World Jewish Congress, wrote that "the repeated interventions of the Holy Father on behalf of Jewish communities in Europe has provoked the profoundest sentiments of appreciation and gratitude from Jews throughout the world."[132] On July 31, 1944, Judge Joseph Proskauer, the president of the American Jewish Committee, declared in a speech at a Madison Square Garden rally: "We have heard . . . what a great part the Holy Father [has played] in the salvation of the Jewish refugees in Italy, and we know from sources that must be credited that this great pope has reached forth his mighty and sheltering hand to help the oppressed of Hungary."[133] Rabbi Louis Finkelstein, the chancellor of the Jewish Theological Seminary of America, stated: "No keener rebuke has come to Nazism than from Pope Pius XI and his successor, Pope Pius XII."[134]

Moshe Sharett, who would become Israel's first foreign minister and second prime minister, reinforced these feelings of gratitude when he met with Pius in the closing days of World War II: "I told him that my first duty was to thank him, and through him the Catholic Church, on behalf of the Jewish public for all they had done in the various countries to rescue Jews. . . . We are deeply grateful to the Catholic Church."[135]

So, too, in 1945, Rabbi Isaac Herzog, the chief rabbi of Israel, sent a message to Monsignor Angelo Roncalli expressing his gratitude for the actions taken by Pope Pius XII on behalf of the Jewish people. "The people of Israel," wrote Rabbi Herzog, "will never forget what His Holiness and his illustrious delegates, inspired by the eternal principles of religion, which form the very foundation of true civilization, are doing for our unfortunate brothers and sisters in the most tragic hour of our history, which is living proof of Divine Providence in this world."[136]

Dr. Alexander Safran, the chief rabbi of Romania, expressed the gratitude of the Jewish community for the Vatican's help and support for prisoners in the concentration camps. In September 1945, Dr. Leon Kubowitzky, the secretary general of the World Jewish Congress, personally thanked the pope in Rome for his interventions on behalf of Jews, and the World Jewish Congress donated $20,000 to Vatican charities "in recognition of the work of the Holy See in rescuing Jews from Fascist and Nazi persecutions."[137] Also in 1945, Maurice Edelman, a member of the British parliament and president of the Anglo-Jewish Association, met with the pope to thank him, on behalf of the Jewish community of England, for saving tens of thousands of Jews.[138]

Dr. Raffael Cantoni, head of the Italian Jewish community's wartime Jewish Assistance Committee, who would subsequently become the president of the Union of Italian Jewish Communities, similarly expressed his gratitude to the Vatican, stating that "six million of my co-religionists have been murdered by the Nazis, but there could have been many more victims had it not been for the efficacious intervention of Pius XII."[139]

Grateful testimonials to Pius XII came from American Jewish communal leaders as well. During a 1946 conference on the plight of displaced Jewish refugees in St. Louis, William Rosenwald, the national chairman of the United Jewish Appeal and one of American Jewry's preeminent philanthropists, said, "I wish to take this opportunity to pay tribute to Pope Pius for his appeal on behalf of the victims of war and oppression. He provided aid for Jews in Italy and intervened in behalf of refugees to lighten their burdens."[140]

Many other Jewish tributes to Pius came in the years just preceding, and in the immediate aftermath, of the pontiff's death. In 1955, when Italy celebrated the tenth anniversary of its liberation, the Union of Italian Jewish Communities proclaimed April 17 a day of gratitude for the pope's wartime assistance in defying the Nazis. Dozens of Italian Catholics, including several priests and nuns, were awarded gold medals for their outstanding rescue work during the war.

A few weeks later, on May 26, 1955, the Israeli Philharmonic Orchestra flew to Rome to give a special performance of Beethoven's Seventh Symphony at the Vatican's Consistory Hall, expressing the State of Israel's enduring gratitude for the help that the pope and the Catholic Church had given to the Jewish people.[141] That the Israeli Philharmonic Orchestra so joined the rest of the Jewish world in warmly honoring the achievements and legacy of Pope Pius XII is of more than passing significance. As a matter of state policy, the Israeli Philharmonic has never played the music of nineteenth-century composer Richard Wagner because of Wagner's well-known reputation as an anti-Semite and as Hitler's favorite composer. Wagner was also one of the cultural patron saints of the Third Reich, and his music was played at Nazi party functions and ceremonies. Despite requests from music lovers, the official state ban on Wagner has never been lifted. During the 1950s and 1960s, a significant sector of the Israeli public—hundreds of thousands of whom were survivors of the Nazi concentration and death camps—still viewed his music, and even his name, as a symbol of Hitler's regime.

That being the case, it is inconceivable that the Israeli government would have paid the travel expenses for the entire Philharmonic to travel to Rome for a special concert to pay tribute to a church leader who was considered to have been Hitler's pope. On the contrary, the Israeli Philharmonic's historic visit to Rome to perform for Pius XII at the Vatican was a unique gesture of collective recognition and gratitude to a great world leader and friend of the Jewish people for his instrumental role in saving the lives of hundreds of thousands of Jews.[142]

On the day of Pius XII's death in 1958, Golda Meir, Israel's foreign minister, cabled the following message of condolence to the Vatican: "We share in the grief of humanity. . . . When fearful martyrdom came to our people in the decade of Nazi terror, the voice of the pope was raised for the victims. The life of our times was enriched by a voice speaking out on the great moral truths above the tumult of daily conflict. We mourn a great servant of peace."[143] Before beginning a concert of the New York Philharmonic Orchestra, conductor Leonard Bernstein called for a minute of silence "for the passing of a very great man, Pope Pius XII."[144]

In the weeks following Pius XII's death, many Jewish organizations and newspapers throughout the world mourned his passing and paid tribute to his wartime efforts to rescue Jews. The *Canadian Jewish Chronicle* recalled that

Pius XII "made it possible for thousands of Jewish victims of Nazism and Fascism to be hidden away." In the November 6, 1958, edition of the *Jewish Post* in Winnipeg, William Zuckerman, the former *American Hebrew* columnist, wrote that no other leader "did more to help the Jews in their hour of greatest tragedy, during the Nazi occupation of Europe, than did the late pope."[145]

Similar sentiments were expressed in the many tributes and eulogies for Pius by numerous rabbis and Jewish communal leaders, as well as by most of the Israeli press—several readers even suggested in open letters that a "Pope Pius XII forest" be planted in the hills of Judea "in order to perpetuate fittingly the humane services rendered by the late pontiff to European Jewry."[146] During and for close to two decades after World War II, Jewish praise and gratitude for Pius XII's efforts on behalf of European Jewry were virtually unanimous. Indeed, as Pinchas Lapide has so aptly stated: "No pope in history has been thanked more heartily by Jews for having saved or helped their brethren in distress."[147]

Conclusion:
Pius XII as a "Righteous Gentile"

In the conclusion of her book *Under His Very Windows: The Vatican and the Holocaust in Italy*, Susan Zuccotti disparages and dismisses—as wrongheaded, ill-informed, or even devious—the praise that Pius XII received from contemporary Jewish leaders and scholars such as Golda Meir, Moshe Sharett, Isaac Herzog, Pinchas Lapide, and Albert Einstein, as well as other expressions of gratitude from the Jewish military chaplains and Holocaust survivors who bore personal witness to the assistance and compassion of the pope. That she does so is unfortunate and deeply disturbing. To thus dismiss and deny the legitimacy of their collective gratitude to Pius XII is tantamount to denying the credibility of their personal testimony and judgment about the Holocaust itself. To so deny and delegitimize their collective memory and experience of the Holocaust, as Zuccotti does, is to engage in a subtle yet profound form of Holocaust denial.

In her effort to vilify Pius XII, Zuccotti also ignores, disparages, or rejects the compelling firsthand testimony of several Italian Catholic Church leaders and priest-rescuers who have testified that Pius XII gave them explicit instructions to rescue and shelter Jews. To cite but two examples: First, she dismisses the testimony of a priest who says that Bishop Giuseppe Nicolini of Assisi approached him holding a letter and declaring that the pope had written to request his help in rescuing and sheltering Jews. Because the priest did not actually read the letter, Zuccotti says his testimony should be rejected.[148] Also, the well-documented firsthand testimony of the priest-rescuer Monsignor John Patrick Carroll-Abbing—who testified to Pope Pius XII's direct personal instructions to rescue and shelter Italy's Jews—is completely ignored by Zuccotti.

Implicit in Zuccotti's vilification of Pius XII is her attempt to dismiss and disparage Jewish scholars such as Pinchas Lapide, who have written in Pius's defense, as part of an effort of "Jews dedicated to the creation of the state of Israel" to solicit Vatican recognition of the Jewish state.[149] For Zuccotti, Jewish praise for Pius and Jewish scholarship in his defense are merely political ploys to win Vatican recognition of Israel. While this was "a desirable objective" for Lapide and other Jewish writers devoted to Israel, she maintains, it took precedence over "the task of establishing historical truth."[150] To so question and attack the motives and credibility of Jewish leaders and scholars as a group solely because they are Jews dedicated to the State of Israel is especially unfortunate and disturbing. Given the historical record, it is intellectually irresponsible as well.

But Zuccotti is not alone. The recent campaign waged by Zuccotti, Cornwell, and other recent papal critics to vilify Pius XII and to defame his memory is itself popularizing the historical falsehood that Pius XII was a Nazi sympathizer and an anti-Semite. In truth, Pius XII was a true friend of the Jewish people—at a moment in history when such friendship mattered most.

Writing in *Yad Vashem Studies* in 1983, John S. Conway—the leading authority on the Vatican's eleven-volume *Acts and Documents of the Holy See During the Second World War*—concluded: "A close study of the many thousands of documents published in these volumes lends little support to the thesis that ecclesiastical self-preservation was the main motive behind the attitudes of the Vatican diplomats. Rather, the picture that emerges is one of a group of intelligent and conscientious men, seeking to pursue the paths of peace and justice, at a time when these ideals were ruthlessly being rendered irrelevant in a world of 'total war.'"[151] These neglected volumes (which the English reader can find summarized in Pierre Blet's *Pius XII and the Second World War*) "will reveal ever more clearly and convincingly"—as the late pope John Paul II told a group of Jewish leaders in Miami in 1987—"how deeply Pius XII felt the tragedy of the Jewish people, and how hard and effectively he worked to assist them."[152]

The Talmud, the great sixth-century compendium of Jewish religious law and ethics, teaches Jews that "whosoever preserves one life, it is accounted to him by Scripture as if he had preserved a whole world." More so than most other twentieth-century leaders, Pius XII effectively fulfilled this Talmudic dictum when the fate of European Jewry was at stake. Today, close to sixty years after the Holocaust, it needs to be more widely recognized and appreciated that Pius XII was a true friend of the Jewish people, who indeed saved more Jewish lives than any other person, including Raoul Wallenberg and Oskar Schindler—men who are often, and rightly, treated as heroes for their efforts. It needs to be remembered that Jewish leaders in Israel, Europe, and America praised the pope's efforts during and after the Holocaust, and promised never to forget. It needs to be remembered that no other pope in history had been so universally praised by Jews. The compelling reason for this unprecedented praise needs to be better remembered. It is hard to imagine that so many of the world's greatest Jewish leaders, on several continents, were all misguided or mistaken in praising the pope's wartime record. The enduring gratitude of Holocaust survivors to Pius XII was genuine and profound.

The time has come, I believe, for Pius XII to receive formal recognition from Yad Vashem as one of the "righteous gentiles." In enacting the law establishing Yad Vashem in 1953, the Israeli parliament stipulated that it was "making it the duty of the State of Israel to recognize the work done by non-Jews in saving Jewish lives during the Second World War. An 'expression of honour' was awarded, in the name of the Jewish people, to every non-Jewish person or family who took the risk of hiding or saving Jews."[153] The Hebrew phrase chosen for those to be honored was *Sderot hassidei umot haolam*, the "righteous among the nations." They have come to be known, and deservedly admired, as "righteous gentiles."[154]

The concept of "righteous among the nations," as Martin Gilbert has noted, "is an ancient one in Jewish tradition."[155] The term "righteous among the nations" has its origins in Jewish lore, "and has known various interpretations, including the popular one of non-Jews who showed favor to Jews during periods of distress and persecution."[156] The Israeli parliament, therefore, chose this ancient Jewish title to honor non-Jewish rescuers of Jews during the Holocaust.[157]

In 1962, Yad Vashem created a public commission chaired by Israeli supreme court justice Moshe Landau, who a year earlier had presided over the trial of the Nazi war criminal Adolf Eichmann. The commission's task was to define the criteria for bestowing the title of "righteous among the nations" to non-Jewish rescuers of Jews, and to decide whom to recognize.[158] This Commission for the Designation of the Righteous, which meets periodically and is composed of eighteen Israeli judges and experts, examines the evidence of rescue activity contained in both eyewitness accounts and archival sources and solicits firsthand, eyewitness testimony from Jewish Holocaust survivors and Christian rescuers. At Yad Vashem's Avenue of the Righteous, every non-Jew honored plants a tree or has a tree planted in his or her name.[159]

By the beginning of 2002, fifty-six years after the end of World War II, more than nineteen thousand non-Jews had been honored as "righteous gentiles" at Yad Vashem. "As one century gave way to another," Martin Gilbert has poignantly noted, "more than eight hundred non-Jews were being identified and honored every year."[160] Over the last two decades, several Catholic Church leaders—priests, nuns, and cardinals—have been honored as "righteous gentiles," including Monsignor Angelo Rotta, the Vatican's wartime ambassador to Hungary, and Cardinal Pietro Palazzini, who, according to a Yad Vashem spokesperson, "had endangered his life" and gone "above and beyond the call of duty to save [Italian] Jews during the Holocaust."[161] However, Pius XII has not yet been honored as a "righteous gentile," although he, like Palazzini, went "above and beyond the call of duty" to save and shelter Italian Jews during the Nazi occupation of Rome.

When he was honored by Yad Vashem as a "righteous gentile" in 1985, Palazzini testified that Pius XII had personally ordered him to save and shelter Jews. The well-documented firsthand testimony of Palazzini, John Patrick Carroll-Abbing, Tibor Baranski, Father Benoit, and other Catholic rescuers contain extensive details about Pius's rescue efforts on behalf of the Jews of Rome and elsewhere that should, by itself, qualify Pius XII as a "righteous gentile."

As I have demonstrated, there is abundant firsthand, eyewitness testimony from Jewish contemporaries of Pius XII to further verify his historic role in rescuing Jews, as does the fact that he sheltered Jews at Castel Gandolfo and at the Vatican during the Nazi roundup of Italian Jews. "More than all others," recalled Elio Toaff, an Italian Jew who lived through the Holocaust and later became chief rabbi of Rome, "we had the opportunity of experiencing the great compassionate goodness and magnanimity of the pope during the unhappy years of the persecution and terror, when it seemed that for us there was no longer an escape."[162] The perspective and judgment of Pius's Jewish contemporaries, such as Rabbi Toaff and numerous other Italian Jewish Holocaust survivors, are crucial to understanding how Pius's pontificate and legacy should be viewed and evaluated by Jews and historians today.

We also have the personal testimonies of Jewish military chaplains serving with the Allied forces. For example, Rabbi Andre Zaoui, a Jewish chaplain with the French Expeditionary Forces in Italy, wrote on June 22, 1944, to express his gratitude to the pope "for the immense good and incomparable charity that your Holiness extended generously to the Jews of Italy and especially the children, women, and elderly of the community of Rome."[163]

Four weeks later, David de Sola Pool, a preeminent New York rabbi who chaired the National Jewish Welfare Board's Commission on Jewish Chaplaincy, which coordinated the work of America's Jewish military chaplains, wrote to the pope, conveying the same message of public recognition and gratitude: "We have received reports from our army chaplains in Italy of the aid and protection given to so many Italian Jews by the Vatican and by priests and institutions of the Church during the Nazi occupation of the country. We are deeply moved by this extraordinary display of Christian love—the more so as we know the risk incurred by those who afforded shelter to Jews. . . . From the bottom of our hearts we send you the assurances of undying gratitude."[164]

At the Thanksgiving service at Tempio Israelita, the synagogue of the chief rabbi of Rome, on July 30, the American 5th Army Division's Jewish chaplain, stationed in Italy, stated: "If it had not been for the truly substantial assistance and the help given to Jews by the Vatican and by Rome's ecclesiastical authorities, thousands of Jewish refugees would have undoubtedly perished before Rome was liberated."[165]

Pope Pius XII's critics sweep aside the reports of Jewish chaplains, of Holocaust survivors, and Catholic rescuers. They prefer their own ideological prejudices to testimony of those who were there. They would deprive future generations of an accurate historical memory of the Holocaust.

As we approach the fiftieth anniversary of the death of Pius XII, it would be both historically just and morally appropriate for Yad Vashem to posthumously recognize and honor Pius XII as one of the "righteous among the nations." During the pontificate of John Paul II, some Catholic and Jewish leaders, including Rome's chief rabbi (and Holocaust survivor) Elio Toaff, began discussing and promoting the cause of Pius XII to receive such posthumous recognition from Yad Vashem. Catholic and Jewish leaders and scholars should, during the next few years, continue to work together to support and promote the cause of recognizing and honoring Pius XII as a "righteous gentile."

As we shall see in the next chapters, there are ramifications of recognizing the historical truth about Pope Pius XII, both in the contemporary culture wars and in the clash of civilizations.

CHAPTER FIVE

THE LIBERAL MEDIA
AND THE CULTURE WARS

HE LIBERAL MEDIA, IN POPULARIZING and perpetuating the myth of Hitler's pope, have made it a focal point of the culture wars. Indeed, it began as part of the culture wars—as a way to attack the late Pope John Paul II because he supported the possible canonization of Pope Pius XII. James Carroll penned a virulent attack on Pius XII in the June 1999 *New Yorker* precisely to challenge and derail the cause of Pius XII's candidacy for sainthood.[1] Liberal papal critics such as Carroll have been at least partially successful. As Daniel Jonah Goldhagen has reflected, with evident satisfaction, "The spate of recent books dwelling on the misconduct of Pius XII during the Holocaust has put the [Catholic] Church under pressure, as it wishes formally to begin the process that would typically lead to his canonization."[2]

To discredit Pius XII is to discredit the judgment of a pope whom prominent liberals disliked. Thus Garry Wills goes beyond condemning "Hitler's pope," to condemn John Paul II's decision to canonize Catholics martyred by the Nazis, especially Edith Stein and Maximilian Kolbe, arguing that his decision to do so "represents a cynical attempt to de-Judaize the Holocaust."[3]

Goldhagen not only vilifies Pius XII for what he claims is the pope's "criminal role during the Holocaust . . . and quite probably afterward,"[4] but also goes on to assert that "it should now be clear that the Church should cease efforts to canonize Pius XII."[5] Indeed, "any canonization would look like granting an official approval to anti-Semitism, and even a retroactive Church blessing of the Holocaust."[6] As historian Philip Jenkins has aptly noted, "the stakes in this debate are very high."[7]

The liberal media employ a double standard in the Pius wars, popularizing and perpetuating the myth of Hitler's pope and downplaying or ignoring the substantive historical evidence to the contrary. Most recently, this bias of the liberal media found expression in its slanted coverage of the outrageous new anti-papal allegation that the Catholic Church "kidnapped Jewish children after the Holocaust."[8] Specifically, it was falsely alleged that the French Catholic Church, on a direct order from Pius XII, forbade French Catholic families that had hidden Jewish children during the Holocaust to return these children to their Jewish families if they had been baptized.[9]

This new anti-Pius controversy began on December 28, 2004. The liberal Italian daily newspaper *Il Corriere della Sera* made the nightmarish claim that in 1946, Pius XII sent explicit instructions to his papal nuncio in France, Archbishop Angelo Roncalli, ordering him *not* to return Jewish children to their parents, if the children had been baptized while being sheltered by Catholic families or institutions during the Holocaust. The article, written by left-wing anti-papal Italian journalist and historian Alberto Melloni, further alleged that Roncalli ignored Pius XII's "stone-hearted instructions" and circumvented them, ordering that the Jewish families that had survived the Holocaust be reunited.[10]

Before anyone could check the accuracy of these allegations, the world media had plastered them across the globe. On January 9, 2005, the *New York Times* published its own article, "Saving Jewish Children: But at What Cost?" based on Melloni's allegations.[11] Liberal papal critics had added a new sin to Pius XII's pontificate: papal kidnapping. Not since the infamous Mortara affair of the late 1850s had a pope ever been accused of "kidnapping" a baptized Jewish child and refusing to return the child to his family.

It is true that during the Holocaust, Jewish children sheltered by Catholic families had to "pass" as Catholics. Some Catholics did indeed baptize these children—perhaps out of their own faith convictions, or as an effort to further deceive the Nazis.[12] After the war, there were 10,000 to 20,000 orphaned Jewish children in France alone (of which only a small percentage had been baptized) who were still living with Catholic families or in Catholic Church–related institutions.

In the immediate aftermath of the Holocaust, in March 1946, Dr. Isaac Herzog, the chief rabbi of Palestine, met with Pius XII to ask what might be done to turn these Jewish orphans over to Jewish families or philanthropic institutions, so that they could be raised in a Jewish environment. By all accounts, this meeting went exceptionally well: The pope promised Rabbi Herzog that he would inquire into the situation, and the chief rabbi "expressed his profound thanks," both for the pope's promise and for the heroic work done by Pius and the Catholic Church to rescue and shelter Jews during the war.[13]

Herzog noted that Pius XII "worked to banish anti-Semitism in many countries," and concluded with an invocation: "God willing, may history remember that when everything was dark for our people, His Holiness lit a light of hope for them."[14]

On March 31, 1946, the *Palestine Post* reported that Rabbi Herzog "told of his audience with the pope, who had received him on a Sunday early in March. Their conversation . . . was mainly on the subject of the 8,000 Jewish children in Poland, France, Belgium, and Holland who were [being] brought up in monasteries and by Christian families. He had the Vatican's promise of help to bring those children back into the Jewish fold."[15] The pope must have come through on his promise, because Rabbi Herzog "continued to praise his conduct toward the Jewish community throughout the pope's life."

The testimony of other Jewish leaders confirms this assumption. Dr. Leon Kubowitzky of the World Jewish Congress said in 1965: "I can state now that I hardly know of a single case where Catholic institutions refused to return Jewish children."[16] More recently, French Jewish Holocaust historian and anti-Nazi attorney Serge Klarsfeld has emphatically stated that this new

controversy over the fate of Jewish children hidden by Catholic families during the Holocaust is "a storm in a teacup," because "almost none were with-
held from their Jewish families afterward."[17] Klarsfeld, who has studied the fate
of Jewish children during the Holocaust and has been involved in the prosecution of several Nazi war criminals who operated in France, said that most
baptized "hidden children" probably went back to Judaism when they were
reunited with relatives after the war. "They never stopped being Jews," he said.
"They simply had a paper in their pockets saying they had been baptized."[18]

In fact, soon after his March 1946 meeting with Herzog, Pius instructed
the Vatican's Holy Congregation of the Holy Office to draw up guidelines on
how the Church could best work with Jewish families and institutions that
wanted to reclaim or adopt Jewish children still residing in Catholic homes.
Basing his words on the Holy Office's guidelines, one of Pius XII's assistants,
Monsignor Domenico Tardini, sent a memo dated September 28, 1946, in
Italian to Nuncio Roncalli in France, explaining how French Church officials
should deal with this issue.

In his article, Melloni quotes a French translation (by an unknown writer)
of Tardini's instructions. The French memo, dated October 23, 1946, mis-
translates a key phrase about the claims that surviving Jewish relatives had
on Jewish children under the Church's care. Unlike the original Tardini document, which explicitly encourages French Catholic officials and laymen to
return all rescued Jewish children, baptized or not, to their appropriate surviving relatives or to Jewish institutions, the French translation leaves "the
impression that the Church should hold on to these children, especially if
they were baptized, even if the surviving parents now came back to reclaim
them."[19] The French translation directly contradicts Tardini's original version
of Pius XII's instructions. Subsequent actions by both Pius XII and Roncalli,
as well as by the French Catholic hierarchy, all "make clear that Pius's postwar policy was to support reuniting Jewish children with their surviving relatives, as quickly and humanely as possible."

Why this contradiction? Because it turns out that the French memo—an
alleged "papal document"—is not authentic. Alberto Melloni's article, as
Robert J. Rychlak has pointed out, "was based on a bad translation (perhaps

an intentional fraud)." The memo is a "fabricated" document, definitely "not from the Vatican."[20]

This purported papal document "was not signed, not on the Vatican letterhead, and Vatican officials immediately noted that the words used were not typical for directives from the Vatican." Indeed the very fact that the letter was in French and not Italian is enough to show that it was no authentic "instruction from the pope to his nuncio."[21]

The credibility of Melloni's sensational anti-Pius allegations, which were uncritically reported by the *New York Times* and other liberal media in the United States, has been categorically refuted by two of Italy's preeminent authorities on Pius XII and his pontificate. They are Andrea Tornielli, the respected Vatican correspondent for the Milan newspaper *Il Giornale*, and the diplomatic historian Matteo L. Napolitano. Tornielli and Napolitano co-authored the recent book *Il Papa che salvo gli Ebrei* (*The Pope Who Saved the Jews*).[22]

Alberto Melloni did not identify the Church archive in France from which his alleged papal document came, but Tornielli found the original and authentic papal instructions in the Centre National des Archives de l'Eglise de France. In a front-page article in *Il Giornale*, "Ecco il vero documento su Pio XII e i bimbi Ebrei,"[23] Tornielli compared the original Vatican document to Melloni's version and proved Melloni's allegations against Pope Pius XII false.[24] The amazing thing, notes one scholar who has read this authentic papal document, is that the instructions from Pius XII "are almost exactly the opposite of Melloni's account, which was so enthusiastically embraced by the papal critics. Nowhere do they suggest that Jewish children should be kept from their families—precisely the opposite!"[25]

Similarly, in a separate article in *Il Giornale*, Matteo Napolitano "severely chastises Melloni for rushing to judgment, and for rushing to publish an incomplete, totally misleading story based upon a dubious memo unrelated to Pius XII—something that no serious historian would ever do."[26] For Melloni, a leftwing critic of Pius XII and John Paul II, no evidence was too dubious to further the myth of Hitler's pope. The liberal American media asked no questions.

For example, the *New York Times* merely reiterated the unverified anti-Pius allegations. Much of the liberal media followed suit. The *Jewish Forward*, the

New Republic, and National Public Radio produced editorials, articles, op-ed pieces, and broadcasts based on Melloni's discredited article. Daniel Jonah Goldhagen, writing in both the *Jewish Forward* and the *New Republic*, called for the Vatican to create and fund an independent international commission "to determine how many Jewish children the Church kidnapped across Europe and the precise role that Pius XII . . . played."[27]

Rather than thank the Catholic Church for saving the lives of Jewish children, the liberal media attacked the Church and Pope Pius XII, leaping to judge and condemn on the basis of a fraudulent memo. Goldhagen attacks Pius XII as an "anti-Semitic pope . . . one of the most rampant would-be kidnappers in modern times."[28] Goldhagen argued that Melloni's memo "reveals that the pope's and the Church's policy was, in effect, to kidnap Jewish children, perhaps by the thousands. . . . Its plain purpose was to implement a plan that would cruelly victimize the Jews a second time, depriving these bodily and spiritually survivors of the Nazi hell of their own children."[29] Goldhagen concludes this attack on Pius by asserting that the Catholic Church "should cease efforts to canonize Pius XII."[30] In his *New Republic* tirade, he went even further, arguing that "the chilling directive of Pope Pius XII points to what may have been a continental criminal conspiracy."[31]

It is depressing that such wild-eyed hysteria is accepted as fact by the liberal media. But while the liberal media continues to offer further grotesque distortions to its myth of Hitler's pope, it ignores what could be equally compelling stories—ones that are true—about Pope Pius XII based on newly released documents. Consider, for instance, the documents about the Nazi plot to kidnap Pius XII.

It has long been known that Hitler had plans to kidnap Pius XII and that Pius knew such plans existed. But now we have more details. In January 2005, the Italian Catholic daily newspaper *Avvenire d'Italia* offered a thoroughly documented account of how General Karl Otto Wolff, the SS commander of Nazi-occupied Rome, was ordered by Hitler to kidnap the pope. It was to happen in 1944, shortly before the Germans retreated from the city. But Wolff thought the kidnapping was a bad idea and told Pius about Hitler's plan in a secret audience at the Vatican.[32] According to *Avvenire d'Italia*, which is published by the Italian Bishops' Conference, after Wolff received his orders in May 1944, he arranged a secret meeting with the pope and "went to the Vatican in civilian clothes at night with the help of a priest."[33] At this meeting, "Wolff assured the pope that no kidnapping would occur, but warned him" that Hitler considered Pius a "friend of the Jews," and an obstacle to the Nazi "plan for global domination."[34] Wolff told the pope "to be on guard, because, even if in no case he would have carried out the order, the situation was in any case confused and bristling with risks." Pius then asked Wolff, "as a sign of his sincerity," to free Italians condemned to be executed by the Nazis.[35] This was done, on Wolff's orders, before the German retreat from Rome.

Avvenire d'Italia's well-documented account of the Nazi plot to kidnap Pius was published only a few weeks after the liberal *Corriere della Sera* ran its story about the French memo. The *Corriere della Sera* story, of course, caused a liberal media explosion. The *Avvenire d'Italia* story received little, if any, attention at all, perhaps because reminding readers that Hitler planned to kidnap Pius and indeed regarded him as an enemy flies in the face of the myth of Hitler's pope. Readers of the *New York Times* and the *New Republic*, for example, have yet to read any substantive commentary about Hitler's plot. Liberal papal critics like James Carroll, Garry Wills, and Daniel Jonah Goldhagen have never explained why Hitler should want to kidnap "his" pope, whom, in fact, he detested as a "friend of the Jews." Perhaps, as William Donohue has suggested, the *New York Times* might wish to provide "one of these professional Pius bashers an opportunity to explain himself on its op-ed pages."[36]

There are other examples of the liberal media's double standard in its coverage of Pius XII. While the *New York Times*, the *New Yorker,* the *New York Review of Books*, the *New Republic,* and the *Jewish Forward* have been quick to publish lengthy (and often uncritical) reviews of books attacking Pius XII and the Vatican's role during the Holocaust, none of these publications has seen fit to review, critically or otherwise, any of the scholarly books written in Pius's defense.

This double standard is especially evident in coverage of John Cornwell. In his book *The Pontiff in Winter*, published in the United States in late 2004, Cornwell acknowledged that he had erred in his book *Hitler's Pope*. He was wrong to have ascribed evil motives to Pius and now found it "impossible to judge" the wartime pope.[37] Cornwell's about-face received only slight notice in the liberal media, which of course had completely ignored previous scholarly refutations of *Hitler's Pope*.

Hitler's Pope and the Hollywood Culture Wars

The myth of Hitler's pope hit Hollywood with Constantin Costa-Gavras's virulently anti-Pius movie *Amen* (2002), based on Rolf Hochhuth's 1963 infamously anti-papal play *The Deputy*. The sensationalized poster promoting *Amen* had a red cross twisted into a swastika along with photos of the film's protagonists, an SS officer and a Jesuit priest, implying "an amalgam of Nazi and Christian beliefs."[38] German bishops meeting in Stuttgart called the poster promoting *Amen* an "outright defamation and a distortion of history."[39] Cardinal Jean-Marie Lustiger, the archbishop of Paris, compared the poster "to pro-Nazi graffiti scrawled on synagogues and Jewish graves."[40] A French Catholic organization tried to have it banned, claiming the poster was "a gratuitous, unnecessary, and public assault on respectable religious feelings." Several of France's most prominent Jewish leaders, including the chief rabbi of France, joined in the complaint.[41]

The Catholic Church is no stranger to cinematic hostility, however. It has endured a wave of hostile movies and media coverage since the 1980s, beginning with such films as *Monsignor* and *Agnes of God*. These films, as historian Philip Jenkins notes, "dabbled in other familiar anti-clerical themes, exploring the far-reaching hypocrisy that was said to lurk behind the mask of saintliness."[42] But in the case of *Amen*, there was a deliberate falsification of established historical fact in order to preach an anti-Catholic message.

The movie plot follows the efforts of two men to expose the horrors of the Holocaust. One of the movie's protagonists is a Catholic priest based in Berlin. This character, Father Riccardo Fontana, is completely fictitious. The other is based on a real person, the devout German Protestant chemist Kurt Gerstein, who helped develop the lethal Zyklon B poison gas used for the mass murder of Jews at Auschwitz and other Nazi death camps.[43] Despite his early opposition to Nazism, Gerstein became an SS officer and was placed in charge of distributing Zyklon B to the camps.[44] When he learns that the lethal gas, which he thought was being used to decontaminate and purify drinking water for German soldiers, was also being used to exterminate Jews in Polish death camps, he is horrified and futilely tries to expose the Nazi extermination plans to the outside world. In the film's "climactic scene," Gerstein meets with another historical character, Monsignor Orsenigo, the papal representative in Berlin, seeking to enlist his help on behalf of the Jews in Poland. Orsenigo refuses to cooperate.

In the movie, Gerstein and the fictional Father Fontana travel to Rome, hoping for an audience with the pope. They arrive when the Nazis are rounding up Roman Jews and deporting them to Auschwitz. Father Fontana meets with Pius, (portrayed, as in Hochhuth's play, as an avaricious, cold-hearted Nazi collaborator and anti-Semite), and seeks to persuade him to intervene on behalf of Rome's Jews. When the young Jesuit priest fails to convince the "silent" pope to take immediate action, he places a star of David on his clerical garb and joins the Jews of Rome, who are rounded up and deported to the death camp. Gerstein tries to rescue him, but the priest refuses to leave Auschwitz. Gerstein subsequently tries to meet with Pius XII, who callously refuses to grant him an audience. Not long thereafter, a horrified and disillusioned Gerstein commits suicide.

While this plot line of the movie is interesting, it is completely untrue. As Ronald J. Rychlak has pointed out, "the real Kurt Gerstein never met with the papal nuncio in Berlin, nor did he ever claim to have done so. He tried to meet with Monsignor Orsenigo, yes, and he was denied entry to the nunciature— but this was primarily because he was wearing an SS officer's uniform. Contrary to what the film would have us believe, Church officials did not cavort with Nazi officials."[45] Similarly, the real Gerstein was never turned away by Pope Pius XII in Rome; in fact, he never made it to Rome and died in a French military jail.[46]

Ronald J. Rychlak rightly concludes that while *Amen* claims to have "historical honesty, its thesis, its facts, and its promotional materials run counter to virtually every historical discovery that has been made since Hochhuth wrote *The Deputy*. Like the 1963 play, it emphatically is not history. Or it is history à la Oliver Stone."[47] Worse that that, actually, it is history according to Rolf Hochhuth, who recently acknowledged that he was a long-standing friend of Holocaust denier David Irving, whom Hochhuth praised as a "fabulous pioneer of contemporary history," an "honorable man" "much more serious than many German historians."[48]

Amen was not a box-office success. But another movie about Christianity and Judaism that came out only two years later broke box-office records. It was Mel Gibson's *The Passion of the Christ*, and, strangely enough, it tied directly into the Pius controversy.

Mel Gibson and the Culture Wars

In response to heated criticism from liberal Jews and Catholics, who attacked *The Passion of the Christ* as anti-Semitic, Mel Gibson repeatedly denied that the movie's approach or message was potentially disparaging to Jews. "This is not a Christian versus Jewish thing," Gibson asserted. Jesuit Father William J. Fulco, a professor of ancient Mediterranean studies at Loyola Marymount University in Los Angeles, who translated the movie script into Aramaic and Latin, said he saw no hint of anti-Semitism in the film. "I would be aghast at any suggestion that Mel is anti-Semitic,"[49] Fulco added.

Interestingly, some of Gibson's harshest critics are the same writers who have attacked Pope Pius XII. Their reasoning is that traditional Catholicism, even the Gospels themselves—let alone the head of the Catholic Church or a traditionalist Catholic filmmaker—are virtually by definition anti-Semitic. James Carroll, for example, denounced Gibson's use of the New Testament. "Even a faithful repetition of the Gospel stories of the death of Jesus can do damage exactly because those sacred texts themselves carry the virus of Jew hatred," wrote Carroll.[50]

Such extremism typifies the work of Carroll and, of course, Daniel Jonah Goldhagen. But it is widely accepted in the liberal media. Carroll, in fact, emerged as one of the most prominent liberal Catholic critics of the Gibson movie, going so far as to call it an "obscene portrayal of Christ's passion." "*The Passion of the Christ*," alleges Carroll, "is an obscene movie. It will incite contempt for Jews. It is a blasphemous insult to the memory of Jesus Christ. It is an icon of religious violence." Jews, Carroll concludes, "have every reason to be offended by *The Passion of the Christ*. Even more so, if possible, do Christians."[51] In the left-liberal Jewish magazine *Tikkun*, Carroll similarly denounces the movie as "an anti-Jewish twisting of the Gospel story."[52]

Carroll's indictment of Gibson is predicated on his assumption, spelled out in *Constantine's Sword*, that anti-Semitism is a direct outgrowth of Christianity and that "Christian anti-Semitism has its roots in the text of [New Testament] Scripture."[53] As Philip Jenkins remarks, "Carroll argues that anti-Semitism is central to the making of Christianity—literally, its original sin. Christian theology is founded upon anti-Semitism."[54] So, in Carroll's view, a traditional Catholic like Pope Pius XII, or Mel Gibson filming an account of Christ's passion taken from the Gospel texts, must believe and fundamentally espouse anti-Semitic doctrines. It is a definition that doesn't need to make room for facts. Carroll's historical linkage between Catholicism and anti-Semitism can be disputed at countless points. Jenkins asserts that Carroll is "weakest on the critical era of the New Testament itself" and correctly notes that Carroll "relies too heavily on the work of John Dominic Crossan, the most prolific and influential member of the Jesus Seminar group, who represent a radical fringe of New Testament scholarship."[55] Crossan also emerged as an outspoken critic of Gibson. For both Crossan and Carroll, "a praiseworthy wish to purge possibly anti-Semitic elements leads them to reject the historicity of many [New Testament] incidents and passages," such as those relating to Jesus' passion, "that most mainstream scholars would accept as authentic."[56]

Carroll specifically condemns *The Passion of the Christ* as a product of Gibson's "ultra-conservative brand of Catholicism."[57] Papal critic Garry Wills agrees. Writing in the *New York Review of Books*, Wills combined a review of Gibson's movie with a review of a book titled *Vows of Silence: The Abuse of Power in the Papacy of John Paul II*.[58] So Wills gets to vilify not only Gibson, but Pope John Paul II as well. He also attacks the conservative Catholic group the Legion of Christ (an orthodox congregation of priests) specifically for its adherence to the Catholicism of Pope Pius XII.

Like Carroll, Daniel Jonah Goldhagen sees anti-Semitism as inherent in Catholicism. Goldhagen writes that Gibson's depiction of *The Passion* is "centrally animated by the notion that all Jews were Christ-killers" and implies that most orthodox Catholics believe that Jews today are indictable for the crucifixion of Jesus.

In attacking what he calls "Mel Gibson's Cross of Vengeance," Goldhagen acknowledges his indebtedness to Carroll, who, in *Constantine's Sword*, "made manifest how historically the Church had turned the cross into a symbol of many things unwholesome and unholy, not the least of which were a martial, conquering spirit, and the demonizing of the Jews as Christ-killers."[59] Goldhagen argues that for those who view *The Passion of the Christ*, it will be "hard to lament the unjust death of a beloved [Jesus]" without blaming the Jews as his killer, "without feeling anger and the desire for punishment or vengeance." Proof of this, claims Goldhagen, is found "both in the history of the cross, a martial symbol brandished by Crusaders and other Christians in their assaults on Jews, and of renditions of the passion during Holy Week, which often led Christian mobs to attack local Jews."[60]

While liberal critics feared that *The Passion of the Christ* would create an anti-Semitic frenzy, the only frenzy, in fact, was their own hysteria. As several Jewish defenders of Gibson have pointed out, "none of the dire predictions of Gibson's film inspiring outbreaks of anti-Semitic violence ever came true, in the United States or around the world."[61] Although "record-breaking multitudes over a span of many weeks have now viewed Mel Gibson's *The Passion of the Christ* in every major and far-flung U.S. locale," noted Rabbi Aryeh Spero, "not one American synagogue has been torched or Jewish cemetery vandalized by the Christian faithful who have seen the movie." He continued:

> Having been forewarned that in medieval Europe, passion plays and
> Easter sermons roused the public to immediate pillaging of Jews and

their property, Americans should be proud that the warnings of [liberal] Jewish organizations, such as the Anti-Defamation League, of anti-Semitic outbreaks did not materialize here.... Instead of affirming its critics' nightmares, *The Passion* has proved just the opposite, namely, how generously disposed American Christians are toward their Jewish neighbors. If latent anti-Semitism dwelled in the hearts of American Christians, the movie would have been a convenient catalyst for expressing it. Since that has not happened, the record-breaking crowds are telling us that they are moved by the positive, the religious, and the inspirational, not by prejudice or prurience.

Spero concluded, "*The Passion* should be now seen as a watershed event announcing once and for all that anti-Semitism barely exists in American Christian communities.... For the Jewish community, the results should be cause for celebration, not anxiety."[62] A public opinion poll seemed to underline Rabbi Spero's point, as seen in the headline: "*Passion* Having Unexpected Impact; Film and Surrounding Debate Might Be Lessening Hostility Toward Jews."[63] So, too, a nationwide survey of one thousand people conducted by the Institute for Jewish and Community Research reported that by a margin of more than two to one, respondents said that viewing the movie made them "less likely to hold today's Jews responsible for the death of Jesus."[64]

Gibson's movie had prominent Jewish defenders, including not only Rabbi Spero, but Rabbi Daniel Lapin, president of the Seattle-based Jewish group Toward Tradition; David Klinghoffer, a leading Orthodox Jewish intellectual and the former literary editor of *National Review*; and the conservative Jewish media critic and talk-show host Michael Medved. Lapin pointed out the hysteria of liberal Jewish organizations who "have squandered both time and money" protesting against *The Passion of the Christ*, "ostensibly in order to prevent pogroms in Pittsburgh." He also noted their "remarkably selective... ire. It is ... bizarre that the new movie *Luther,* which champions someone who was surely one of history's most eloquent anti-Semites, gets a free pass from our self-appointed Jewish guardians."[65]

Writing in the *Los Angeles Times*, Klinghoffer challenged Gibson's critics and defended the historicity of the Gospel account of the crucifixion based on Talmudic sources. Medved defended Gibson and the film "from hysterical and destructive charges of anti-Semitism." "The only relevant question about *The Passion of the Christ*," he wrote, "is whether or not its portrayal of the last hours of Jesus falls within the mainstream of Christian interpretation and finds support within the Gospel text. The enthusiastic embrace of this movie by leaders of every Christian denomination, including the leading Catholic authorities, provides a definitive answer to that question."[66] Lapin, Klinghoffer, and Medved, it should be noted, have been vocal Jewish defenders of Pius XII.

Jewish religious conservatives increasingly see Christian religious conservatives as their allies on issues such as freedom of religious expression in the public square, the importance of faith in life, support for traditional marriage, opposition to abortion, and support for religious schools. Indeed, many Orthodox Jews, as Jewish historian David Berger has pointed out, "feel a commonality" with Evangelical Protestants and conservative Catholics.[67]

Another important issue that links Christian and Jewish religious conservatives is their shared opposition to the resurgent anti-Semitism (and anti-Americanism) of militant Islam and the anti-religious Left. "Above all, the misguided agony over *The Passion of the Christ*," laments Medved, "serves as a tragic distraction at a time when we need unity and allies more than ever before. Let us never forget that the menacing recent wave of anti-Semitism in the Middle East and around the world arises from the Islamic community and the anti-religious Left, not from traditional Christians. In this context, the challenge to Christian orthodoxy implicit in the more intemperate attacks on Mel Gibson's movie serve no constructive purpose and work to foment, rather than deflect, anti-Semitic attitudes."[68]

While liberals attack traditionalist Catholics like Gibson, defame the memory of Pope Pius XII, and practice the virulent anti-Catholicism that, in Will Herberg's phrase, is the anti-Semitism of liberal intellectuals, there is a real threat to Jews and indeed to Judeo-Christian civilization. "Right now," Rabbi

Lapin maintains, "the most serious peril threatening Jews, and indeed perhaps all of Western civilization, is Islamic fundamentalism. In this titanic twenty-first-century struggle that links Washington, D.C., with Jerusalem, our only steadfast allies have been Christians. In particular, those Christians who most ardently defend Israel, and most reliably denounce anti-Semitism, happen to be those Christians most fervently committed to their faith. Jewish interests are best served by fostering friendship with [these] Christians [rather] than cynically eroding them."[69]

In Pius XII's time as well, the fundamental threats to Jews came not from devoted Christians—they were the prime rescuers of Jewish lives in the Holocaust—but from anti-Catholic Nazis, atheistic Communists, and, as we'll see, from Hitler's mufti in Jerusalem.

HITLER'S MUFTI: MUSLIM ANTI-SEMITISM AND THE CONTINUING ISLAMIC WAR AGAINST THE JEWS

O NE OF THE MOST DAMAGING SIDE EFFECTS of the myth of Hitler's pope is that it perpetuates the myth that the Catholic Church, rather than radical Islam, has been and remains the preeminent source of anti-Semitism in the modern world.

The undeniable historical fact remains, however, that it is in the Muslim, rather than the Christian, world that "the ancient and modern strands of anti-Semitism have been most successfully fused today, and from there the hatred of Jews receives its main propulsion outward," as Gabriel Schoenfeld notes in his recent book *The Return of Anti-Semitism*.[1] Numerous other Jewish scholars, intellectuals, and communal leaders agree. "The fact is," asserts Abraham H. Foxman of the Anti-Defamation League, "that virulent anti-Semitism is widespread throughout the Arab Middle East.... Anti-Semitism is tolerated or openly endorsed by Arab governments, disseminated by the Arab media, taught in [Muslim] schools and universities, and preached in mosques. No segment of [Islamic] society is free of its taint."[2] Bernard Lewis, perhaps the twentieth century's preeminent historian of Islam and the Middle East, writes that "classical anti-Semitism is an essential part of Arab intellectual life at the present time—almost as much as happened in Nazi Germany and considerably more than in late nineteenth- and early twentieth-century France."[3]

The roots of Islamic anti-Semitism run deep—and they were invigorated by radical Islamic and Nazi collaboration during World War II. As Robert S. Wistrich of the Hebrew University, one of the world's preeminent authorities on the history of anti-Semitism, has persuasively argued, the anti-Jewish legacy of Nazism "has proven to be especially potent" in the Arab-Islamic world, "where anti-Semitism is once again acquiring a potentially lethal charge."[4] Wistrich demonstrates that there is an anti-Jewish "culture of hatred that permeates books, magazines, newspapers, sermons, videocassettes, the Internet, television, and radio in the Arab Middle East that has not been seen since the heyday of Nazi Germany."[5]

Contemporary Muslim anti-Semitism is deeply rooted in Islamic religious teachings and political tradition. Since the founding of Islam, Jews have had to live "with the legacy of Muhammad's historical interaction with their co-religionists from Medina."[6] The "ire he felt at Jewish opposition to his expanding influence" recorded in the Koran "was followed by his triumph over them and their subjugation to his word."[7] As Abraham H. Foxman has suggested, "this hostility and triumphalism set the tone for Islam's subsequent attitude toward the Jews. As descendants of those who distorted God's truth and opposed his Prophet, Jews would rightly be humbled before Muslims."[8]

The roots of present-day Muslim anti-Semitism can thus be traced to the maliciously anti-Jewish teachings of Muhammad himself. "After being rebuffed by the Jews of Medina following his arrival there in 622," notes Gabriel Schoenfeld, Muhammad "successfully conquered the city, expelling or massacring the recalcitrant Jewish tribes."[9] This "seminal clash" between Muhammad and the Jews of Medina set the stage for "a foundation of continuing theological antipathy," on which Islam would subsequently erect "an indelibly fixed notion of the Jews as a great enemy of the Muslims and their god, Allah."[10] In modern times, "Muhammad's conflict with the Jews has been portrayed as a central theme in his career, and their enmity to him given a cosmic significance,"[11] which has in turn been used to legitimize and encourage Muslim anti-Jewish hostility and violence.

Contemporary Islamic anti-Semitic speakers and publications echo Muhammad's teaching in the Koran (5:82) that the Jews are the greatest enemies of mankind.[12] As Kenneth R. Timmerman has pointed out, this verse, "as well as other Koranic verses singling out Jews for special vilification" by the Islamic faithful "have become extremely popular in recent years with Muslim clerics from Riyadh to Richardson, Texas."[13] The Koran, as one scholar of Islam has aptly put it, "is laced with anti-Jewish pronouncements."[14] Jews are said to be "laden with God's anger" for having rejected Muhammad as a prophet of God, and for failing to accept Muhammad's vision of a submissive faith. Cowardice, greed, and chicanery "are but a few of the characteristics ascribed to the Jews by Muhammad, who asserted that they were accursed by God."[15] The "unbelievers of the children of Israel," according to Muhammad's teachings in the Koran, were allegedly cursed by King David and "in punishment were transformed into monkeys and pigs."[16] Elsewhere in the Koran, the Jews are "accused of falsehood" and condemned "for their distortion" and for being "corrupters of Scripture."[17]

These and other maliciously anti-Jewish accusations, "articulated by Muhammad as reactions to the Jewish rejection of him, have ever since been regarded by Muslims as God's word. As such they have formed the basis of Muslim anti-Semitism until the present day. Though originally directed against specific Jews of a specific time, these statements often have been understood by succeeding generations as referring to all Jews at all times."[18] In this way, as Dennis Prager and Joseph Telushkin have concluded, "Muhammad's angry reactions to the Jews," recorded in the Koran, gave "millions of Muslims throughout history divinely based antipathy to the Jews."[19] Indeed, in 2002, the Los Angeles public schools withdrew a translation of the Koran from library shelves "because of the violent anti-Jewish commentaries that accompanied the text."[20] In recent decades, moreover, the late Yasser Arafat and other anti-Jewish Muslim terrorists have continued to invoke Muhammad's "divinely based antipathy to the Jews," contained in the Koran and in "violent anti-Jewish commentaries that accompany the text," to justify their call for a *jihad*, or holy war, that every "good Muslim" is obligated to carry out against the Jews.[21] For Arafat and his comrades, as for the grand mufti before him, Muhammad's "divinely based antipathy to the Jews," has been the all-important pretext for the continuing Islamic war of terrorism against the Jewish people and the Jewish state.

Since the time of Muhammad, Jews have been denigrated as *dhimmis*—second-class citizens—in Muslim societies, and were required to "always acknowledge their subservient position to Muslims."[22] While Jews were permitted to live in Muslim lands as dhimmis, "tolerated minorities," and were often free to practice their religion, they were always "subject to the humiliation of second-class status."[23] In 897, the caliph of Baghdad, Harun al-Rashid, "legislated that Jews must wear a yellow belt and a tall conical cap." As Prager and Telushkin have pointed out, "this Muslim decree provided the model for the yellow badge associated with the degradation of the Jews in [medieval] Europe and most recently utilized by the Nazis."[24] The failure of Jews to wear this yellow belt and dunce cap, and to thus "demonstrate the proper obsequiousness" to their Muslim rulers, could result in death.[25] And even in the relatively tolerant Islamic Ottoman Empire, where many Jewish refugees were welcomed after their expulsion from Spain in 1492, there were still laws "restricting the number and location of synagogues, which could not be built in close proximity to mosques."[26]

In the centuries that followed, there was a rising tide of hostility and violence toward Jews throughout the Muslim world. During the nineteenth century, especially, "Jews were massacred periodically throughout the Muslim Middle East." Muslims attacked Jews as "drinkers of Muslim blood" in Aleppo in 1853, Damascus in 1848 and 1890, Cairo in 1844 and 1901–1902, and Alexandria in 1870 and 1881.[27] On the Tunisian island of Djerba in 1864, "Arab bands pillaged the Jewish communities, burned and looted synagogues, and raped the women."[28] In Tunis itself, in 1869, eighteen Jews were murdered in the space of a few months by Muslims. Between 1864 and 1880, as Robert S. Wistrich has documented, more than five hundred Jews were murdered by Muslims in Morocco, often in broad daylight.[29] At the beginning of the twentieth century, rampages against Jews by Muslims also occurred in the Moroccan cities of Casablanca and Fez.[30] Indeed, in Fez, on April 18, 1912, Muslim riots resulted in the killing of sixty Jews and the sacking of the Jewish quarter.[31]

Thus, as several scholars have recently documented, the tradition of Muslim anti-Semitism is venerable indeed. In recent decades, as Wistrich has suggested, the dehumanizing images of Jews and Israel, the Islamic revival of the blood libel charge, the wide airing in the Islamic world of anti-Semitic conspiracy theories, the historic support of radical Islam for the Nazis, and the rise of support for radical Islam constitute, amongst radicalized Arabs, a new "warrant for genocide" against the Jews.[32]

In the Arab world, the effects of radical Islam's wartime alliance with Hitler have been long-lasting. They are also in stark contrast to the experience of the Catholic Church in World War II. To put it bluntly, while Pope Pius XII was saving Jewish lives, Hajj Amin al-Husseini, the grand mufti of Jerusalem, was supporting Hitler's Final Solution.

In Hitler's Service:
Hajj Amin al-Husseini, the Grand Mufti of Jerusalem

Today, sixty years after the Holocaust, the wartime career and historical significance of Hitler's mufti, Hajj Amin al-Husseini, should be better remembered and understood. The "most dangerous" cleric in modern history, to use John Cornwell's phrase, was not Pope Pius XII but Hajj Amin al-Husseini, whose anti-Jewish Islamic fundamentalism was as dangerous in World War II as it is today. While in Berlin, al-Husseini met privately with Hitler on numerous occasions, and called publicly—and repeatedly—for the destruction of European Jewry. The grand mufti was the Nazi collaborator *par excellence*. "Hitler's mufti" is truth. "Hitler's pope" is myth.

The scion of a wealthy and influential Palestinian Arab family, Hajj Amin al-Husseini was born in Jerusalem in 1893.[33] Living in Jerusalem during the 1920s, al-Husseini emerged as the recognized leader of the Palestinian Arabs, who were governed by the British under the authority of the British mandatory government in Palestine. From his earliest years, al-Husseini was known as a virulent anti-Semite and as an opponent of Jewish immigration to Palestine. His hatred of the Jewish people (and of the British) was unrelenting. His career as an anti-Semitic agitator and terrorist began on April 4, 1920, when he and his followers went on a murderous rampage and, "inflamed by anti-Jewish diatribes, began attacking Jewish passersby and looting Jewish stores."[34] He was subsequently convicted by a British military tribunal of inciting the anti-Semitic violence that had resulted in the killing of five Jews and in the wounding of 211 others. Because of his status as a leader among the Palestinian Arabs, however, British officials disregarded his record of anti-Semitic violence and incitement and appointed him to the prestigious post of grand mufti of Jerusalem in 1922.[35] As grand mufti, he was in effect both the religious and political leader of the Palestinian Arabs. Only two months after al-Husseini's appointment, a second anti-Jewish riot broke out in Palestine, "instigated by the mufti's propaganda, including a translation in the Arab press of the anti-Semitic *Protocols of the Elders of Zion*."[36] On August 23, 1929, al-Husseini led a massacre of the Jews in Hebron, "where Jewish immigrants had established a thriving community on the site of Judaism's second most holiest city."[37] Sixty Jews were slaughtered in Hebron, and a few days later the tragedy was repeated in Safad, where forty-five Jews were murdered.[38] In 1936, still in his capacity as grand mufti, he incited and led another massacre of Jewish settlers.[39]

Throughout the 1930s, al-Husseini continued to incite violence against the Jews of Palestine, while at the same time beginning to make overtures to the new Nazi government of Adolf Hitler in Berlin. During World War II, as Dennis Prager and Joseph Telushkin have correctly noted, "most Arab leaders were pro-Nazi."[40] The unholy alliance between Adolf Hitler and radical Islam was initiated and forged by the grand mufti at the very beginning of the new Nazi regime. In late March 1933, shortly after Hitler's accession to power, al-Husseini approached the consul general in Jerusalem, Dr. Heinrich Wolff, and "offered his services."[41] His objectives, "as he explained on numerous occasions to German officials, were far-reaching. His immediate aim was to halt and terminate the Jewish settlement in Palestine. Beyond that, however, he aimed at much vaster purposes, conceived not so much in pan-Arab as in pan-Islamic terms, for a Holy War of Islam in alliance with Germany against world Jewry, to accomplish the final solution of the Jewish problem everywhere."[42] In 1938, after British prime minister Neville Chamberlain's infamous capitulation to Hitler at Munich, al-Husseini's overtures to Nazi Germany were officially reciprocated and became the basis of a nascent Islamic-Nazi alliance. But in the intervening years, the influence of Nazi ideology had already grown significantly throughout the Arab Middle East.

Several of the new Arab political parties founded during the 1930s betrayed shades of the Nazi model.[43] In 1934, when the anti-Jewish Nuremberg laws were first promulgated, telegrams of congratulations to the Führer were sent from all over the Islamic world, especially from Morocco and Palestine, where German propaganda had been most active. Between 1933 and 1938, political parties such as the Syrian Popular Party and the Young Egypt Society, which were organized throughout the Arab Middle East, were explicitly anti-Semitic in their ideology and programs. The leader of Syria's Socialist Nationalist Party, Anton Sa'ada, styled himself as the Führer of the Syrian nation, and the party's banner even featured the swastika.[44] So, too, the anti-Semitic program of the Young Egypt Society included "support for Nazi philosophy, viciously anti-Jewish propaganda in the party press, and the organization of boycotts and harassment directed against the Jewish community in Egypt."[45] The pro-Nazi milieu and increasingly anti-Jewish worldview shared by al-Husseini and his cohorts among the new Arab leadership, who would ally themselves with Nazi Germany during the 1930s, was recounted in an autobiographical memoir by a leader of the pro-German Islamic fundamentalist Ba'ath Party in Syria:

> We were racists, admiring Nazism, reading its books and the source of its thought, particularly Nietzsche ... Fichte and H. S. Chamberlain's

Foundations of the Nineteenth Century, which revolves on race. We were the first to think of translating *Mein Kampf*. Whoever lived during this period in Damascus would appreciate the inclination of the Arab people to Nazism, for Nazism was the power which could serve as its champion, and he who is defeated will by nature love the victor.[46]

Between 1938 and 1941, it was this already emergent predisposition of the Arab people toward Nazism that al-Husseini effectively exploited in shaping the new alliance between the radical Islamic parties of the Middle East and Hitler's Nazi regime. During the 1930s and early 1940s, their hatred of Jews and Jewish nationalism, and their opposition to the creation of a Jewish state in Palestine, was so intense that most Arab leaders were eager to embrace Nazi anti-Semitism and to support an alliance with Nazi Germany in its war against the Jews. Central to the political agenda of this new alliance from its inception was al-Husseini's underlying objective to curtail all European Jewish immigration to Palestine and to prevent the establishment of a Jewish state. For al-Husseini, the valued Nazi ally and propagandist, the Final Solution (to the "Jewish problem") advocated by Hitler was the instrumental means to the end of eliminating a Jewish National Home in Palestine. He embarked on his campaign to establish an alliance between Nazi Germany and the radical Islamic fundamentalist leadership of the Arab world "for the ultimate purpose of conducting a Holy War of Islam against international Jewry."[47]

By 1938, the grand mufti of Jerusalem had moved his base of operations to Lebanon and subsequently, in October 1939, to Iraq, where he continued his pro-Nazi propaganda activities. As an articulate Nazi propagandist and political organizer within the Arab Middle East, al-Husseini gained the role of a loyal Axis ally and valued supporter of Hitler's anti-Semitic ideology. Al-Husseini's part in helping establish the strongly pro-German regime of Rashid Ali al-Gaylani, who became prime minister of Iraq in March 1940, was much applauded by the Nazi leadership in Berlin, who soon thereafter invited al-Husseini to move his base of operations to the German capital.[48] On the very day that he arrived in Berlin, November 6, 1941, al-Husseini met with Ernst von Weizsacker, the German foreign minister. He discussed his proposal that as a provision of their new Nazi-Arab alliance, the Axis powers should declare themselves "ready to give their approval for the elimination (*Beseitigung*) of the Jewish National Home in Palestine."[49]

Three weeks later, on November 28, 1941, al-Husseini met with Hitler in the first of several meetings that he would have with the Nazi leader. As Kenneth R. Timmerman has correctly argued, "al-Husseini owes his place in history" to this meeting: "He had gone to convince Adolf Hitler of his total dedication to the Nazi goal of exterminating the Jews, and offered to raise an Arab legion to carry out that task in the Middle East."[50] The new Muslim-Nazi alliance that the mufti forged with Hitler marks the beginning of a "Nazi-style anti-Semitism as a mass movement in the Arab world," that, under the initial leadership of the mufti and his protégé, Yasser Arafat, continues to this day.[51] "The mufti's close ties to Hitler, and his total embrace of Hitler's Final Solution," concludes Timmerman, "provides the common thread linking past to present. If today's Muslim anti-Semitism is like a tree with many branches, its roots feed directly off of Hitler's Third Reich."[52]

From the very outset of his stay in Berlin, it became apparent that the Nazis planned to employ al-Husseini as their chief mouthpiece in the Middle East. Nazi propaganda portrayed him as the spiritual and religious leader of Islam. On January 8, 1942, Radio Berlin reported that the mufti had announced in a telegram to Hitler his adherence to the Tripartite Pact against the British, the Jews, and the Communists.[53] The impression given was that the mufti was the recognized leader of the Arabs, just as Hitler was of the Germans and Mussolini of the Italians. This impression was also given in a front-page picture of a November 21, 1941, meeting between al-Husseini and Hitler in the *Volkischer Beobachter*, the official organ of the Nazi Party.[54]

An honored guest in Berlin throughout the war years, al-Husseini would be warmly received by the Muslim leaders of Germany, who welcomed him as the "Führer of the Arabic world."[55] He called the Jews the "most fierce enemies of the Muslims" and an "ever corruptive element" in the world.[56] Participating in a broad range of activities on behalf of the Nazi war machine, the mufti personally collaborated, through a friendship with Heinrich Himmler, in the bureaucratic apparatus at work on the extermination of European Jewry.[57] From his office in Berlin, beginning in 1941, al-Husseini mobilized political and military support for the Nazi regime and organized networks of German spies throughout the Arab Middle East. During his long sojourn in Nazi Germany, al-Husseini paved the way for other pro-Nazi Arab leaders to find a safe haven in the German capital. As Bernard Lewis has reminded us, even former Egyptian president Anwar Sadat spied for Germany in British-occupied Egypt.[58]

There is also direct evidence that al-Husseini advised and assisted the Nazis in pursuing Hitler's Final Solution. In June 1944, Adolf Eichmann's deputy Dieter Wisliceny told Dr. Rudolf Kastner, the Hungarian Jewish leader and representative of the Budapest rescue council, that he was convinced that the mufti had "played a role in the decision to exterminate the European Jews."[59] The importance of the mufti's role, insisted Wisliceny, "must not be disregarded.... The mufti had repeatedly suggested to the various authorities with whom he was maintaining contact, above all to Hitler, Ribbentrop, and Himmler, the extermination of European Jewry."[60]

At the Nuremberg trials, Wisliceny (who was subsequently executed as a war criminal) was even more explicit. "The mufti was one of the initiators of the systematic extermination of European Jewry and had been a collaborator and adviser of Eichmann and Himmler in the execution of this plan," he testified. "He was one of Eichmann's best friends and had constantly incited him to accelerate the extermination measures. I heard him say that, accompanied by Eichmann, he had visited incognito the gas chamber of Auschwitz."[61] On this visit to Auschwitz, al-Husseini reportedly urged the guards in charge of the chambers to "work more diligently."[62]

In 1943, al-Husseini traveled to Bosnia several times. There he helped to recruit a Bosnian Muslim Waffen SS company, the notorious "Hanjar troopers" who slaughtered 90 percent of Bosnia's Jews and burned countless Serbian Catholic churches and villages.[63] The mufti sent other Bosnian Muslim units to Croatia and Hungary, where they aided in the killing of Jews.[64] SS chief Heinrich Himmler even established a special mullah military school in Dresden for the Bosnian Muslim recruits.[65] A U.S. army officer who seized the mufti's wartime archives in Berlin "found a photograph of Himmler and the mufti raising wineglasses to each other in a chummy toast." Himmler had personally inscribed the photograph: "In remembrance to my good friend, Haj Amin Husseini."[66]

Throughout World War II al-Husseini appeared regularly on German radio broadcasts to the Middle East. On November 2, 1943, fewer than three weeks after the initial Nazi roundup of Roman Jews, al-Husseini used German radio to broadcast one of his most virulently anti-Semitic messages: "The overwhelming egoism which lies in the character of Jews, their unworthy belief that they are God's chosen nation and their assertion that all was created for them and that other people are animals," al-Husseini declared, "[makes them] incapable of being trusted. They cannot mix with any other nation but live as parasites among the nations, suck out their blood, embezzle their property, corrupt their morals. . . .The divine anger and curse that the Holy Koran mentions with reference to the Jews is because of this unique character of the Jews."[67]

Time and again throughout the Nazi occupation of Rome, as Pius XII was saving thousands of Jews from deportation to Auschwitz, sheltering them in the monasteries and convents of Rome, the grand mufti was using German radio to call for European Jewry's death and destruction. "Kill the Jews wherever you find them," the mufti told his growing Arab radio audience, "this pleases God, history, and religion."[68]

There is a great deal on the public record about Hajj Amin al-Husseini's efforts. In his 1965 book *The Mufti and the Fuhrer*, Joseph B. Schechtmann pointed out that "it is hardly accidental that the beginning of the systematic physical destruction of European Jewry by Hitler's Third Reich roughly coincided with the mufti's arrival in the Axis camp."[69] Indeed, only two months after the mufti's initial meeting with Hitler on November 28, 1941, the

infamous Wannsee Conference took place, in which the Nazi leadership produced their plan to systematically exterminate European Jewry. More recently,
Israeli historian Zvi Elpeleg has concluded that "it is impossible to estimate
the extent of the consequences of Hajj Amin's efforts to prevent the exit of the
Jews from countries under Nazi occupation, nor the number of those whose
rescue was foiled and who consequently perished in the Holocaust."[70] These
conclusions, and the compelling scholarship upon which they are based, suggest that it was al-Husseini who contributed—not insignificantly—to Hitler's
ability to execute the Holocaust, not, as John Cornwell had it before he
retracted the accusations of his own book, Pope Pius XII.

While "there was surely no more committed devotee of Nazi Germany
among the Arab leaders than Hajj Amin,"[71] much of the Arab Muslim leadership in the Middle East shared his pro-Nazi allegiance, which from Gamal
Abdul Nasser to Yasser Arafat to today's radical Islamic leaders has inspired
militant Arabs to continue Hitler's war against the Jews.

The Mufti and His Protégés: Al-Husseini, Yasser Arafat, and the Legacy of Islamic Terrorism

After the defeat of Nazi Germany, Hajj Amin al-Husseini barely escaped
indictment and trial for war crimes by fleeing to Egypt in 1946, where he
received political asylum and where he met the young Yasser Arafat shortly
after his arrival.[72] Arafat and al-Husseini were, in fact, distantly related:
Arafat's mother was the daughter of the mufti's first cousin. Arafat became a
devoted protégé of al-Husseini, who "indoctrinated him with hatred toward
Israel"[73] and a burning desire to wage terrorist war against the Jews. The
grand mufti—who had promoted Arab terrorism against Jewish immigrants
to Palestine between the two world wars—"secretly imported a former Nazi
commando officer into Egypt to teach Arafat and other teenage recruits the
fine points of guerrilla warfare."[74] Arafat killed his first Jew during terrorist
raids against Israel in 1947.[75]

During the 1950s, with al-Husseini's encouragement, Arafat began recruiting followers for Fatah, his Palestinian terrorist guerrilla group. In 1964,

Arafat's Fatah terrorists, based in Syria, began murdering Israelis, the same year that Egyptian dictator Gamal Abdul Nasser created the Palestine Liberation Organization (PLO).[76] Nasser also orchestrated the 1967 war against Israel—the Six-Day War—the explicit agenda of which was the elimination of an Israeli state.[77] Nasser, like Arafat, regarded al-Husseini as his hero and mentor. In 1968, Arafat merged Fatah with the PLO. And in 1970, Arafat succeeded al-Husseini as the leader of the Palestine National Movement.

Arafat continued the mufti's Nazi legacy by recruiting Nazis and neo-Nazis for Fatah and the PLO. In 1969, for example, the PLO recruited two former Nazi instructors, Erich Altern, a leader of the Gestapo's Jewish affairs section, and Willy Berner, an SS officer in the Mauthausen extermination camp.[78] Another former Nazi, Johann Schuller, was found supplying arms to Fatah. Belgian Jean Tireault, secretary of the neo-Nazi La Nation Europeenne, also went on the Fatah payroll. Another Belgian, neo-Nazi Karl van der Put, recruited volunteers for the PLO.[79] German neo-Nazi Otto Albrecht was arrested in West Germany with PLO identity papers after the PLO had given him $1.2 million to buy weapons.[80]

The Father of Modern Terrorism

Yasser Arafat—implicated in the murders of thousands of Christians, Jews, Israelis, and Americans—well deserved his reputation as "the father of modern terrorism," and as "an inspiration for Osama bin Laden."[81] In condemning Arafat as "a cold-blooded premeditated murderer," Harvard Law School professor Alan Dershowitz reminds us that in 1973, "Palestinian terrorists invaded a diplomatic reception at the Saudi Arabian embassy in Khartoum, Sudan, and kidnapped two American diplomats and a Belgian diplomat.... The U.S. government has hard evidence that when the Americans refused the demands of the Palestinian terrorists—to free Sirhan Sirhan, the murderer of Robert Kennedy—Yasser Arafat personally ordered the murder of the three diplomats."[82]

As Dershowitz and others have noted, Arafat has also claimed credit for the massacre of eleven Israeli athletes at the 1972 Munich Olympics, a brutal deed that shocked the world. In his forty-year career as the founder and leader of the PLO, Arafat was involved with innumerable terrorist attacks against Israeli and other Jewish civilians, ranging from the hijacking of planes to the recruitment and training of terrorist bombers.[83] Arafat, like Osama bin Laden, targeted Jews just because they were Jews.[84] These targets included Jews at prayer in synagogues throughout Israel and Europe, and even helpless children in nurseries and school buses.[85] His direction and sponsorship of terrorist attacks against Israeli civilians as well as Jewish students and tourists in Israel became an almost daily occurrence during the eighteen-month Intifada (the Palestinian uprising against Israel), between 2000 and 2002, as "suicide bombers with explosives strapped to their bodies... detonated themselves in crowded markets, outdoor cafes, pizza parlors, and public buses."[86] These Arafat-orchestrated killings claimed the lives of more than 640 Israeli civilians in 2001 and 2002 alone. Also between 2000 and 2002, Arafat and his Palestinian Authority were implicated in the bombing of French synagogues and other acts of anti-Semitic violence and terrorism against Jewish communal leaders and institutions in France.

History will remember Arafat as "the most prominent (and the most richly rewarded) face of terrorism in the latter decades of the last century."[87] In this regard, it might well be said that with regard to terrorism Arafat "was a true pioneer of this century. It is a dubious distinction, and not only because it describes the murder of many innocent people. After all, there were many leaders of national liberation movements who resorted to political violence.... But many of them eventually renounced political violence for the responsibilities of sovereignty. Not Arafat."[88] From the founding of the PLO in 1964 until his death in 2004, Yasser Arafat remained a terrorist leader.

In this, Arafat was true to al-Husseini, the "central figure in the pantheon of the PLO... the founding father of the PLO in both spirit and practice."[89] No one had more influence on Arafat or on the minds of Arab leaders after World War II.[90] In a major address in April 1985, Arafat expressed that he felt great pride in being the mufti's student, and emphasized that the PLO was following the course al-Husseini had set.[91] In an August 2002 interview,

Arafat referred to "our hero al-Husseini" as a heroic "symbol of withstand-
ing world pressure, having remained an Arab leader in spite of demands to
have him replaced because of his Nazi ties." Arafat compared al-Husseini's
ability to withstand world pressure to that of the Palestinians in the face of
pressure for reform of the Palestinian Authority. This "pressure," of course,
included the American demand that Arafat be replaced as leader of the Palestinian Authority.[92] As scholar Carl K. Savich notes, "the grand mufti was a
precursor of both the Palestine Liberation Organization and of the Palestine
national struggle and movement. . . . The terrorism, fanaticism, and ruthless-
ness of that movement reflect [his] enduring legacy and influence."[93]

Anwar Sadat, Nasser's successor as president of Egypt, and for many years
Arafat's ally, also boasted a long history of pro-Nazi sympathies and anti-
Semitic speeches.[94] A member of the radically anti-Semitic Muslim Brother-
hood in his youth, Sadat had ties to the Third Reich during World War II.[95]
His attitude did not change after the war. On April 25, 1972, celebrating the
anniversary of Muhammad's birth, Sadat declared: "We shall not only liber-
ate the Arab lands in Jerusalem and break Israel's pride of victory, but we will
return [the Jews] to the state in which the Koran described them before: to
be persecuted, suppressed and miserable."[96] In the years before he concluded
a peace treaty with Israel, Sadat often quoted anti-Semitic verses from the
Koran to illustrate what kind of treatment Muslims would impose on Jews
when Egypt defeated Israel.[97]

The Long Legacy of Muslim Anti-Semitic Literature

Hatred of the Jews is fanned in the Islamic world by the mass circulation of
notoriously anti-Semitic publications, including the *Protocols of the Elders of
Zion* and Hitler's viciously anti-Jewish autobiography *Mein Kampf*. The *Protocols*, an infamous forgery dating from Czarist Russia, purports to document
a worldwide Jewish conspiracy "to rule the world through treachery, fraud,
and secret violence."[98] Unfortunately, it is treated as authoritative scholarship
in the Arab world. Egyptian president Gamal Abdul Nasser praised the book
and recommended that it be widely read. Nasser told an interviewer from an

Indian newspaper, "I will give you an English copy. It proves clearly, to quote from the *Protocols*, that 'three hundred Zionists, each of whom knows all the others, govern the fate of the European continents and they elect their successors from their entourage.' "[99] King Faisal of Saudi Arabia often gave copies of the *Protocols* to the guests of his regime. When he presented the *Protocols*, along with an anthology of anti-Semitic writings, to French journalists who accompanied French foreign minister Michel Jobert on his visit to Saudi Arabia in January 1974, officials noted that it was among the king's favorite books.[100] Anwar Sadat, Muammar Qadafi of Libya, and, of course, Yasser Arafat, have enthusiastically endorsed and promoted the *Protocols* as well.[101] Spokesmen for the government of Iran, from the era of Ayatollah Khomeini to the present, have embraced the *Protocols* and often serialized the book in daily newspapers.[102] Today, many Arabic translations of the *Protocols* are available, many published repeatedly by Egyptian government presses.[103]

Hundreds of Arab periodicals regularly quote or summarize the *Protocols*, referencing them as the "authority" on the "perfidy of the Jews."[104] The Lebanese newspaper *Al-Anwar* reported that a recent edition of the book hit the top of its nonfiction bestseller list.[105] As the great Middle East historian Bernard Lewis has pointed out, the *Protocols* "remain a staple not just of propaganda, but even of academic scholarship," within the radical Islamic world.[106]

Hitler's *Mein Kampf*, a favorite anti-Semitic publication of the grand mufti and his protégés, has similarly enjoyed a wide and appreciative radical Islamic audience in recent decades. Indeed, if the *Protocols* is the most popular anti-Semitic tract in the Arab world, *Mein Kampf* could be considered a close second.[107] Hitler's hate-filled and virulently anti-Jewish autobiography has been published in Arabic since 1963 and is a perennial bestseller in several Islamic countries.[108] After the Six-Day War in 1967, Israeli soldiers discovered that many Egyptian prisoners carried small paperback editions of *Mein Kampf*, translated into Arabic by an official of the Arab Information Center in Cairo. The translator, who was known as el-Hadj, had been a leading official in the Nazi propaganda ministry under the name Luis Heiden.[109] Like his friend

Hajj Amin al-Husseini, Heiden had fled to Egypt after World War II. He took
this new name after converting to Islam. When *Mein Kampf* was republished
by Yasser Arafat's Palestinian Authority in 2001, it achieved immediate bestseller status throughout the Arab world. While *Mein Kampf* continues to
enjoy a wide and appreciative Arab audience, *Schindler's List*, a film portray-
ing the suffering of Jews under Nazi rule, is banned in Arab countries.[110]

The Arab media has also resurrected the blood libel that so many popes,
medieval and modern, categorically condemned and rejected. Since the early
1960s, the Arab media has routinely charged Jews with committing ritual
murders. In 1962, the Egyptian ministry of education reissued *Talmudic
Sacrifices* by Habib Faris, first published in 1890 in Cairo. In the introduction, the editor notes that the book constitutes "an explicit documentation
of indictment, based upon clear-cut evidence that the Jewish people permitted the shedding of blood as religious duty enjoined in the Talmud."[111] On
April 24, 1970, Yasser Arafat's Fatah radio broadcast that "reports from the
captured homeland tell that the Zionist enemy has begun to kidnap small children from the streets. Afterwards the occupying forces take the blood of the
children and throw away their empty bodies. The inhabitants of Gaza have
seen this with their own eyes."[112] And, as Abraham H. Foxman has pointed out,
similar blood libel accusations continue to appear in the Arab media.[113]

Some Arab political leaders, meanwhile, have thrown their weight behind
the blood libel and charges of Jewish ritual murder. In August 1972, for example, King Faisal of Saudi Arabia reported in the Egyptian magazine *al-
Musawar* that while he was in Paris "the police discovered five murdered
children. Their blood had been drained and it turned out that some Jews had
murdered them in order to take their blood and mix it with the bread that
they eat on that [Passover] day."[114] The following year, in November 1973,
Faisal stated that "it was necessary to understand the Jewish religious obligation to obtain non-Jewish blood in order to comprehend the [Jewish]
crimes of Zionism."[115]

Similarly, in 1984, Syrian defense minister Mustafa Tlass published a book
called *The Matzah of Zion*, in which he discussed the infamous Damascus

Affair of 1840, in which the Jews of Damascus, Syria, were falsely accused of ritual murder after a Capuchin friar and his Muslim servant had mysteriously disappeared.[116] In *The Matzah of Zion*, Tlass claimed that the Jews of Damascus had indeed murdered the friar and his servant to use their blood to make the holiday matzah for Passover. In the book's preface, Tlass warns: "The Jew can . . . kill you and take your blood in order to make his Zionist bread. . . . I hope that I will have done my duty in presenting the practices of the enemy of our historic nation. Allah aid this project."[117] In 2001, an Egyptian producer announced that he was adapting Tlass's book into a movie. "It will be," he said, "the Arab answer to *Schindler's List*."[118]

In the light of this continual use of the Koran, the blood libel, and the mass circulation of *Mein Kampf* by radical Muslim Arabs to incite hatred against the Jews, it is particularly irresponsible and outrageous for liberal papal critics like Goldhagen, Cornwell, Kertzer, and Carroll to blame the Catholic Church for anti-Semitism, to falsify the Church's efforts to save Jews during the Holocaust, and to ignore the fact that popes since the twelfth century have rejected the blood libel. It is not in the Catholic world that anti-Semitism thrives, or where religion is used to justify the Holocaust, or where the blood libel is promoted. It is in the radical Islamic world.

Anti-Semitic Arab leaders like Mahmood Abbas, Yasser Arafat's chief deputy and designated successor, can go to the extent of denying the Holocaust even happened. From its inception, Holocaust denial has attracted widespread support in the Muslim Middle East. The government of Saudi Arabia, as Deborah Lipstadt has documented, paid for publication of a number of books accusing Jews of creating a myth of the Holocaust in order to win support for Israel.[119] The Cyprus-based PLO publication *El Istiqlal* trumpeted the Holocaust denial thesis under the headline "Burning of the Jews in the Nazi Chambers Is the Lie of the Twentieth Century."[120]

Mahmood Abbas is the author of a 1983 book titled *The Other Side: The Secret Relationship Between Nazism and the Zionist Movement*, which claims that the Nazis killed "only a few hundred thousand" Jews, not six million, and that the Zionist movement "was a partner in the slaughter of the Jews" during the Third Reich.[121] Abbas, who is considered a Palestinian "moderate" and was appointed by Arafat as the Palestinian Authority's first prime minister in March 2003, has repeatedly refused to retract these claims.[122] Indeed, shortly after his appointment as Arafat's prime minister, Abbas reasserted his views in a May 28, 2003, interview with journalists from the Israeli daily *Yediot Aharonot*.[123] And, as Kenneth R. Timmerman has documented, other Palestinian leaders have followed suit, espousing Abbas's line. Holocaust denial is regularly broadcast through the official Palestinian Authority media. It has become another standard radical Islamic calumny against the Jews.[124]

Such anti-Semitic attitudes do not echo from the Vatican—and never have. As we have seen, the papacy of the Catholic Church has a long philo-Semitic tradition that goes back at least to the pontificate of Gregory the Great in the sixth century. And, as I'll show in the next chapter, during the pontificate of John Paul II, the contrast between Islamic and Catholic attitudes to the Jews was as dramatic as ever.

CHAPTER SEVEN

JOHN PAUL II AND PAPAL
CONDEMNATION OF ANTI-SEMITISM

IN CONTRAST TO HAJJ AMIN AL-HUSSEINI and his doctrine of radical Islamic anti-Semitism, Pope John Paul II expanded the philo-Semitic traditions of the papacy. From his election as pope in 1978, as George Weigel has noted, John Paul II "invested enormous energy in building a new conversation between Catholics and Jews."[1] At his very first meeting with representatives of Rome's Jewish community, on March 12, 1979, John Paul noted that "our two religious communities are connected and closely related at the very level of their respective religious identities."[2] Jewish-Catholic dialogue, from a Catholic perspective, was a religious obligation.

John Paul II made it a practice to meet with representatives of Jewish communities in his extensive travels. Addressing representatives of the German-Jewish community of Mainz in November 1980, he spoke of "the depth and richness of our common inheritance bringing us together in mutually trustful collaboration."[3] Imbued with a deep understanding of Judaism, he described the religion as a "living legacy" that needed to be understood by

Christians. He also spoke of a dialogue between "today's churches and today's people of the covenant concluded with Moses."[4] The pope described Jews as "the people of God and of the Old Covenant, which has never been revoked by God," and emphasized the "permanent value" of both the Hebrew Scriptures and the Jewish community.[5]

In subsequent addresses, he deplored the terrible persecutions suffered by the Jewish people. Indeed, in Australia in 1986, he called anti-Jewish discrimination and persecution "sinful." He confirmed that as Christians and Jews, "Our common spiritual heritage is considerable, and we can find help in understanding certain aspects of the Church's life by taking into account the faith and religious life of the Jewish people."[6]

As Eugene Fisher has noted, the pope's abhorrence of anti-Semitism was "not simply theoretical. John Paul II lived under Nazism in Poland and experienced personally the malignancy of the ancient evil of Jew-hatred."[7] In his first papal audience with Jewish leaders, he reaffirmed the Second Vatican Council's repudiation of anti-Semitism "as opposed to the very spirit of Christianity," and "which in any case the dignity of the human person alone would suffice to condemn."[8] John Paul II often repeated this message in meetings with Jewish leaders at the Vatican and in country after country throughout the world. Speaking at Auschwitz, in a homily commemorating the six million Jews who perished during the Holocaust, he called on Catholics to remember "in particular, the memory of the people whose sons and daughters were intended for total extermination."[9] From the intensity of his own personal experience, the pope was able to articulate the uniqueness of the Jewish experience of the Shoah while never forgetting the memory of Nazism's millions of other victims. The pope would agree unreservedly with the formulation of Elie Wiesel: "Not every victim of the Holocaust was a Jew, but every Jew was a victim."[10]

Throughout his pontificate, John Paul II "persistently, vigorously and unambiguously condemned the Shoah."[11] Meeting with Jews in Paris on May 31, 1980, John Paul made a point of mentioning the great suffering of the Jewish community of France "during the dark years of the occupation."

Their sacrifice, he said, "we know, has not been fruitless."[12] Speaking as a Pole and as a Catholic on the fortieth anniversary of the uprising of the Warsaw Ghetto, in April 1983, the pope termed "that horrible and tragic event" a "desperate cry for the right to life, for liberty, and for the salvation of human dignity."[13] On the twentieth anniversary of *Nostra Aetate*, in October 1985, the pope stated that "anti-Semitism, in its ugly and sometimes violent manifestations, should be completely eradicated."[14] Speaking to the leadership of Australia's Jewish community in Sydney on November 26, 1986, John Paul II said "this is still the century of the Shoah," and declared that "no theological justification could ever be found for acts of discrimination or persecution against Jews. In fact, such acts must be held to be sinful."[15] Perhaps the most eloquent papal statement condemning the Holocaust came at a meeting with Jewish leaders in Warsaw on June 14, 1987, when he described the Holocaust as a universal icon of evil:

> Be sure, dear brother, that . . . this Polish Church is in a spirit of profound solidarity with you when she looks closely at the terrible realization of the extermination—the unconditional extermination—of your nation, an extermination carried out with premeditation. The threat against you was also a threat against us; this latter was not realized to the same extent, because it did not have time to be realized to the same extent. It was you who suffered this terrible sacrifice of extermination: one might say that you suffered it also on behalf of those who were in the purifying power of suffering. The more atrocious the suffering, the greater the purification. The more painful the experience, the greater the hope. . . .
>
> [Because] of this terrible experience . . . you have become a warning voice for all humanity, for all nations, all the powers of this world, all systems and every person. More than anyone else, it is precisely you who have become the saving warning. I think that in this sense you continue your particular vocation, showing yourselves still to be the heirs of that election to which God is faithful. This is your

mission in the contemporary world before all the peoples, the nations, all of humanity, the Church.[16]

In the years following this dramatic statement, John Paul worked to keep the memory of the Shoah alive in the center of world Catholicism. Addressing the leaders of the Jewish community of Strasbourg in 1988, the pope said: "I repeat again with you the strongest condemnation of anti-Semitism," which is "opposed to the principles of Christianity."[17] In commemorating the fiftieth anniversary of the uprising in the Warsaw Ghetto, at Saint Peter's Square on April 18, 1993, he spoke of the Shoah as "a true night of history, with unimaginable crimes against God and humanity."[18]

The following year, on April 7, 1994, John Paul II hosted a Holocaust memorial concert in the Paul VI Audience Hall of the Vatican. The Royal Philharmonic Orchestra was conducted by Gilbert Levine, a Brooklyn-born American Jew who served as director of the Krakow Philharmonic in 1987.[19] On this occasion, the pope sat in the audience hall with the chief rabbi of Rome, Elio Toaff, himself a Holocaust survivor, and Italian president Oscar Luigi Scalfàro. Rabbi Toaff "had brought his congregation with him, the first time that many had been inside the Vatican except as tourists. Two hundred Holocaust survivors from twelve different countries attended, along with diplomats from all over the world."[20]

This concert, as John Paul's biographers have pointed out, was a "unique and unprecedented moment" in the history of the Catholic Church and of John Paul II's personal mission to keep the memory of the Holocaust alive in the center of world Catholicism.[21] In addition to hosting the concert, the pope also arranged for the traditional Jewish prayer for the dead—the Kaddish— to be recited and for six candlesticks of the menorah to be lit in his presence at the Vatican.[22] In so doing, "the pope chose to publicly honor the memory of those Jews who died in the name of freedom" during the Holocaust—in a way that "the [Catholic] Church had never done before."[23]

In April 1986, John Paul II became the first pope to visit Rome's chief synagogue. No pope had ever set foot in the synagogue for 1,900 years, although

John XXIII had once stopped (in his car) to bless Jews leaving their Sabbath worship services.[24] And, yet, even John XXIII, who was revered in the Jewish community for convening the Second Vatican Council (which publicly repudiated anti-Semitism and had expunged from the Catholic liturgy the insulting reference to the Jews as "perfidious"), had never actually entered Rome's great synagogue. In this meeting, when the pope honored the memory of the Jews killed in the Holocaust, John Paul II changed history.[25]

Yet this historic event goes completely unmentioned in the books of liberal papal critics like Daniel Jonah Goldhagen. Goldhagen's anti-Catholic diatribe *A Moral Reckoning* actually attributes anti-Semitism to John Paul II. Goldhagen writes that "neither John Paul II nor any other pope has seen fit to make . . . a direct and forceful public statement about Catholics' culpability and the need for all the members of the Church who have sinned during the Holocaust to repent for their many different kind of offenses and sins against Jews."[26] In fact, however, John Paul II made just such a public statement during his visit to Rome's synagogue. After Rabbi Elio Toaff welcomed him, John Paul II responded with an eloquent address in which he publicly acknowledged, and apologized for, the Church's sins against the Jews during the Holocaust and in the centuries that preceded it. John Paul II declared that the Church condemned anti-Semitism "by anyone—I repeat: by anyone." He did precisely what Goldhagen claims he never did: He admitted, in public, the Church's "culpability."[27] Moreover, time and again, the pope cited the Thirteenth International Catholic-Jewish Liaison Committee meeting held in Prague, with its call for Christian *teshuvah* (repentance) for anti-Semitism over the centuries and its statement that anti-Semitism is "a sin against God and humanity."[28]

In the late 1980s, Rabbi Elio Toaff asked John Paul II to establish Vatican-Israeli diplomatic relations. Six years later, over the objections of some of the bureaucrats in the Vatican's Secretariat of State, which was waiting for the government of Israel to first reach an accord with the Palestinians, the pope personally took the initiative to do so. In 1994, the Vatican established full diplomatic relations with Israel.[29] In taking this initiative, once again, John

Paul II changed history, and radically transformed the Vatican's relationship with Zionism and the Jewish state.

On December 30, 1993, representatives of the Holy See and the State of Israel signed the Fundamental Agreement, which would lead the way to full diplomatic "normalization" of relations between the two.[30] On August 16, 1994, in Jerusalem, Archbishop Andrea Montezemolo presented his credentials to President Chaim Herzog of Israel as the first ambassador of the Holy See to the Jewish state. The following month, in Rome, Shmuel Hadas presented his credentials to Pope John Paul II as the first ambassador of Israel to the Holy See.

As the Fundamental Agreement acknowledged, "This was not just a moment of international diplomacy between two tiny Mediterranean states."[31] It was, rather, as Eugene Fisher has noted, a historic and "theologically significant moment in the nearly two-millennia-long history of relationship between the Jewish people and the Catholic Church."[32] The Fundamental Agreement "was widely regarded as one of the diplomatic master strokes of John Paul II's pontificate and a historic turning point in Jewish-Catholic relations."[33]

In his historic visit to Israel in March 2000, John Paul II continued to condemn anti-Semitism, and Jews and Catholics alike were profoundly moved by his tearful meeting with Holocaust survivors from his hometown in Poland. The pope saluted an Israeli flag, listened to the "Hatikvah," the Israeli national anthem, and was welcomed as an honored guest.[34]

These were unique and unprecedented moments in the history of Catholic-Jewish relations, as was the pope's prayer at the Western Wall, one of Judaism's holiest sites. For nearly two millennia, Jews have prayed at the Western Wall, which is all that remains of the temple compound after the Romans destroyed the city in AD 70. Now came the bishop of Rome, the successor of Saint Peter, to pray at the Western Wall, as a humble pilgrim acknowledging the full validity of Jewish prayer, on its own terms, at the site.[35] For Jews, the Western Wall is the central physical remnant of biblical Israel, "the central symbolic referent for Jews as a people and for Judaism as a four-to-five-thousand-year-old faith tradition."[36]

Profoundly moving, especially—and perhaps the highlight of John Paul's Israel visit—was the pope's impassioned and emotional talk in the Hall of Remembrance at Israel's Holocaust Memorial, Yad Vashem. After observing a moment of prayerful silence, John Paul began by saying:

> In this place of memories, the mind and heart and soul feel an extreme need for silence. Silence in which to remember. Silence in which to try to make some sense of the memories which come flooding back. Silence because there are no words strong enough to deplore the terrible tragedy of the Shoah. My own personal memories are of all that happened when the Nazis occupied Poland during the war. I remember my Jewish friends and neighbors, some of whom perished while others survived.

Remembrance, he continued after a moment, must be in the service of a noble cause: "We wish to remember for a purpose," he said, "to ensure that never again will evil prevail, as it did for the millions of innocent victims of Nazism."

He then made what no one listening could doubt was a heartfelt statement of repentance: "As bishop of Rome and successor of the Apostle Peter, I assure the Jewish people that the Catholic Church, motivated by the Gospel law of truth and love and by no political considerations, is deeply saddened by the hatred, acts of persecution, and displays of anti-Semitism directed against the Jews by Christians at any time and in any place."[37] At the conclusion of the pope's address, many Israelis in attendance, Holocaust survivors and politicians, religious leaders and army officers alike, cried. In his own address that followed, Israeli prime minister Ehud Barak, himself a former army general "not given to sentimentality," told the pope, "You have done more than anyone else to bring about the historic change in the attitude of the Church toward the Jewish people ... and to dress the gaping wounds that festered over many bitter centuries."[38]

This goodwill continued throughout John Paul II's visit. The pope's unprecedented meeting in Jerusalem with the two chief rabbis of Israel was, as one Catholic commentator pointed out, "a meeting of dialogue not diatribe."[39] In initiating this meeting, Pope John Paul II had "seized the opportunity not just of a lifetime but of the millennium."[40]

While the pope was meeting in Jerusalem with Israel's two chief rabbis, the Muslim grand mufti of Jerusalem, Sheik Ikrima Sabri, provided a notable contrast. In a series of interviews, he engaged in "Holocaust denial and Jewbaiting"[41] and publicly rejected an invitation to meet with the pope and the two chief rabbis.

A Lonely Voice in the Wilderness: John Paul II vs. the New Muslim Anti-Semitism

Throughout the 1980s, John Paul II "issued strong statements of condemnation of acts of terrorism against synagogues and Jewish communities," in Vienna and Rome, "sending messages of sympathy for their victims."[42] He condemned, for example, the August 29, 1981, bomb-throwing attack on a synagogue in Vienna, Austria, as "a bloody and absurd act, which assails the Jewish community in Austria and the entire world," and warned against a "new wave of that same anti-Semitism that has provoked so much mourning throughout the centuries."[43] During the October 1985 seizure by Muslim Palestinian terrorists of the Italian cruise ship *Achille Lauro,* in which a Jewish passenger was singled out for killing, the pope condemned what he called "this grave act of violence against innocent and defenseless persons."[44]

John Paul II always condemned European anti-Semitism. But other European leaders have been less willing to take a stand against the resurgent Muslim anti-Semitism that is part of the "Islamization of Europe."[45] This is especially true in France, where Muslims make up about 10 percent of France's population and outnumber French Jews ten to one.[46]

Between 2000 and 2003, Yasser Arafat and his Palestinian Authority were implicated in the bombing of French synagogues and other acts of anti-Semitic violence and terrorism against Jewish communal leaders and institutions in France. The year 2000 witnessed an alarming eruption of anti-Jewish violence carried out almost exclusively by Arab Muslims.[47] During the last three months of 2000 alone, violence aimed at French Jews included forty-four fire bombings, forty-three attacks on synagogues, and thirty-nine assaults on Jews as they were leaving their places of worship.[48] Between January and May 2001, there were more than three hundred attacks against Jews. Synagogues were destroyed, school buses stoned, and even innocent Jewish children assaulted. Yet very few of the incidents were reported in the French media, which has an evident pro-Palestinian bias.[49]

On January 12, 2001, Palestinian journalist Raymonda Hawa-Tawil (whose daughter Souha is Yasser Arafat's wife) spoke on the public radio station France Culture, attacking the "racism of the Jews of France" and the "influence of the Jewish lobby."[50] During 2002 and 2003, the violent anti-Semitic attacks against French Jews continued to increase. In December 2003, a young Jewish disc jockey was killed by his Muslim neighbor, who "slit his throat and mutilated his face." Returning to his apartment, the murderer reportedly said, "I killed my Jew. I will go to heaven."[51]

In the face of this resurgence of Islam-inspired French anti-Semitism, John Paul II often seemed to be a lonely voice in the wilderness, consistent and unequivocal in his condemnation of Europe's new anti-Semitic, post-Christian Left, while other European leaders and intellectuals—politicians, journalists, and leftist religious activists alike—chose to remain silent. Often alone among European leaders, Pope John Paul II issued strong statements condemning acts of Islamic terrorism against synagogues and other Jewish communal buildings and institutions in France and elsewhere, calling these incidents un-Christian and reprehensible. On April 3, 2002, moreover, Bishop Jean-Pierre Ricard, president of the French Conference of Catholic Bishops, issued a forceful condemnation of French anti-Semitism. Speaking in the spirit of John Paul II's many vocal protests against anti-Semitism, Ricard declared: "In recent days, attacks were committed against several synagogues in France, in Lyon, in Marseilles, and in Strasbourg. The Jewish communities are deeply struck in their most precious places of worship. Such acts of violence make one fear the worst.... To strike a community, whichever it is, in its religious sensibilities and faith, is a particularly grave act, which affects our democratic life with full force. In condemning these attacks with the greatest firmness, the Catholic Church in France expresses its profound sympathy and solidarity with the Jewish communities."[52]

While almost all French politicians and liberal journalists were silent or equivocating concerning the wave of arson and violence against French synagogues and other Jewish institutions, the French bishops were the only French leaders—religious or political—to unequivocally condemn the new anti-Semitism resurgent in France. As Michel Gurfinkiel pointed out, the response of France's liberal political elite to these and other anti-Semitic incidents that occurred on a daily basis, in 2000 and 2001, was "minimal or mute."[53] Not so that of the Vatican, the Conference of French Bishops, and the Church leadership in France. As Jewish leaders have appreciatively noted, their response has been forthright and forceful.

Apologists for Evil: Liberal Papal Critics and the New Muslim Anti-Semitism

As Yasser Arafat was the spiritual heir of the grand mufti of Jerusalem, Pope John Paul II was the spiritual heir of Pope Pius XII. During the 1970s, 1980s, and 1990s, while Yasser Arafat was promoting anti-Semitism, John Paul II was condemning it. While John Paul II was condemning the Nazis and the Holocaust, Arafat and other radical Islamic extremists were praising Hitler and denying that the Holocaust ever took place.

While John Paul II was making his historic 2000 visit to Israel and memorializing the victims of the Holocaust at Yad Vashem, Yasser Arafat was ordering terrorist attacks against Israeli civilians, sabotaging the Middle East peace process, and continuing his jihad against the Jewish state and the Jewish people. Between 1980 and 2000, Arafat and his fellow Islamic extremists were murdering innocent Jews and seeking to destroy Israel while John Paul II and the leadership of his Catholic Church were charting new and more cordial vistas in Vatican-Israel relations. While John Paul II honored Jewish victims of the Holocaust, Mahmood Abbas, Yasser Arafat's deputy and designated successor, denied the Holocaust ever occurred.

The liberal papal critics who have been so quick to condemn the alleged anti-Semitism of Pius XII and John Paul II have been much slower to condemn the very real and well-documented anti-Semitic violence and terrorist activity in both Israel and France. Indeed, they have hardly condemned it at all. One can thoroughly search the extensive recent writings of Goldhagen, Carroll, Wills, and Cornwell without finding any criticism of Islamic anti-Semitic violence and terrorist activity against Israel and its Jewish citizens, or of the increasingly numerous anti-Semitic incidents—including synagogue arsons and vandalism and vicious attacks upon individual Jews—perpetrated by Islamic fundamentalists against the Jews of France.

The same liberal papal critics who have been all too ready to condemn and vilify Pius XII for his alleged silence during the Holocaust have been conspicuously silent themselves on the issue of the frightening resurgence of anti-Semitism on the part of Islamic fundamentalists in France. Why haven't Carroll or Wills, for example, taken to the pages of the *New Yorker* or the *New York Review of Books*, in which they frequently write, to express their outrage and condemnation about synagogue arsons and bombings in Paris, Strasbourg, and Marseilles, or about the numerous Muslim Arab terrorist attacks in Israel, which have killed or wounded hundreds of innocent Israeli civilians? Their silence has been deafening. Why didn't they write essays or op-ed pieces to denounce the anti-Semitic terrorist activities of Yasser Arafat, as they denounced the alleged papal "sins" of Pius II and John Paul II? Why hasn't James Carroll devoted even one column in the *Boston Globe*, for which he is a twice-weekly columnist, to documenting and condemning the new Islamic anti-Semitism resurgent in France and the negligible response of the Chirac government and of France's liberal political elite to this new Islamic anti-Semitism? Why hasn't Carroll devoted even one of his numerous columns to documenting and condemning the numerous acts of terrorist violence and destruction perpetrated as part of the Islamic fundamentalist war of terrorism against the Jewish people and the Jewish state?

Despite Arafat's legacy as a terrorist dedicated to the destruction of Israel and the extermination of the Jewish people, a dedication inspired by the murderous ideology of the grand mufti Hajj Amin al-Husseini and of Hitler himself, the liberal papal critics who have done so much to perpetuate the myth of Hitler's pope have not condemned and vilified him, as they have been so quick to vilify and condemn both Pius XII and John Paul II. Worse, some of these liberal papal critics condone or apologize for the murderous acts of anti-Jewish terrorism perpetrated by Arafat's Palestinian Authority. Take, for example, James Carroll. As Andrea Levin, a thoughtful critic of the liberal media's coverage of the Arab-Israeli conflict and of Islamic anti-Jewish terrorism, has noted, "Carroll minimizes Palestinian enthusiasm for terrorism. In a June 2003 column devoted almost entirely to Palestinian grievances... he asserted that 'a mere fraction of the Palestinian population' supports terrorism. Yet a respected Palestinian polling agency, the Jerusalem Media and Communication Center, just weeks earlier had found a substantial majority of 59.9 percent of Palestinians supported suicide bombings against Israeli civilians."

How, asks Levin, is it possible for Carroll to confront the Catholic Church for its alleged anti-Semitic actions, "but to deny virulent hate-mongering by the Palestinian Authority?"[54] Perhaps "most inexplicable," notes Levin, given Carroll's "awareness of the lethal impact of the inculcation of hatred against Jews in Europe, is his apparent refusal to credit Palestinian hate-indoctrination as the underlying cause of the savage attacks against Jews in Israel.... Carroll is evidently unwilling to hold accountable the Palestinian Authority, which from its inception has stoked anti-Jewish hatred through schools, media, mosques, summer camps, and political rallies that have painted Jews as alien, thieving conquerors, to be driven out or destroyed."[55] Moreover, concludes Levin, "in placing the onus on Israel for the ongoing violence and characterizing as illegitimate its efforts at defense," Carroll "does a disservice to Israel no less unfair than the anti-Jewish campaigns of the past"[56] that he has so vocally and passionately criticized.

Daniel Jonah Goldhagen seems to go even further in drawing a moral equivalence between Arab terrorism and Israeli-Jewish efforts at self-defense. "People of good faith," argues Goldhagen in *A Moral Reckoning*, "can have different opinions about how to apportion responsibility and blame for the conflict between Israel and Jewish Israelis on the one hand, and various Arab states and their peoples and the Palestinian Authority and Palestinians on the other. Whatever the range of reasonable conclusions may be . . . Israel and Israelis have certainly committed their fair share of criminal, political and moral offenses."[57]

In their unwillingness to condemn or vilify Arafat or his Palestinian Authority for their murderous terrorist activities, which have stolen the lives of so many Israelis and other Jews, Carroll and Goldhagen have cast their lot with the other liberal apologists for Palestinian terrorism who "pretend that there is no connection between the religion of Islam and those who practice terror in its name."[58]

Reestablishing the Truth

Hitler's wartime Islamic ally Hajj Amin al-Husseini inspired two generations of radical Islamic leaders to admire Nazi anti-Semitism. Yet liberal papal critics with their own agenda against conservative Catholics and the papacy have falsely and maliciously attacked Pope Pius XII as an anti-Semite and Nazi collaborator. In doing so, they have not only propagated a pernicious myth, but have deflected blame from the overtly pro-Nazi Islamic fundamentalists who were Hitler's allies in World War II and who today carry on his war against the Jews.

As Philip Jenkins notes, "there is no question that anti-Semitism is far more widespread amongst Muslims than Christians. Anti-Semitism is as normal and unexceptional in the Muslim world today as it was in the Europe of the 1920s." Copies of the *Protocols of the Elders of Zion*, he writes, "are as easily available in the contemporary Middle East as they were in Europe between the two world wars, and pseudo-learned volumes on the alleged Jewish practice of ritual murder are just as accessible. Across the Muslim world, even allegedly reputable news media peddle the lie that the September 11 massacres were the work of Jews, operating through the Israeli Mossad. Besides parlor bigotry, armed mobs call for direct action against Jews. The slogan 'Kill the Jews!' is commonplace among Middle Eastern radicals and Islamists and also in Arab immigrant communities across Europe. . . . At every point, Islam seems as fundamentally and pervasively anti-Jewish as Catholicism has ever been accused of being."[59]

Today, sixty years after the Holocaust, it needs to be better remembered that, contrary to the myths perpetuated by liberal papal critics, it has been the radical leaders of Islam and their terrorist networks, and not the modern papacy and the contemporary leadership of the Catholic Church, who have played a disproportionate and fundamental role in the resurgence and spread of the new anti-Semitism.

John Paul II and Pope Pius XII both came from the philo-Semitic tradition of the Catholic Church, and they were staunch friends of the Jewish people. So, too, is John Paul II's successor, Pope Benedict XVI. As Cardinal Joseph Ratzinger, he wrote of "the gift of Christmas" as "the heritage of Abraham"[60] and condemned both Christian anti-Semitism and the Shoah, which, he noted accurately, was "perpetrated in the name of an anti-Christian ideology, which tried to strike the Christian faith at its Abrahamic roots in the people of Israel."[61]

Jewish leaders, including Abraham H. Foxman, director of the Anti-Defamation League, have praised the new pope, saying that "he has shown this sensitivity [to Jews and the Holocaust] countless times, in meetings with Jewish leadership and in important statements condemning anti-Semitism and expressing profound sorrow for the Holocaust."[62] Rabbi David Rosen of the American Jewish Committee said that Cardinal Ratzinger's election as pope meant a continuity with the philo-Semitic policies of John Paul II, and noted that as Cardinal Ratzinger the new pope had been "supportive of the establishment of full relations between the Holy See and Israel, and he cares deeply about the welfare of the State of Israel."[63] Rabbi Israel Singer of the

World Jewish Congress added that Cardinal Ratzinger had, in fact, been "the architect of the ideological policy to recognize, to have full relations with Israel."[64]

As it is in 2005, so it was in the 1930s and 1940s: The papacy was and is a friend of the Jewish people. Those who would deny that would deny history and, worse, they provide a cover for the true anti-Semitic evil of our times.

Acknowledgments

―――――

THIS BOOK HAD ITS GENESIS IN AN ESSAY that I wrote on Pius XII and the Jews that was published in the *Weekly Standard* on February 26, 2001. I owe a special debt of gratitude to my friend Joseph Bottum, the former Books & Arts editor of the *Weekly Standard*, who invited me to write this essay as well as two subsequent essays relating to Pius XII that were also published in the *Weekly Standard*. I remain grateful for his continuing encouragement and numerous constructive suggestions throughout the writing and revising of these essays, which have been incorporated into the present volume. I also owe a special debt of gratitude to the *Weekly Standard*'s editor William Kristol, for his continuing encouragement and support of my writing.

The publication of this book provides me a welcome opportunity to acknowledge my thanks to three friends and colleagues who took time out of their busy schedules to read and comment on my *Weekly Standard* essays, and on the present manuscript as well. My good friend Robert George, the

McCormick Professor of Jurisprudence at Princeton University, and the director of Princeton's James Madison Program in American Ideals and Institutions, has read and commented on all of my writing about Pius XII. At Robby George's invitation, I had the opportunity to spend the 2002–2003 academic year as a Visiting Fellow with his James Madison Program at Princeton University, where I began the research and writing of this book. I remain grateful to Professor George for his continuing advice, encouragement, and friendship over the past many years. I am most grateful to Michael Novak, the George Frederick Jewett Scholar in Religion and Public Policy at the American Enterprise Institute, who has also read and encouraged my ongoing research and writing about Pius XII, and has been the source of much good advice for many years. Over occasional lunches with Michael Novak at AEI, I was able to critically discuss, rethink, and refine many of the ideas and arguments contained in this book. I am also indebted to William Doino, Jr. for sharing with me (through telephone conversations and e-mails), his encyclopedic knowledge about Pius XII and the twentieth-century papacy, and for his critical reading of several of the chapters in the present volume.

During the course of researching and writing this book, I have benefited enormously from the advice and encouragement of several other friends and colleagues who took the time to speak with me about material relating to the subject of this book, and/or to read and comment on sections of this manuscript. I would like to express my appreciation to each of following individuals, whose sharing of their thoughts and insights surely has helped to make this a better book: Marshall Breger, Gerard V. Bradley, William F. Buckley, Jr., William Donohue, Mary Ann Glendon, Nicholas J. Healy, Jr., Russell Hittinger, David Klinghoffer, Rabbi Daniel Lapin, Matthew Levering, Roger McCaffrey, Joseph Pearce, Rev. Richard John Neuhaus, Rabbi David Novak, John F. Rothmann, Ronald J. Rychlak, Jonathan D. Sarna, Paola Tartakoff, Andrea Tornielli, and Robert Louis Wilken.

I would also like to express my gratitude to the Earhart Foundation, the William E. Simon Foundation, and the Our Sunday Visitor Institute for their generous financial support that made the research and writing of this book possible.

Finally, I would like to thank my editors at Regnery Publishing for their careful reading and editing of my book manuscript and their many excellent suggestions for its improvement. I would especially like to express my appreciation to Regnery's executive editor, Harry Crocker III, for his confidence in, and encouragement of, this project from its inception. His continuing good advice and numerous constructive suggestions have been invaluable throughout. I am also indebted to Regnery's managing editor, Paula Decker, for her advice and assistance during the proofreading and editing process. I remain grateful to Harry and Paula for their skillful editing of my manuscript, and for their unfailing patience and good humor in answering my many questions as this book neared completion.

NOTES

Chapter One: The Myth of Hitler's Pope and Why It Matters

1. Jose M. Sanchez, *Pius XII and the Holocaust: Understanding the Controversy* (Washington, D.C.: Catholic University of America Press, 2002), 1.
2. Ibid.
3. Joseph Bottum, "Introduction," in Joseph Bottum and David G. Dalin, eds., *The Pius War: Responses to the Critics of Pius XII* (Lanham, Maryland: Lexington Books, 2004), 3; the views of Alfred Kazin, Karl Jaspers, Hannah Arendt, and other scholars and public intellectuals on *The Deputy* and on the public debate it precipitated can be found in: Eric Bentley, *The Storm Over* The Deputy: *Essays and Articles about Hochhuth's Explosive Drama* (New York: Grove Press Inc., 1964).
4. Daniel Jonah Goldhagen, *A Moral Reckoning: The Role of the Catholic Church in the Holocaust and Its Unfulfilled Duty of Repair* (New York: Knopf, 2002).
5. Thus, for example, the critique of Goldhagen by Fritz Stern, Columbia University's distinguished historian of modern Germany: Fritz Stern, "The Goldhagen Controversy," *Foreign Affairs*, November/December 1996. See also Franklin H. Littell, ed., *Hyping the Holocaust: Scholars Answer Goldhagen* (Merion Station, Pennsylvania: Merion Westfield, 1997); Norman G. Finklestein and Ruth Bettina Birn, *A Nation on Trial: The Goldhagen Thesis and Historical Truth* (New York: Henry Holt, 1998);

and Richard John Neuhaus, "Daniel Goldhagen's Holocaust," *First Things*, August/September 1996.

6.   The dates Goldhagen provides for the establishment of European ghettos are found in *A Moral Reckoning*, 36.

7.   Quoted in David G. Dalin, "History as Bigotry: Daniel Goldhagen Slanders the Catholic Church," *Weekly Standard*, February 10, 2003, 41.

8.   Ibid.

9.   Daniel Jonah Goldhagen, "What Would Jesus Have Done?" *New Republic*, January 21, 2002.

10. Michael Berenbaum, "Indicting the Church: A Rush to Judgment," *Forward*, January 18, 2002, 9.

11. John Cornwell, *The Pontiff in Winter: Triumph and Conflict in the Reign of John Paul II* (New York: Doubleday, 2004), 193.

12. Eugene J. Fisher, "What Is Known Today: A Brief Review of the Literature," in Carol Rittner and John K. Roth, eds., *Pope Pius XII and the Holocaust* (London: Leicester University Press, 2002), 77.

13. Ibid.

14. Ibid.

15. William D. Rubenstein review of David Kertzer, *The Popes Against the Jews: The Vatican's Role in the Rise of Modern Anti-Semitism*, in *First Things*, February 2002, 54–58.

16. Quoted in Philip Jenkins, *The New Anti-Catholicism: The Last Acceptable Prejudice* (New York: Oxford University Press, 2003), 198.

17. Ibid., 201.

18. Ibid., 202.

19. Garry Wills, *Why I Am a Catholic* (Boston: Houghton Mifflin, 2002), 282.

20. Jenkins, 202.

21. Richard Rorty, "Acting Fallible," *New York Times Book Review*, June 11, 2000.

22. Eamon Duffy, *Commonweal*, July 14, 2000, 24–26.

23. William Doino, Jr., "Bibliography of Works on Pius XII, the Second World War and the Holocaust," in Bottum and Dalin, 2005.

24. Quoted in ibid., 202.

25. Robert M. W. Kempner, introduction to Jeno Levai, *Hungarian Jewry and the Papacy: Pius XII Did Not Remain Silent* (London: Sands, 1968), ix–x.

26. Ibid., epilogue.

27. "Jewish Historian Praises Pius XII's Wartime Conduct," Zenit News Agency, October 26, 2000; also quoted in Doino, in Bottum and Dalin, 143.

28. "Jewish Historian Praises Pius XII's Wartime Conduct"; Doino, in Bottum and Dalin, 144.

29. David G. Dalin, "Pius XII and the Jews," *Weekly Standard*, February 26, 2001, 34.

30. Quoted in Thomas Craughwell, "Pius XII and the Holocaust," www.catholictradi-
    tion.org/piusxii.
31. William Doino, Jr., "Stories of the Righteous: Jews, Catholics and the Holocaust—
    an Interview with Sir Martin Gilbert," *Inside the Vatican* (August 2003), 31.
32. Ibid.
33. Homily of Pope Benedict XVI at his inauguration, April 24, 2005.

Chapter Two: Popes in Defense of the Jews

1. James Carroll, *Constantine's Sword: The Church and the Jews—A History* (Boston:
   Houghton Mifflin, 2001), 22.
2. Quoted in David G. Dalin, "History as Bigotry: Daniel Goldhagen Slanders the
   Catholic Church," *Weekly Standard*, February 10, 2003, 41.
3. Israel Abrahams, *Jewish Life in the Middle Ages* (Philadelphia: The Jewish Publication Society of America, 1896), 400.
4. Thomas F. Madden, "The Church and the Jews in the Middle Ages," *Crisis* (January
   2003), 25.
5. Ibid., 22.
6. Ibid., 25.
7. David B. Ruderman, "Cecil Roth, Historian of Italian Jewry: A Reassessment," in
   David N. Myers and David B. Ruderman, eds., *The Jewish Past Revisited: Reflections
   on Modern Jewish Historians* (New Haven, Connecticut: Yale University Press,
   1998), 129–30.
8. David Goldstein, *Jewish Panorama*, (Boston: Catholic Campaigners for Christ,
   1940), 200.
9. Sam Waagenaar, *The Pope's Jews* (La Salle, Illinois: Open Court Publishers, 1974),
   71–72.
10. Elliot Rosenberg, *But Were They Good for the Jews? Over 150 Historical Figures from
    a Jewish Perspective* (Secaucus, New Jersey: Carol Publishing Group, 1997), 35.
11. Norman Roth, "Church and Jews," in Norman Roth, ed., *Medieval Jewish Civiliza-
    tion: An Encyclopedia* (New York and London: Routledge, 2003), 165.
12. Carroll, 269.
13. Solomon Grayzel, "Papal Bulls," *Encyclopedia Judaica*, Vol. 4 (Jerusalem: Keter Pub-
    lishing House, 1971), 1495.
14. Carroll, 270.
15. Bernhard Blumenkranz, "Gregory X," *Encyclopedia Judaica*, Vol. 7 (Jerusalem: Keter
    Publishing House, 1971), 920.
16. Paul Johnson, *A History of the Jews* (New York: HarperPerennial, 1988), 216; on the
    subject of the Black Death and anti-Semitism, see Mordechai Breuer, "The 'Black
    Death' and Anti-Semitism," in Shmuel Almog, ed., *Anti-Semitism Through the Ages*
    (Oxford: Pergamon Press, 1988), 139–51.

17. Edward A. Synan, *The Popes and the Jews in the Middle Ages* (New York: Macmillan, 1967), 133.

18. Carroll, 339.

19. Ibid., 132.

20. Waagenaar, 114.

21. Nicholas de Lange, "Martin V," *Encyclopedia Judaica*, Vol. 11 (Jerusalem: Keter Publishing House, 1971), 1063–64.

22. Synan, 136.

23. Lange, "Martin V," 1064.

24. Waagenaar, 108.

25. Ibid.

26. Cecil Roth, *The History of the Jews of Italy* (Philadelphia: The Jewish Publication Society of America, 1946), 158.

27. Ibid., 160.

28. Ibid.

29. Cecil Roth, "Popes," *Encyclopedia Judaica*, Vol. 13 (Jerusalem: Keter Publishing House, 1971), 855.

30. Cecil Roth, *The Jews in the Renaissance* (Philadelphia: The Jewish Publication Society of America, 1977), 215; and Ariel Toaff, "Elijah ben Shabbetai Be'er," *Encyclopedia Judaica*, Vol. 6 (Jerusalem: Keter Publishing House, 1971), 649.

31. Roth, *The Jews in the Renaissance*, 213–14.

32. Richard P. McBrien, *Lives of the Popes: The Pontiffs from St. Peter to John Paul II* (San Francisco: HarperCollins, 1997), 264.

33. Roth, *The Jews in the Renaissance*, 151.

34. Ibid.

35. Waagenaar, 104.

36. Ibid., 232.

37. Synan, 146–47.

38. Rosenberg, 68.

39. Cecil Roth, *A Short History of the Jewish People* (London: The East and West Library of the Horovitz Publishing Co., 1969), 263.

40. Roth, "Popes," 856.

41. Waagenaar, 134.

42. Roth, "Popes," 856.

43. Waagenaar, 147.

44. Ibid.

45. Shmuel Ettinger, "David Reuveni," *Encyclopedia Judaica*, Vol. 14 (Jerusalem: Keter Publishing House, 1971), 114.

46. Waagenaar, 148; Raphael Loewe, "Egidio Da Viterbo," *Encyclopedia Judaica*, Vol. 6 (Jerusalem: Keter Publishing House, 1971), 475.

47. Waagenaar, 149.

48. Roth, *The Jews in the Renaissance*, 218.
49. Ibid.
50. Renato Spiegel, "Sarfati," *Encyclopedia Judaica*, Vol. 14 (Jerusalem: Keter Publishing House, 1971), 878–79; Roth, *The Jews in the Renaissance*, 218.
51. Roth, *The Jews in the Renaissance*, 40.
52. Ibid., 158.
53. Ibid., 22–23.
54. Waagenaar, 104.
55. Johnson, 243.
56. Leon Poliakov, *The History of Anti-Semitism: From the Time of Christ to the Court Jews*, Richard Howard, trans. (New York: The Vanguard Press, Inc., 1965), 57–60.
57. Edward H. Flannery, *The Anguish of the Jews: Twenty-Three Centuries of Anti-Semitism* (New York: Macmillan, 1965), 120.
58. Ibid., 120–21.
59. Ibid., 121.
60. Marc Saperstein, *Moments of Crisis in Jewish-Christian Relations* (Philadelphia: Trinity Press International, 1989), 21.
61. Roth, *A Short History of the Jewish People*, 190.
62. Synan, 114.
63. Saperstein, 21.
64. Synan, 114.
65. Ibid.
66. Saperstein, 21.
67. Quoted in Cecil Roth, ed., *The Ritual Murder Libel and the Jews: The Report by Cardinal Lorenzo Ganganelli (Pope Clement XIV)* (London: Woburn Press, 1935), 21–22.
68. Ibid., 22.
69. Ibid., 22–23.
70. Ibid., 23.
71. Ibid., 26.
72. Ibid., 26, 29; McBrien, 325.
73. Roth, ed., *The Ritual Murder Libel and the Jews*, 26.
74. Poliakov, 272.
75. McBrien, 348.
76. Quoted in David G. Dalin, "Popes and Jews: Truths and Falsehoods in the History of Catholic-Jewish Relations," *Weekly Standard*, November 5, 2001, 36–38.
77. David I. Kertzer, *The Popes Against the Jews: The Vatican's Role in the Rise of Modern Anti-Semitism* (New York: Knopf, 2001), 222.
78. Ibid., 224; Andrew M. Canepa, "Pius X and the Jews: A Reappraisal," *Church History* 61 (1992).
79. Canepa, "Pius X and the Jews: A Reappraisal."

80. Kertzer, 224.
81. Canepa, "Pius X and the Jews: A Reappraisal."
82. Ibid.
83. Sergio I. Minerbi, *The Vatican and Zionism: Conflict in the Holy Land, 1895–1925* (New York: Oxford University Press, 1990), 101.
84. Theodore Herzl, *Diaries*, Marvin Lowenthal, trans. (New York: Dial Press, 1956), 427–30.
85. Kertzer, 240–41.
86. Pinchas E. Lapide, *Three Popes and the Jews* (New York: Hawthorn Books, Inc., 1967), 84.
87. Ibid., 83–84.
88. Florian Sokolow, "Nahum Sokolow and Pope Benedict XV," *Jewish Chronicle*, November 25, 1949.
89. McBrien, 358.
90. Lord William Clonmore, *Pope Pius XI and World Peace* (London: E. P. Dutton & Co., 1938), 54.
91. Ibid.
92. Lapide, 91–92.
93. Ewa Kozerska, "Pius XI and German Anti-Semitism," in Marcin Wodzinski and Janosf Spyra, eds., *Jews in Silesia* (Cracow: University of Wroclaw Research Centre for the Culture and Languages of Polish Jews, 2001), 194.
94. Ibid., 98.
95. Quoted in "Pius XI Considered Hitler an Antichrist," Zenit News Agency, March 6, 2001.
96. "Pope Assails Fascism," *National Jewish Monthly*, February 1939, 207.
97. Waagenaar, 457.
98. Michael Phayer, *The Catholic Church and the Holocaust, 1930–1965* (Bloomington, Indiana: Indiana University Press, 2000), 2.
99. Ibid.
100. Garry Wills, *Papal Sin: Structures of Deceit* (New York: Image, 2001), 29.
101. Kertzer, 280.
102. Ibid.
103. Phayer, 2–3.
104. Lapide, 114.
105. Ibid., 114–15.
106. Pius XI's secret encyclical is discussed in Georges Passelecq and Bernard Suchecky, *The Hidden Encyclical of Pius XI*, translated from the French by Steven Randall (New York: Harcourt Brace, 1997), and in Wills, *Papal Sin*, 29–33.
107. Henri de Lubac, *Christian Resistance to Anti-Semitism* (San Francisco: Ignatius Press, 1990), 32–33.

108. Lapide, 115–16.
109. Ibid., 116.
110. "Pope Assails Fascism," 207.

Chapter Three: The Future Pope

1. Alden Hatch and Seamus Walshe, *Crown of Glory: The Life of Pope Pius XII* (New York: Hawthorn Books, Inc., 1957), 24.
2. Ronald J. Rychlak, *Hitler, the War, and the Pope* (Huntington, Indiana: Our Sunday Visitor, 2000), 5.
3. John Cornwell, *Hitler's Pope: The Secret History of Pius XII* (New York: Penguin, 2000),13.
4. Hatch and Walshe, 24–25.
5. Susan Zuccotti, *The Italians and the Holocaust: Persecution, Rescue, and Survival* (New York: Basic Books, 1987),16.
6. Andrew Canepa, "Christian-Jewish Relations in Italy from Unification to Fascism," in Ivo Herzer, Llaus Voigt, and James Burgwyn, eds., *The Italian Refuge: Rescue of Jews During the Holocaust* (Washington, D.C.: The Catholic University of America Press, 1989),14.
7. Sam Waagenaar, *The Pope's Jews* (La Salle, Illinois: Open Court Publishers, 1974), 276.
8. Ibid.
9. Ibid., 4.
10. Jose M. Sanchez, *Pius XII and the Holocaust: Understanding the Controversy* (Washington, D.C.: The Catholic University of America Press, 2002), 14.
11. Ibid.
12. Ralph McInerny, *The Defamation of Pius XII* (South Bend, Indiana: St. Augustine's Press, 2001), 8.
13. Cornwell, 31–32.
14. Oscar Halecki and James F. Murray, Jr., *Pius XII: Eugenio Pacelli, Pope of Peace* (New York: Farrar, Straus and Young, Inc., 1954), 23.
15. Rychlak, *Hitler, the War, and the Pope*, 5.
16. Cornwell provides a detailed discussion of the background of the Serbian Concordat, and a highly critical (and not unbiased) analysis of Pacelli's role in negotiating it in pages 48–57.
17. Sanchez, 15.
18. Pierre Birnbaum and Ira Katznelson, eds., *Paths of Emancipation: Jews, States and Citizenship*, 227.
19. Zuccotti, 15–16.
20. Ibid., 16–17.

21. Birnbaum and Katznelson, 227.
22. Michael E. Feldkamp, "A Future Pope in Germany: How Eugenio Pacelli Became "il Papa tedesco," unpublished paper delivered at the Millersville University Conference on Pius XII and the Holocaust (April 15, 2002), 2.
23. Ibid., 15.
24. Rychlak, *Hitler, the War, and the Pope*, 6.
25. Ibid.
26. Sanchez, 15.
27. Bruno Walter, *Theme and Variations: An Autobiography* (New York: Knopf, 1966), 221.
28. Howard M. Sachar, *Dreamland: Europeans and Jews in the Aftermath of the Great War* (New York: Knopf, 2002), 220.
29. Ibid., 248–49.
30. Ibid., 251.
31. Harry Kessler, *Walter Rathenau: His Life and Work* (New York: Oxford University Press, 1944), 362.
32. Sachar, 252.
33. Ronald J. Rychlak, "Goldhagen v. Pius XII," *First Things*, June/July 2002, 42.
34. Ibid.
35. On Eugene Levine's career as a revolutionary, socialist politician, and journalist, see "Eugene Levine," *Encyclopedia Judaica*, Vol. 11 (Jerusalem: Keter Publishing House, 1971), 113–14.
36. Rychlak, "Goldhagen v. Pius XII," 42.
37. Cornwell, 74–75.
38. Ibid., 75.
39. Rychlak, "Goldhagen v. Pius XII," 42.
40. Rychlak, *Hitler, the War, and the Pope*, 299.
41. Rychlak, "Goldhagen v. Pius XII," 43.
42. See, for example: "Kurt Eisner," *Encyclopedia Judaica*, Vol. 6 (Jerusalem: Keter Publishing House, 1971), 556–57; "Eugene Levine," *Encyclopedia Judaica*, Vol. 11, 113–14; and Samuel Hugo Bergman, "Gustav Landauer," *Encyclopedia Judaica*, Vol. 10, 1399–1401.
43. Ibid.
44. Rychlak, *Hitler, the War, and the Pope*, 299.
45. The life and career of the physician Dr. Fernando Mendes is discussed in Harry Friedenwald, *The Jews and Medicine*, Vol. 2 (Baltimore: The Johns Hopkins University Press, 1944), 497–502; and Vivian D. Lipman, "Fernando Mendes," *Encyclopedia Judaica*, Vol. 11 (Jerusalem: Keter Publishing House, 1971), 1342–43.
46. Sometimes referred to also as the Liceo Quirino Visconti Gymnasium, it was situated in the Collegio Romano, the former site of the renowned Jesuit university in Rome. Cornwell, 17.

47. Mark Segal, "Ramat Gan Physician Recalls Schooldays with Pius XII," *Jerusalem Post*, October 10, 1958.
48. Ibid.
49. Cornwell, 16–17.
50. Ibid., 16.
51. Ibid., 27.
52. Ibid.
53. Ibid., 28.
54. Rychlak, *Hitler, the War, and the Pope*, 288.
55. For an analysis of Pacelli's involvement in the Vatican's 1916 condemnation of anti-Semitism, as well as the text of the statement, see Rychlak, *Hitler, the War, and the Pope*, 299–300 and 439, footnotes 141–142.
56. Ibid.
57. Abraham A. Neuman, *Cyrus Adler: A Biographical Sketch* (New York and Philadelphia: The American Jewish Committee and the Jewish Publication Society of America, 1942), 143.
58. Rychlak, "Goldhagen v. Pius XII," 43.
59. Cyrus Adler's role in American Jewish public life is discussed in: David G. Dalin, "Cyrus Adler," in Jack Fischel and Sanford Pinsker, eds., *Jewish-American History and Culture: An Encyclopedia* (New York: Garland Publishing, Inc., 1992), 13–14; and in the articles by David G. Dalin, Ira Robinson, and Jonathan D. Sarna in "The Role of Cyrus Adler in American Jewish History," *American Jewish History* (March 1989), 351–94.
60. Cyrus Adler, *I Have Considered the Days* (Philadelphia: The Jewish Publication Society of America, 1941), 319.
61. Ibid.
62. Cornwell, 177.
63. Halecki and Murray, 156.
64. Thomas Maier, *The Kennedys: America's Emerald Kings* (New York: Basic Books, 2003), 102.
65. Ibid., 103.
66. Ibid., 106.
67. Cornwell, 177.
68. Quoted in Maier, 109.
69. Ibid.
70. Appointment by President Roosevelt of Myron C. Taylor as the President's Personal Representative to Pope Pius XII, in *Foreign Relations of the United States, Diplomatic Papers*, 1939, Vol. II, (General, The British Commonwealth and Europe), United States Government Printing Office (Washington, D.C., 1956), 869.
71. This concordat is discussed and analyzed in detail in William Roberts, "Napoleon, the Concordat of 1801 and Its Consequences," in Frank J. Coppa, ed., *Controversial*

Concordats: The Vatican's Relations with Napoleon, Mussolini and Hitler (Washington, D.C.: The Catholic University of America Press, 1999), 34–80.

72. Eamon Duffy, *Saints and Sinners: A History of the Popes* (New Haven, Connecticut: Yale University Press, 1997), 214–15.

73. Stewart A. Stehlin, "The *Reichskonkordat* of 1933," paper delivered at the Millersville University Conference on Pope Pius XII and the Holocaust, April 15, 2002, 5.

74. Ibid., 2. The Lateran Treaties of 1929 with Italy and the Reich Concordat of 1933 are both discussed in detail in Coppa, 193–214.

75. Sanchez, 87.

76. Ibid., 82.

77. Rychlak, *Hitler, the War, and the Pope*, 295.

78. James Carroll, *Constantine's Sword: The Church and the Jews—A History* (New York: Houghton Mifflin Company, 2001), 499.

79. See for instance the historical record compiled by Jose Sanchez of the University of St. Louis; Heinz Hurten, Ludwig Volk, and Konrad Repgen (all Germans); and Stewart Stehlin of New York University, all of whom rely on careful scholarship rather than the headline-grabbing sensationalism of *Hitler's Pope*, *Papal Sin*, and the rest.

80. Quoted in Sanchez, ibid., 86.

81. Report of Ivone Kirkpatrick (the Vatican) to Sir R. Vansittart, August 19, 1933, *Documents on British Foreign Policy, 1919–1939*, Series II, Volume V (London, 1956, No. 342), 524–25.

82. Rychlak, *Hitler, the War, and the Pope*, 329.

83. Report of Ivone Kirkpatrick (the Vatican) to Sir R. Vansittart, August 19, 1933.

84. John Conway, "The Vatican, Germany and the Holocaust," in Kent and J. F. Pollard, eds., *Papal Diplomacy in the Modern Age* (Westport, Connecticut: Praeger, 1994), 106–107.

85. Sanchez, 88.

86. Philip Jenkins, *The New Anti-Catholicism: The Last Acceptable Prejudice* (New York: Oxford University Press, 2003), 198.

87. Ibid.

88. Rychlak, *Hitler, the War, and the Pope*, 285.

89. "1923 Letter Shows the Future Pius XII Opposed to Hitler" Zenit News Agency, March 5, 2003. For an English translation of Pacelli's November 14, 1923, letter, see "Pacelli Denounces the Nazis," *Inside the Vatican*, March 2003, 30–31.

90. "New Proofs of Pius XII's Efforts to Assist Jews: 1933 Letter Targets 'Anti-Semitic Excesses' in Germany," Zenit News Agency, Vatican City, February 17, 2003.

91. Ibid.

92. Robert Lieber, "*Mit brennender Sorge*: Marz 1937–Marz 1962," *Stimmen der Zeit* (the newspaper *Voices of the Times*, published in Germany), March 1962, 420.

93. "New Proofs of Pius XII's Efforts to Assist Jews: 1933 Letter Targets 'Anti-Semitic Excesses' in Germany."

94. Joseph L. Lichten, "A Question of Judgment: Pius XII and the Jews," in *Pius XII and the Holocaust: A Reader* (Milwaukee, Wisconsin: Catholic League for Religious and Civil Rights,1988), 107.

95. Ibid.

96. David G. Dalin, "Pius XII and the Jews," *Weekly Standard*, February 26, 2001, 34.

97. Ibid.

98. Ibid., 35.

99. Ibid.

100. Ibid.

101. His three-hour meeting with Pacelli, and Pacelli's anti-Nazi views, are described in a State Department report filed by Klieforth in 1939, and contained in papers that were donated in 2003 by Jay Pierrepont Moffat, who was chief of European Affairs at the State Department, to Harvard University. Klieworth's report is discussed in: Frances D'Emilio, "Researcher: Wartime pope's anti-Nazi stand was strong in 'private' contacts," Associated Press, August 21, 2003; and in Laurie Goodstein, "New Look at Pius XII's Views of Nazis," *New York Times*, August 31, 2003.

102. Ibid.

103. Ibid.

104. Ibid.

105. Ibid.

106. Ibid.

107. Pinchas Lapide, *Three Popes and the Jews* (New York: Hawthorn Books, Inc., 1967), 118; Ronald J. Rychlak, "Comments on Susan Zuccotti's *Under His Very Windows*," *Journal of Modern Italian Studies*, 7:2, summer 2002.

108. Jacques Maritain, "The Pagan Empire and the Power of God," *Virginia Quarterly Review*, 1939, 161,167.

Chapter Four: A Righteous Gentile:
Pope Pius XII and the Holocaust

1. Ralph McInerny, *The Defamation of Pius XII* (South Bend, Indiana: St. Augustine's Press, 2001), 38.

2. Ronald J. Rychlak, *Hitler, the War, and the Pope* (Huntington, Indiana: Our Sunday Visitor, 2000), 106.

3. Michael O'Carroll, *Pius XII: Greatness Dishonoured* (Dublin: Laetare Press, 1980), 48.

4. Richard McBrien, *Lives of the Popes: The Pontiffs from St. Peter to John Paul II* (New York: HarperCollins, 1997), 342.

5. Rychlak, *Hitler, the War, and the Pope*, 108.
6. Ibid.
7. O'Carroll, 47.
8. Ibid., 24.
9. Ibid.
10. McBrie, 343.
11. Quoted in Rychlak, *Hitler, the War, and the Pope*, 110.
12. Ibid.
13. Meir Michaelis, "Fascist Policy Toward Italian Jews: Tolerance and Persecution," in Ivo Herzer, Klaus Voigt, and James Burgwyn, eds., *The Italian Refuge: Rescue of Jews During the Holocaust* (Washington, D.C.: The Catholic University of America Press, 1989), 53.
14. Cecil Roth, *The History of the Jews of Italy* (Philadelphia: The Jewish Publication Society of America, 1946), 528.
15. Susan Zuccotti, *The Italians and the Holocaust: Persecution, Rescue, Survival* (New York: Basic Books, 1987), 18.
16. Roth, 527.
17. Edward D. Kleinlerer, "The Pope's Jewish Scholars," *B'nai B'rith National Jewish Monthly*, May 1940, 269.
18. Ibid.
19. Ibid.
20. McInerny, 44, 47.
21. Kleinlerer, "The Pope's Jewish Scholars," 269.
22. Ibid.
23. Ibid.
24. Ibid.
25. Joseph L. Lichten, "A Question of Judgment: Pius XII and the Jews," in Katherine T. Hargrove, ed., *The Star and the Cross: Essays on Jewish-Christian Relations* (Milwaukee: Bruce Publishing Company, 1966), 201.
26. Mark Segal, "Ramat Gan Physician Recalls Schooldays with Pius XII," *Jerusalem Post*, October 10, 1958.
27. Lichten, "A Question of Judgment: Pius XII and the Jews," 201–02.
28. Ronald J. Rychlak, "Comments on Susan Zuccotti's *Under His Very Windows*," *Journal of Modern Italian Studies*, 7:2, summer 2002, 227.
29. Ibid.
30. David G. Dalin, "Pius XII and the Jews," *Weekly Standard*, February 26, 2001, 34.
31. Margherita Marchione, *Consensus and Controversy: Defending Pope Pius XII* (Mahwah, New Jersey: Paulist Press, 2002), 48.
32. Dalin, "Pius XII and the Jews," 34.
33. Ibid.
34. Ibid., 35.

35. Ibid., 35–36.

36. Ibid.

37. Rychlak, *Hitler, the War, and the Pope*, 166.

38. Anthony Rhodes, *The Vatican in the Age of the Dictators, 1922–1945* (New York: Holt, Rinehart and Winston, 1973), 272–73; this German Foreign Office analysis of the pope's Christmas address is also quoted in Owen Chadwick, *Britain and the Vatican during the Second World War* (Cambridge: Cambridge University Press, 1986), 219.

39. Eamon Duffy, *Saints and Sinners: A History of the Popes* (New Haven, Connecticut: Yale University Press, 1997), 264.

40. Rychlak, *Hitler, the War, and the Pope*, 264.

41. McBrien, 332.

42. Ibid., 345.

43. Rychlak, *Hitler, the War, and the Pope*, 265.

44. Dalin, "Pius XII and the Jews," 36.

45. Rhodes, 342.

46. Pinchas E. Lapide, *Three Popes and the Jews* (New York: Hawthorn Books, Inc., 1967), 230.

47. Rhodes, 342–43.

48. Ibid.

49. Ibid., 266.

50. Dalin, "Pius XII and the Jews," 37.

51. Lapide, 202.

52. Dalin, "Pius XII and the Jews," 37.

53. Robert Royal, *The Catholic Martyrs of the Twentieth Century: A Comprehensive World History* (New York: Crossroad Publishing Company, 2000), 194.

54. Quoted in Dalin, "Pius XII and the Jews," 37.

55. Ronald J. Rychlak, "Goldhagen v. Pius XII," *First Things*, June/July 2002, 43.

56. Susan Zuccotti, "Pius XII and the Holocaust: The Case in Italy," in Herzer, Voigt, and Burgwyn, eds., 254.

57. Michael Tagliacozzo. "La Comunita di Roma Sotto l'Incubo della Svastica: Le Grande Razzia del 16 Ottobre 1943," in *Gli Ebrei in Italia durante il fascismo: Quaderni del Centro di Documentazione Ebraica Contemporanea*, III, November 1963, 8–37; and Michael Tagliacozzo, "Ebrei rifugiati nelle zone extraterritoriali del Vaticano," prepared for Israeli historian Meir Michaelis, June 16, 1975.

58. Meir Michaelis, *Mussolini and the Jews: German–Italian Relations and the Jewish Question in Italy, 1922–1945* (Oxford: The Clarendon Press, 1978), 365.

59. "Jewish Historian Praises Pius XII's Wartime Conduct," Zenit News Agency, October 26, 2000.

60. Ibid.

61. Rychlak, "Goldhagen v. Pius XII," 43.

62. Ibid, 44.

63. Rychlak, "Comments on Susan Zuccotti's *Under His Very Windows*," 222.

64. Ibid, 222.

65. Susan Zuccotti, *Under His Very Windows: The Vatican and the Holocaust in Italy* (New Haven: Yale University Press, 2000), 202.

66. Ibid.

67. Ibid.

68. Ibid., 204.

69. Ibid., 205.

70. Ronald J. Rychlak, "A Righteous Gentile Defends Pius XII," Zenit News Agency, October 5, 2002.

71. In his memoir *But for the Grace of God* (New York: Delacorte, 1965), Carroll-Abbing describes the pope's protests against the Nazi seizure of Jews, his extensive relief efforts, and also documents Pius XII's direct orders to his subordinates, to rescue and shelter Jews (55–56). In his earlier book, *A Chance to Live: The Story of the Lost Children of the War* (London: Longmans, Green, 1952), Carroll-Abbing had already recorded his own assistance to victims of the war, Jewish and Catholic alike, and given many examples of the pope's direct assistance (77–86).

72. *Inside the Vatican*, August/September 2001, 10–11.

73. Ibid.

74. Harvey Rosenfeld, *Raoul Wallenberg, Angel of Rescue: Heroism and Torment in the Gulag* (Buffalo, New York: Prometheus Books, 1982), 74.

75. Rosenfeld, 75–76.

76. Ibid., 76.

77. Ibid., 78.

78. Ibid., 76.

79. Rychlak, "A Righteous Gentile Defends Pius XII."

80. Ibid.

81. Ibid.

82. Ibid.

83. Rosenfeld, 81.

84. Rychlak, "A Righteous Gentile Defends Pius XII."

85. Ibid.

86. Ibid.

87. Ibid.

88. Henri de Lubac, *Christian Resistance to Anti-Semitism* (San Francisco: Ignatius Press, 1990).

89. Martin Gilbert, *The Righteous: The Unsung Heroes of the Holocaust* (New York: Henry Holt and Company, 2003), 389.

90. Michael Burleigh, "'Hitler's Pope' Tried to Rescue Jews, Say Documents," *Sunday Telegraph*, February 16, 2003.

91. Ibid.

92. Ibid.

93. Ibid.

94. Mordecai Paldiel, *The Path of the Righteous: Gentile Rescuers of Jews During the Holocaust* (Hoboken, New Jersey: KTAV Publishing House, Inc., 1993), 56.

95. Ibid., 57.

96. Ibid.

97. Ibid., 58.

98. William Doino Jr., Interview with Monsignor John Patrick Carroll-Abbing, *Inside the Vatican*, August/September 2001, 10–11.

99. Zuccotti, *The Italians and the Holocaust: Persecution, Rescue, Survival*, 210.

100. Fernande Leboucher, *The Incredible Mission of Father Benoit* (London: William Kimber, 1969), 167–68.

101. George Weigel, *Witness to Hope: The Biography of Pope John Paul II* (New York: HarperCollins, 1999), 484.

102. "Castel Gandolfo Celebrates 400 Years as Papal Residence," *Catholic World News*, December 31, 1996.

103. Alden Hatch and Seamus Walshe, *Crown of Glory: The Life of Pope Pius XII* (New York: Hawthorn Books, Inc., 1957), 188.

104. Dalin, "Pius XII and the Jews," 36.

105. Lapide, 149.

106. Quoted in Lapide, ibid.

107. Raul Hilberg, *The Destruction of the European Jews* (Chicago: Quadrangle Books, 1961), 548.

108. Christian Feldman, *Pope John XXIII* (New York: The Crossroad Publishing Company, 2000), 61.

109. Peter Hebblethwaite, *Pope John XXIII: Shepherd of the Modern World* (Garden City, New York: Doubleday & Co., 1985), 193.

110. Ibid.

111. "To the president of the Council of Romanian Jews, Bucharest," wrote an official of the Romanian foreign ministry, which acted as the intermediary in transferring the money, "I have the honour of enclosing hereby… the pope's contribution—which has been transmitted to the deputy prime minister by his excellency the papal nuncio, with his sentiments of particular affection, for the assistance of the Jews of Transnistria." Lapide, 167.

112. Quoted in Lapide, ibid.

113. Letter from Rabbi Isaac Herzog to Monsignor Angelo Roncalli, February 28, 1944, quoted in Hebblethwaite, 193.

114. Lawrence Elliott, *I Will Be Called John: A Biography of Pope John XXIII* (New York: Reader's Digest Press/E. Dutton & Co., Inc., 1973), 164.

115. Ibid.

116. Lichten, "A Question of Judgment: Pius XII and the Jews," 130.

117. Lapide, 181.

118. Saul Friedlander, *Pius XII and the Third Reich* (New York: Knopf, 1966), 206.

119. Elliott, 164.

120. Lapide, 152–53.

121. Ibid., 153.

122. Lichten, "A Question of Judgment: Pius XII and the Jews," 108.

123. Lapide, 139.

124. Ibid., 141.

125. Ibid.

126. Ibid., 147.

127. Lichten, "A Question of Judgment: Pius XII and the Jews," 110.

128. Leon Poliakov, "The Vatican and the Jewish Question," *Commentary*, November 1950.

129. *Time*, December 23, 1940, 38–40.

130. My following discussion of, and citations for, the many tributes to Pius XII from various Jewish leaders who praised him for his role in saving Jews during the Holocaust is based on my article "Pius XII and the Jews," 38–39; Pinchas Lapide, *Three Popes and the Jews*, 224–28; and Dimitri Cavalli, "The Good Samaritan: Jewish Praise for Pope Pius XII, *Inside the Vatican*, October 2000, 72–77.

131. Quoted in Dalin, "Pius XII and the Jews," 38.

132. Cavalli, "The Good Samaritan: Jewish Praise for Pope Pius XII," 75.

133. Marchione, 50.

134. Ibid., 131.

135. Lapide, 226.

136. Quoted in Cavalli, "The Good Samaritan: Jewish Praise for Pope Pius XII," 75–76.

137. Lapide, 226.

138. Ibid., 225.

139. Ibid., 133.

140. Quoted in Cavalli, "The Good Samaritan: Jewish Praise for Pope Pius XII," 75–76.

141. As the *Jerusalem Post* noted, three days later, in its front-page article about the Israeli Philharmonic Orchestra's concert at the Vatican, the Israeli Philharmonic's "Conductor Paul Klecki had requested that the Orchestra on its first visit to Italy play for the pope as a gesture of gratitude for the help his Church had given to all those persecuted by Nazi fascism." (*Jerusalem Post*, May 29, 1955). Articles about the Israeli Philharmonic Orchestra's concert in tribute to Pius XII at the Vatican also appeared in the Vatican newspaper *L'Osservatore Romano*, May 27, 1955, and in the Catholic newspaper *Tablet* of London, in its June 11, 1955, and June 30, 1955, issues.

142. The unsubstantiated allegation of some of Pius XII's critics that the Israeli Philharmonic's May 26, 1955, concert at the Vatican was held to honor the Italian people

and not the pope—that the Vatican was simply the venue—is categorically refuted by the statement of the Orchestra's conductor, Paul Klecki, noted above.

143. Quoted in Marchione, 117.
144. Lapide, 228.
145. Cavalli, "The Good Samaritan: Jewish Praise for Pope Pius XII," 76.
146. Lapide, 228.
147. Ibid., 229.
148. Zuccotti, *Under His Very Windows: The Vatican and the Holocaust in Italy*, 259–63.
149. Ibid., 303–04.
150. Ibid.
151. John S. Conway, "Records and Documents of the Holy See Relating to the Second World War," *Yad Vashem Studies* 15, 1983, 327–45.
152. Ibid.
153. Martin Gilbert, *Never Again: A History of the Holocaust* (New York: Universe Publishing, 2000), 104.
154. Ibid.
155. Gilbert, *The Righteous: The Unsung Heroes of the Holocaust*, xv.
156. Mordecai Paldiel, *Saving the Jews: Amazing Stories of Men and Women Who Defied the Final Solution* (Rockville, Maryland: Schreiber Publishing, 2000), 28.
157. Ibid.
158. Ibid., 29; and Emmy E. Werner, *A Conspiracy of Decency: The Rescue of Danish Jews During World War II* (Cambridge, Massachusetts: Westview Press, 2002), 167.
159. Gilbert, *Never Again: A History of the Holocaust*, 104.
160. Gilbert, *The Righteous: The Unsung Heroes of the Holocaust*, xvi.
161. Yad Vashem spokeswoman Lisa Davidson quoted in an Associated Press obituary of Cardinal Palazzini in the *Toronto Globe and Mail*, October 16, 2000, which is quoted by Martin Gilbert in *The Righteous: The Unsung Heroes of the Holocaust*, 365.
162. Quoted in Zuccotti, *Under His Very Windows: The Vatican and the Holocaust in Italy*, 301; and also in Lapide, 228.
163. Lapide; and Robert A. Graham, S.J., "Relations of Pius XII and the Catholic Community with Jewish Organizations," in Herzer, Voigt, and Burgwyn, eds., 231.
164. Quoted in Lapide, 131–32.
165. Quoted in Rychlak, *Hitler, the War, and the Pope*, 217; and in Marchione, 76.

Chapter Five: The Liberal Media and the Culture Wars

1. James Carroll, "The Saint and the Holocaust," *New Yorker*, June 7, 1999, 52–57.
2. Daniel Jonah Goldhagen, *A Moral Reckoning: The Role of the Catholic Church in the Holocaust and Its Unfulfilled Duty of Repair* (New York: Knopf, 2002), 197.
3. Philip Jenkins, *The New Anti-Catholicism: The Last Acceptable Prejudice* (New York: Oxford University Press, 2003), 201.

4.   Daniel Jonah Goldhagen, "Hide and Seek: Questions for the Vatican," *New Republic*, January 31, 2005, 13.

5.   Daniel Jonah Goldhagen, "The Unsaintly Acts of Pius XII," *Jewish Forward*, February 7, 2005, 7.

6.   Jenkins, 193.

7.   Ibid.

8.   Goldhagen, "Hide and Seek: Questions for the Vatican,"13.

9.   My discussion of this allegation, and the public controversy it has precipitated, is based primarily on the comprehensive analysis found in William Doino, Jr., "Another Anti-Papal Hoax," *Inside the Vatican*, January/February 2005, 8–11; and Ronald J. Rychlak, "Postwar Catholics, Jewish Children and a Rush to Judgment: Pius XII Never Told Catholic Groups to Keep 'Hidden' Jewish Children from Their Families after World War II," www.beliefnet.com, January 19, 2005.

10.   Doino, "Another Anti-Papal Hoax."

11.   A critique of the credibility of this *New York Times* article, and the anti-Pius allegations it contains, can be found in P. Thierry, "*New York Times* Wrong: Pius XII Saved Jews," www.newsmax.com, January 27, 2005.

12.   Rychlak, "Postwar Catholics, Jewish Children and a Rush to Judgment."

13.   Doino, "Another Anti-Papal Hoax."

14.   Rabbi Herzog is quoted in Rychlak, "Postwar Catholics, Jewish Children and a Rush to Judgment."

15.   The *Palestine Post* report of Rabbi Herzog's meeting with the pope is discussed in Pinchas Lapide, *Three Popes and the Jews* (New York: Hawthorn Books, Inc., 1967), 210.

16.   Ibid.

17.   "French Nazi hunter deflates Jewish war children row," *Haaretz*, January 20, 2005.

18.   Ibid.

19.   Doino, "Another Anti-Papal Hoax."

20.   Rychlak, "Postwar Catholics, Jewish Children and a Rush to Judgment."

21.   Ibid.

22.   Andrea Tornielli and Matteo L. Napolitano, *Il Papa che salvo gli Ebrei* (Italy: Piemme, 2004).

23.   Andrea Tornielli, "Ecco il vero documento su Pio XII e i bimbi Ebrei," ("The real/true document of Pius XII and the Jewish Children"), *Il Giornale*, January 11, 2005.

24.   Thierry, "*New York Times* Wrong: Pius XII Saved Jews."

25.   Ibid.

26.   Matteo L. Napolitano, "The Hasty Scoop of Professor Melloni," *Il Giornale*, January 11, 2005.

27.   Goldhagen, "The Unsaintly Acts of Pius XII."

NOTES   185

28. Ibid.; quoted also in Rychlak, "Postwar Catholics, Jewish Children and a Rush to Judgment."

29. Goldhagen, "The Unsaintly Acts of Pius XII."

30. Ibid.

31. Goldhagen, "Hide and Seek: Questions for the Vatican."

32. "Newspaper Publishes Pope Pius XII Account," AP News Services, January 15, 2005.

33. William Donohue, "Hitler's Plot to Kidnap Pope Leaves Some Mute," news release, Catholic League for Religious and Civil Rights, January 18, 2005.

34. Ibid.

35. "Newspaper Publishes Pope Pius XII Account."

36. Donohue, "Hitler's Plot to Kidnap Pope Leaves Some Mute."

37. John Cornwell, *The Pontiff in Winter: Triumph and Conflict in the Reign of John Paul II* (New York: Doubleday, 2004), 193.

38. See A. O. Scott, "An Inventor Trapped in Nazi Evil," *New York Times*, January 24, 2003; Rex Reed, "The Pope, the Fuhrer, A Secret Shame," *New York Observer*, February 10, 2003; Annette Insdorf, "Extreme Close-up: The Shoah as the Subject of a Lifetime," *Forward*, January 3, 2003; and Tom Tugend, "Silent Witnesses: Costa-Gavras's 'Amen' brings to light the story of those who, during the Holocaust, saw all but said nothing," *Jewish Journal of Greater Los Angeles*, January 31, 2003.

39. Ibid.

40. Archbishop Jean-Marie Lustiger of Paris is quoted in Paul Webster, "New shocker from the man who invented death-row chic: the Christian Swastika," *Observer*, Paris, February 17, 2002.

41. Ibid.

42. Jenkins, 160.

43. Gerstein's role in helping to develop the lethal poison gas used for the mass murder of Jews in the Nazi death camps is mentioned in the following reviews of the Costa-Gavras movie *Amen*: Reed, "The Pope, The Fuhrer, A Secret Shame"; A. James Rudin, "Probing the Holocaust and World War II With Film," *Commentary*, January 31, 2003); Insdorf, "Extreme Close-up"; and Tugend, "Silent Witnesses."

44. Ronald J. Rychlak, "The Church and the Holocaust," *Wall Street Journal Europe*, March 28, 2002.

45. Ibid.

46. Ibid.

47. Ibid.

48. http://www.holocaust-education.de/news/stories/storyReader$1243.

49. Bettijane Levine, "Scholars Express Concern Over Gibson's 'Passion,'" *Los Angeles Times*, April 27, 2003; quoted in David Limbaugh, *Persecution: How Liberals Are Waging War Against Christianity* (Washington, D.C.: Regnery, 2003), 289.

50. James Carroll, "The True Horror of the Death of Jesus," *Boston Globe*, April 15, 2003.

51. James Carroll, "An Obscene Portrayal of Christ's Passion," *Boston Globe*, February 24, 2004.

52. James Carroll, "Mel Gibson's Passion," *Tikkun*, March/April 2004.

53. Jenkins, 187.

54. Ibid.

55. Ibid., 188.

56. Ibid., 188–89.

57. Carroll, "Mel Gibson's Passion."

58. Garry Wills, "God in the Hands of Angry Sinners," *New York Review of Books*, April 8, 2004, 68–74.

59. Daniel Jonah Goldhagen, "Mel Gibson's Cross of Vengeance," *Forward*, March 5, 2004, 9.

60. Ibid.

61. Michael Medved, *Right Turns: Unconventional Lessons from a Controversial Life* (New York: Crown Forum, 2004), 405.

62. Aryeh Spero, "American Christians Don't Threaten Jews," *Wall Street Journal*, April 5, 2004.

63. Medved, 405–06.

64. Quoted in ibid., 406.

65. Rabbi Daniel Lapin, "Protesting Passion: What happened to 'artistic freedom'?" National Review Online, September 26, 2003.

66. Michael Medved, "Misguided Critics Fall Into The 'Passion' Pit," http://www.toward tradition .org/article_Passion_Medved.htm., March 17, 2004.

67. David Berger, "Jews, Christians and *The Passion*," *Commentary*, May 1, 2004, 25.

68. Medved, "Misguided Critics Fall Into The 'Passion' Pit."

69. Lapin, "Protesting Passion: What happened to 'artistic freedom'?"

Chapter Six: Hitler's Mufti: Muslim Anti-Semitism and the Continuing Islamic War against the Jews

1. Gabriel Schoenfeld, *The Return of Anti-Semitism* (San Francisco: Encounter Books, 2004), 6.

2. Abraham H. Foxman, *Never Again? The Threat of the New Anti-Semitism* (New York: HarperCollins, 2003), 195.

3. Bernard Lewis, *Semites and Anti-Semites: An Inquiry into Conflict and Prejudice* (New York: W. W. Norton, 1999), 256; and quoted in Schoenfeld, 24.

4. Robert S. Wistrich, "The Old-New Anti-Semitism," in Ron Rosenbaum, *Those Who Forget the Past: The Question of Anti-Semitism* (New York: Random House, 2004), 71.

5. Ibid., 71–72.

6. Foxman, 196.
7. Ibid., 196–97.
8. Ibid., 197.
9. Schoenfeld, 32.
10. Ibid.
11. Lewis, *Semites and Anti-Semites*, 128.
12. Dennis Prager and Joseph Telushkin, *Why The Jews? The Reason for Anti-Semitism* (New York: Simon and Schuster, Inc., 1983), 125.
13. Kenneth R. Timmerman, *Preachers of Hate: Islam and the War on America* (New York: Three Rivers Press, 2004), 81.
14. Jane S. Gerber, "Anti-Semitism in the Muslim World," in David Berger, ed., *History and Hate: Dimensions of Anti-Semitism* (Philadelphia: The Jewish Publication Society of America, 1986), 78.
15. Ibid., 78–79.
16. Timmerman, 81.
17. Gerber, "Anti-Semitism in the Muslim World," 78.
18. Prager and Telushkin, 114.
19. Ibid.
20. Philip Jenkins, *The New Anti-Catholicism* (New York: Oxford University Press, 2004), 191.
21. Timmerman, 196.
22. Ibid., 99.
23. Foxman, 196.
24. Prager and Telushkin, 117–18.
25. Timmerman, 99.
26. Foxman, 197.
27. Timmerman, 100.
28. Robert S. Wistrich, *Anti-Semitism: The Longest Hatred* (New York: Pantheon Books, 1991), 205.
29. Ibid., 205–06.
30. Timmerman, 100.
31. Wistrich, *Anti-Semitism*, 205.
32. Ibid., 71–72.
33. Elias Cooper, "Forgotten Palestinian: The Nazi Mufti," *The American Zionist* (March/April 1978), 6.
34. Timmerman, 102.
35. Ibid., 103.
36. Cooper, "Forgotten Palestinian," 7.
37. Timmerman, 103.
38. Cooper, "Forgotten Palestinian," 9.
39. Timmerman, 103.

40. Prager and Telushkin, 123.
41. Bernard Lewis, *The Crisis of Islam* (New York: Random House, 2003), 59–60.
42. Lewis, *Semites and Anti-Semites*, 147.
43. Ibid., 148.
44. Paul Longgrear and Raymond McNemar, "The Arab/Muslim Nazi Connection," Canadian Friends (International Christian Embassy, Jerusalem, 2003) www.cdn-friendsicej.ca/medigest/mayoo/arab.nazi.html.
45. Lewis, *Semites and Anti-Semites*, 148–49.
46. Quoted in Lewis, ibid., 147–48.
47. Foxman, 198.
48. Ibid., 150.
49. Lewis, *Semites and Anti-Semites*, 151–52.
50. Timmerman, 103.
51. Ibid., 104.
52. Ibid.
53. Cooper, "Forgotten Palestinian," 17.
54. Ibid.
55. Ibid., 107.
56. Ibid.
57. Schoenfeld, 37.
58. Lewis, *The Crisis of Islam*, 60.
59. Joseph B. Schechtmann, *The Mufti and the Fuehrer: The Rise and Fall of Haj Amin el-Husseini* (New York: Thomas Yoseloff, 1965), 159.
60. Ibid., 159–60.
61. Ibid., 160.
62. Longgrear and McNemar, "The Arab/Muslim Nazi Connection," 2.
63. Timmerman, 110; al-Husseini's role in recruiting the Bosnian Muslim Waffen SS company is also recounted in Cooper, "Forgotten Palestinian," 23–24.
64. Timmerman, 110.
65. Longgrear and McNemar, "The Arab/Muslim Nazi Connection," 2.
66. Timmerman, 111.
67. Cooper, "Forgotten Palestinian," 26; and quoted in Prager and Telushkin, 123.
68. Zvi Elpeleg, *The Grand Mufti: Haj Amin al-Hussaini, Founder of the Palestinian National Movement*, David Harvey, trans. (London: Frank Cass & Co, 1993), 179; this speech of al-Husseini, which was broadcast over Berlin radio on March 1, 1944, is also quoted in Schoenfeld, 37.
69. Schechtmann, 152.
70. Elpeleg, 72.
71. Ibid., 179.
72. David N. Bossie, "Yasser Arafat: Nazi Trained," *Washington Times*, August 9, 2002.
73. Ibid.

74. Ibid.
75. Ibid.
76. Ibid.
77. David Horowitz, *Unholy Alliance: Radical Islam and the American Left* (Washington, D.C.: Regnery, 2004), 135.
78. Benjamin Netanyahu, "Ending the Legacy of Hate," address delivered at a session called "The Question of Palestine" at the Fortieth General Assembly of the United Nations, December 4, 1985, 6.
79. Ibid.
80. Ibid.
81. Joseph Farah, "Arafat the Nazi," *Between the Lines*, www.worldnetdaily.com, August 14, 2002.
82. Alan M. Dershowitz, "Put Arafat on Trial," *Ha'aretz Daily*, September 13, 2002.
83. Gary Rosenblatt, "No Tears for Arafat," *Jewish Week* (New York), November 5, 2004, 7.
84. Dershowitz, "Put Arafat on Trial."
85. Ibid.
86. "Arab Leaders Glorify Suicide Terrorism," Anti-Defamation League of B'nai B'rith, April 17, 2002.
87. "Arafat," *New Republic*, November 22, 2004, 7.
88. Ibid.
89. Netanyahu, "Ending the Legacy of Hate," 3.
90. Timmerman, 120.
91. Netanyahu, "Ending the Legacy of Hate," 3.
92. Itamar Marcus, "Nazi Ally, Hajj Amin al-Husseini, is Arafat's 'hero,'" *Israel Report*, August 2002.
93. Carl K. Savich, "Islam Under the Swastika: The Grand Mufti and the Nazi Protectorate of Bosnia-Hercegovina, 1941–1945," (online article, 2002), 3.
94. Arnold Forster and Benjamin R. Epstein, *The New Anti-Semitism* (New York: McGraw-Hill Book Company, 1974), 160.
95. Ibid.
96. Ibid., 161.
97. Joseph Telushkin, *Jewish Literacy* (New York: William Morrow & Co., 1991), 161.
98. Foxman, 214.
99. Quoted in Prager and Telushkin, 125.
100. Ibid.
101. As Arnold Forster and Benjamin R. Epstein have documented, Western journalists visiting Libya's colonel have noted that he keeps a pile of the *Protocols* on his desk. (Forster and Epstein, 159.)
102. Bernard Lewis, "Muslim Anti-Semitism," in Ron Rosenbaum, ed., *Those Who Forget the Past: The Question of Anti-Semitism* (New York: Random House Trade Paperbacks, 2004), 551.

103. Foxman, 214.

104. Forster and Epstein, 159.

105. Ibid., 158–59.

106. Lewis, "Muslim Anti-Semitism," in Rosenbaum, ed., 554.

107. Forster and Epstein, 159.

108. Foxman, 198.

109. Forster and Epstein, 159–60.

110. Lewis, "Muslim Anti-Semitism," in Rosenbaum, ed., 558.

111. Prager and Telushkin, 124.

112. Ibid., 124–25.

113. Foxman, 213.

114. Ibid.

115. Cited in Prager and Telushkin, 125.

116. Foxman, 213.

117. Quoted in Timmerman, 71.

118. Foxman, 213–14.

119. Deborah Lipstadt, *Denying the Holocaust* (New York: Plume, 1993), 14. Lipstadt's statement is also quoted in Timmerman, 71.

120. Timmerman, 88.

121. Ibid.

122. Ibid.

123. Interview with Mahmood Abbas by Nahum Barnea and Ronny Shaked in *Yediot Aharonot*, May 30, 2003, as cited in Timmerman.

124. Timmerman, 89.

Chapter Seven: John Paul II
and Papal Condemnation of Anti-Semitism

1. George Weigel, *Witness to Hope: The Biography of Pope John Paul II* (New York: HarperCollins, 1999).

2. Eugene J. Fisher and Leon Klenicki, eds., *Pope John Paul II: Spiritual Pilgrimage— Texts on Jews and Judaism, 1979–1995* (New York: Crossroad Publishing, 1995), xxii.

3. Geoffrey Wigoder, *Jewish-Christian Relations Since the Second World War* (Manchester, England: Manchester University Press, 1988), 87.

4. Ibid.

5. Ibid.

6. Ibid.

7. Eugene J. Fisher, "Pope John Paul II's Pilgrimage of Reconciliation," in Fisher and Klenicki, eds., xxvii.

8. Ibid.

9. Ibid., xxviii.

10. Quoted in ibid.

11. Weigel, 823.

12. Fisher, "Pope John Paul II's Pilgrimage of Reconciliation"; and Pope John Paul II, "Meeting with Jews in Paris, May 31, 1980," in Fisher and Klenicki, eds., 9.

13. Pope John Paul II, "Address on the Fortieth Anniversary of the Warsaw Ghetto Uprising, April 25, 1983," ibid., 27–28.

14. Fisher, "Pope John Paul II's Pilgrimage of Reconciliation."

15. Pope John Paul II, "Address to the Jewish Community of Australia, November 26, 1986," in Fisher and Klenicki, eds. 82–83.

16. Weigel, 823.

17. Avery Dulles, S.J., "Commentary on the Holy See's Document We Remember," in *The Holocaust, Never to be Forgotten: Reflections on the Holy See's Document* We Remember (Mahwah, New Jersey: The Paulist Press, 2001), 53; and Pope John Paul II, "Address to Leaders of the Jewish Community in Strasbourg," in Fisher and Klenicki, eds., 128.

18. John Paul II, "Remarks at St. Peter's Square, April 18, 1993," quoted in *L'Osservatore Romano*, April 21, 1993.

19. Weigel, 823.

20. Ibid.

21. Tad Szulc, *Pope John Paul II: The Biography* (New York: Scribner, 1995), 454; and Weigel, 823.

22. Szulc, 455.

23. Ibid., 454.

24. Weigel, 484.

25. Ibid.

26. Daniel Jonah Goldhagen, *A Moral Reckoning: The Role of the Catholic Church in the Holocaust and Its Unfulfilled Duty of Repair* (New York: Knopf, 2002), 224.

27. Ibid., 221.

28. Fisher, "Pope John Paul II's Pilgrimage of Reconciliation."

29. The signing of the Fundamental Agreement between the Holy See and the State of Israel, in December 1994, which established diplomatic ties between the Vatican and Israel for the first time, is discussed in illuminating detail in the recent book edited by Marshall J. Breger, *The Vatican-Israel Accords*, which brings together essays that analyze the legal, historical, theological, and political meaning of the Accords: Marshall J. Breger, ed., *The Vatican-Israel Accords: Political, Legal and Theological Contexts* (Notre Dame, Indiana: University of Notre Dame Press, 2004).

30. Weigel, 709.

31. Eugene J. Fisher, "Pilgrimage of Reconciliation: From Wadowice to the Wailing Wall," in *New Catholic Encyclopedia*, Jubilee Volume: The Wojtyla Years, 96.

32. Ibid.

33. Weigel, 697.

34. George Weigel, "The Holy Father in the Holy Land," *Weekly Standard*, April 10, 2000.

35. Fisher, "Pilgrimage of Reconciliation," 97.

36. Ibid.

37. Weigel, "The Holy Father in the Holy Land."

38. Fisher, "Pilgrimage of Reconciliation," 96.

39. Ibid.

40. Ibid.

41. George Weigel, "Holy Land Pilgrimage: A Diary," *First Things*, June/July 2000, 33.

42. Fisher, "Pope John Paul II's Pilgrimage of Reconciliation."

43. Ibid.

44. Ibid.

45. David Pryce-Jones, "The Islamization of Europe?" *Commentary*, December 2004, 29–33.

46. Gabriel Schoenfeld, *The Return of Anti-Semitism* (San Francisco: Encounter Books, 2004), 60.

47. Meir Weintrater, "France," in David Singer and Lawrence Grossman, eds., *American Jewish Year Book*, Volume 102 (New York: American Jewish Committee, 2002), 334.

48. Kenneth R. Timmerman, *Preachers of Hate: Islam and the War on America* (New York: Three Rivers Press, 2004), 213.

49. Marie Brenner, "France's Scarlet Letter," in Ron Rosenbaum, ed., *Those Who Forget the Past: The Question of Anti-Semitism* (New York: Random House, 2004), 212.

50. Weintrater, "France," 334.

51. Timmerman, 325.

52. Statement of Bishop Jean-Pierre Ricard, President of the French Conference of Catholic Bishops, April 3, 2002.

53. Michel Gurfinkiel, "France's Jewish Problem," *Commentary*, July/August 2002.

54. Andrea Levin, "The James Carroll Paradox," *Jerusalem Post*, March 9, 2004.

55. Ibid.

56. Ibid.

57. Goldhagen, 219.

58. Pryce-Jones, "The Islamization of Europe?" 31.

59. Philip Jenkins, *The New Anti-Catholicism* (New York: Oxford University Press, 2003), 190–91.

60. Cardinal Joseph Ratzinger, "The Heritage of Abraham: The Gift of Christmas," *L'Osservatore Romano*, December 29, 2000.

61. Ibid.

62. David Brinn, "New pope hailed for strong Jewish ties," *Jerusalem Post*, April 19, 2005.

63. Ibid.

64. Ibid.

INDEX

Get a FREE chapter
of Regnery's latest bestseller!

Visit us at
www.Regnery.com

- Hot New Releases

- Upcoming Titles

- Listings of Author Signings
  and Media Events

- Complete Regnery Catalog

 - Always a Free Chapter
  of a Brand-New Book!

Since 1947
**REGNERY
PUBLISHING, INC.**
An Eagle Publishing Company • Washington, DC
www.Regnery.com